Mediated Youth Cultures

Mediated Youth Cultures

The Internet, Belonging and New Cultural Configurations

Edited by

Andy Bennett
Griffith University, Australia

and

Brady Robards
University of Tasmania, Australia

First published 2014 by
PALGRAVE MACMILLAN

Palgrave Macmillan in the UK is an imprint of Macmillan Publishers Limited,
registered in England, company number 785998, of Houndmills, Basingstoke,
Hampshire RG21 6XS.

Palgrave Macmillan in the US is a division of St Martin's Press LLC,
175 Fifth Avenue, New York, NY 10010.

Palgrave Macmillan is the global academic imprint of the above companies
and has companies and representatives throughout the world.

Palgrave® and Macmillan® are registered trademarks in the United States,
the United Kingdom, Europe and other countries.

ISBN 978–1–137–28701–4

This book is printed on paper suitable for recycling and made from fully
managed and sustained forest sources. Logging, pulping and manufacturing
processes are expected to conform to the environmental regulations of the
country of origin.

A catalogue record for this book is available from the British Library.

A catalog record for this book is available from the Library of Congress.

Typeset by MPS Limited, Chennai, India.

Contents

List of Figures

Acknowledgements

We would like to acknowledge the support of our contacts at Palgrave Macmillan, Felicity Plester and Chris Penfold. Thank you for your patience and your hard work throughout the project. Thanks also to our 17 contributors. Your work kept us motivated and passionate about this project (even through the delays!) and we are proud of this collection of important, innovative research.

We should also acknowledge that this book has its origins in a call for papers for a special issue of the journal *Continuum: Journal of Media and Cultural Studies* on the same topic – mediated youth cultures. We received so many proposed contributions to the special issue that we decided it made sense to also go ahead with an edited collection, for which we chose a set of essays that would cohere to address several key themes that we identify in the part introductions. Although the special issue of *Continuum* (volume 26, issue 3) is not organised thematically as this collection is, the papers in that issue are nonetheless impressive and important pieces of scholarship that contribute to our knowledge in this area. Usefully, several of the papers that appear in that issue also inform and are referred to in this collection, so there is a strong connection between the two projects.

Finally, we acknowledge and thank our loved ones for their continued support. Especially to Monika and Daniel, to Dorothy and Tony – thank you.

Notes on Contributors

Melissa Avdeeff is currently an independent researcher based in Canada. Her research focuses on the intersections of technology, popular music and sociability. Melissa is particularly interested in how music playback technologies influence social behaviour, especially amongst youth. She completed her PhD in Musicology at the University of Edinburgh in 2011, under the direction of Simon Frith. Her thesis, 'Finding Meaning in the Masses: Issues of Taste, Identity, and Sociability', presented findings from a large-scale international study of iPod use. She previously held a lectureship position in the Music Department at the University of Alberta in Camrose, Canada.

Andy Bennett is Professor of Cultural Sociology and Director of the Griffith Centre for Cultural Research at Griffith University. He has authored and edited numerous books including *Music, Style and Aging*, *Popular Music and Youth Culture*, *Cultures of Popular Music*, *Remembering Woodstock*, and *Music Scenes* (with Richard A. Peterson). Bennett was Chief Investigator on a three-year, five-country project funded by the Australian Research Council entitled 'Popular Music and Cultural Memory' (DP1092910). He is also a Faculty Fellow of the Center for Cultural Sociology at Yale University.

Liam Berriman is a Researcher at the Centre for Innovation and Research in Childhood and Youth (CIRCY) at the University of Sussex. He studied for his PhD in the Department of Sociology at Goldsmiths, University of London. His thesis – titled 'Design and Participation Across Young People's Online Spaces' – looked at how and on what terms young people are able to participate in the design and development of virtual worlds and other online media spaces. He is currently involved in an NCRM methodological innovation project called 'Face 2 Face: Tracing the Real and the Mediated in Children's Cultural Worlds'.

Susan Bird is a critical ethnographer and doctoral candidate in the School of Law and Justice at Victoria University. She works as a casual academic when not out exploring the city. Her thesis, 'Playing in Melbourne's Urban Wildscapes', is interdisciplinary and uses innovative methodologies. The complexity of the city lends itself to multiple perspectives, and in her thesis, Susan seeks to uncover subjugated voices and the everyday practices that are an embodied resistance to dominant urban discourses.

Katie Davis is an Assistant Professor at the University of Washington Information School, where she studies the role of digital media technologies in adolescents' academic, social and moral lives. Her work has appeared in a variety of peer-reviewed publications, including the *Journal of Adolescence, New Media & Society* and *Computers in Human Behavior*. She is the co-author with Howard Gardner of *The App Generation: How Today's Youth Navigate Identity, Intimacy, and Imagination in a Digital World* (2013). In addition to publishing and presenting her research in scholarly venues, Katie regularly shares her work with parents, teachers and school administrators in an effort to build connections between educational research and practice.

Kate Douglas is an Associate Professor in the School of Humanities at Flinders University. She is the author of *Contesting Childhood: Autobiography, Trauma, Memory* (2010), and the co-editor (with Gillian Whitlock) of *Trauma Texts* (2009) and (with Kylie Cardell) *Telling Tales: Autobiographies of Childhood and Youth*.

Simone Fullagar is Professor of Physical Cultural Studies, University of Bath, England and an Adjunct Member of the Griffith Centre for Cultural Research, Griffith University, Australia. Simone is an interdisciplinary sociologist who has published widely across the areas of health/wellbeing, leisure, sport and tourism, using post-structuralist and feminist perspectives. Her latest edited book is *Slow Tourism: Experiences and Mobilities* (with K. Markwell and E. Wilson, 2012).

Ian Goodwin is a Senior Lecturer in the School of English and Media Studies at Massey University, New Zealand. With a background in cultural studies, his research focuses on the cultural significance of new media technologies. He is particularly interested in issues of identity, consumption, citizenship and activism. He has published widely on these topics in journals such as *New Media & Society, Information, Communication and Society, Convergence, Communication and Critical/Cultural Studies* and *Gender, Place and Culture*.

Christine Griffin is Professor of Social Psychology at the University of Bath in the UK. Her recent work explores the relationship between social identities and alcohol consumption by young people, with a long-standing interest in young women's lives. Recent ESRC-funded projects include a study of young people's experiences of 'branded' leisure at music festivals and free parties, led by Andrew Bengry-Howell; a project on clubbing and dance cultures as forms of social and political participation, led by Sarah Riley; a major study on the marketing of drinks in relation to young adults' everyday drinking culture; and a study of young adults' drinking cultures and social media use in New Zealand (Marsden Fund). Professor Griffin is a member of the UK Centre for Tobacco and Alcohol Studies funded by the UK Clinical Research Collaboration, investigating the influence of social media on young people's drinking cultures.

Sun Jung is a Research Fellow in the Asia Research Institute at the National University of Singapore. She has published broadly on South Korean popular cultures, lifestyles and transnational media flows, including the monograph *Korean Masculinities and Transcultural Consumption: Yonsama, Rain, Oldboy and K-pop Idols* (2011). Her current projects include 'Social Media and Cross-Border Cultural Transmissions'; 'K-pop: Art of Cultural Capital'; 'Neoliberal Capitalism, Sustainable Lifestyles and Media Representations'; 'Participatory Public Space: A Right to the Networked City'; and 'Sexuality and Gender in Asian Pop Cultures'. Her new book, tentatively titled *K-pop and Korean Popular Culture*, is forthcoming (Ashgate).

Siân Lincoln is Senior Lecturer in Media Studies at Liverpool John Moores University. Her research interests are around contemporary youth culture, young people and private space, teenage 'bedroom culture' and young people and social media. She has published in and edited a variety of journals including *Leisure Studies, Space and Culture, Young, Continuum, Journal of Youth Studies* and *Film, Fashion and Consumption*. She has recently published a monograph, *Youth Culture and Private Space* (2012), and an edited collection, *The Time of Our Lives: Dirty Dancing and Popular Culture* (2013). She is currently working on her second monograph, *Rethinking Youth Cultures* (Palgrave Macmillan).

Antonia Lyons is an Associate Professor in the School of Psychology at Massey University, New Zealand. Her research focuses on issues around gender, health and identity, particularly the social contexts of behaviours related to health and wellbeing. Antonia is a co-author of the text *Health Psychology: A Critical Introduction* (with Kerry Chamberlain, 2006) and is currently a co-editor of the journal *Qualitative Research in Psychology*, an Associate Editor for *Health Psychology Review*, and on the editorial boards of the *Journal of Health Psychology* and *Psychology and Health*.

Tim McCreanor is a social scientist working with SHORE & Whariki Research Group, a public health centre at Massey University, based in Auckland. He has a track record in critical studies of commercial alcohol marketing, supervision of doctoral projects around digital communications within minority groups, innovative approaches to the analysis of racism, and the development of qualitative methods in social science. He was a Principal Investigator on the publicly funded study that supported the development of Chapter 4, where key interests were focused on the incursion of commercial alcohol marketing into social networking systems and the subsequent impacts on drinking practices, consumption and population-level alcohol-related harm.

Raphaël Nowak is a cultural sociologist and Adjunct Member of the Griffith Centre for Cultural Research at Griffith University. Recently graduated with a PhD in sociology, he works on various questions related to music consumption in the digital age, such as the articulation between music technologies' materiality and listening practices, the entanglements of music taste and everyday life, and methodological tools with which to grasp such issues.

Adele Pavlidis has recently been awarded her PhD from Griffith University. She is an interdisciplinary sociologist with an interest in sociocultural theories of affect and has published several articles in the area of sport, leisure and gender studies. Her book (co-authored with Simone Fullagar), provisionally titled *Gender, Sport and Power: The Rise of Roller Derby*, is forthcoming (Ashgate).

Anna Poletti lectures in Literary Studies at Monash University. Her research interests are autobiography beyond the book, life writing in youth cultures, and DIY culture. She is the author of *Intimate Ephemera: Reading Young Lives in Australian Zine Culture* (2008), and co-editor of *Identity Technologies: Constructing the Self Online* with Julie Rak (2014).

Brady Robards is a Lecturer in Sociology at the University of Tasmania. Brady's research explores how young people use and produce the social web. His work appears in journals such as *Sociology, Continuum, Young* and the *International Journal of Educational Integrity*. He is the co-author of *Think Sociology* (2012), *Teaching Youth Studies: Practice, Innovation and Popular Culture* (forthcoming, Australian Clearinghouse for Youth Studies) and the co-editor of *Youth Cultures & Subcultures: Australian Perspectives* (forthcoming, Ashgate). You can follow Brady on Twitter (@bradyjay) and see more of his work at bradyrobards.com.

Carmel L. Vaisman is a Lecturer in the Multidisciplinary Program in the Humanities at Tel Aviv University, researching digital discourse and the online cultures of Israeli girls. She co-authored the book *Hebrew On-Line* and has published in journals such as *Language & Communication* and the *Journal of Children and Media* as well as editing volumes such as *Digital Discourse* and *International Blogging*. She earned her PhD from the Hebrew University in Jerusalem.

Ann Werner is Senior Lecturer in Gender Studies, Södertörn University, Sweden. She wrote her dissertation on teenage girls, music culture and gender identity at Linköping University in Sweden and it was published as a book in 2009. Ann's research is within the field of feminist cultural studies, inspired by media theory, gender theory and ethnographic methods alike. Currently, she is part of the research project 'Music Use in the Online Media Age: A Qualitative Study of Music Cultures Among Young People in Moscow and Stockholm', together with three other researchers. All her work has focused on cultural musical representations and people's uses, experiences and production of them.

Introduction: Youth, Cultural Practice and Media Technologies

Andy Bennett (Griffith University) & Brady Robards
(University of Tasmania)

Since the early 1990s the impacts of digital media have increasingly been felt among different parts of society in both the developed and, progressively, the developing world. Not surprisingly perhaps, young people have been fast to acquire digital media devices and incorporate them into their everyday lives. Such early adoption follows a pattern that has been evident since the 1950s, whereby youth are typically seen to be at ease with and adapt quickly to emerging forms of technology (see Bausinger, 1984; Reimer, 1995). While we would shy away from propping up a 'digital natives' mythology (see Bennett et al., 2008 for a thorough critique), the specific features of digital media have seen their dissemination and uptake by youth proceed at an unprecedented pace. In particular, the interactive features of digital media and their combined capabilities – as communication devices, search engines, cameras, notebooks and so on – have given them a high level of appeal among young consumers.

As a feature of the digital media landscape situated at the centre of young people's engagement with different digital media devices, the internet continues to have a profound effect. Through its intersection with the everyday practices of youth, the internet has brought new dimensions to what has conventionally been referred to as youth culture. In particular, the internet has served to redefine notions of public and private space (Lincoln, 2012) and the relationship between the global and the local (Hodkinson, 2003) while simultaneously giving rise to new ways in which young people frame and understand their interactions and associations with others. As we have argued previously (Robards & Bennett, 2011), rather than assuming that there is an easy distinction to be made between offline and online interactions between youth in the post-digital age, such interactions often

1

embody a merging of offline and online qualities and characteristics in a seamless fashion.

Such discernible shifts in the ways in which young people connect with each other, spatially, temporally and socially, are, in turn, giving rise to new questions about the definition of youth culture. Conventionally, youth culture has been regarded as something bound by geographical proximity and a collective affinity confirmed by collective visual displays of taste, typically through style, clothing and various forms of modification. Such forms of visually spectacular youth culture as this, manifested at the level of the physical neighbourhood or community, provided a focus for much of the early work on youth cultures and, as they were commonly termed, 'subcultures' (see, for example, Brake, 1985; Hall & Jefferson, 1976; Hebdige, 1979). With the increasing importance of the internet as a means through which youth cultural practice is articulated and maintained, it is no longer the case that we can consider youth culture as a purely physical, locally bounded phenomenon. Thus, as Bennett observes,

> we can no longer take it for granted that membership of a youth culture involves issues of stylistic unity, collective knowledge of a particular club scene, or even face-to-face interaction. On the contrary, youth cultures may be seen increasingly as cultures of 'shared ideas', whose interactions take place not in physical spaces such as the street, club or festival field but in the virtual spaces facilitated by the internet. (Bennett, 2004: 163)

At the same time, and as the chapters in this book will presently serve to illustrate, through the medium of the internet the forms of practice that constitute youth culture are diversifying to the extent that youth culture can no longer be regarded as principally bounded by elements of style. On the contrary, it could be argued that through the emergence of the internet a number of those more mundane practices often elided in youth cultural research have become new and significant foci for contemporary youth researchers. The collection of essays in this book is based on highly innovative research conducted in various parts of the world including Oceania, Europe, North America, Asia and the Middle East. Between them they consider a range of topics including friendship, musical taste, cultural production, subversive strategies, sport and leisure as these relate to online contexts. This is the first time that such an internationally diverse group of researchers and a diverse range of research topics have been brought together in a single volume.

That said, many of the themes and issues explored in the pages of this book speak to global and trans-local issues as these are experienced and engaged with by contemporary youth in their everyday interactions with the internet.

The book is divided into three parts. Part 1 focuses on the relationship between online and offline identities. In Chapter 1 Katie Davis considers the significance of friendship among adolescent youth in influencing their use of the internet. In a chapter that challenges some existing accounts of a separation between young people's online and offline identities, Davis illustrates how pre-existing offline friendships among young people both underpin the ways in which they make use of the internet in their daily lives and inform their understanding of what counts as acceptable and unacceptable behaviour online. As Davis also shows, the presence of friendship in an offline context also functions in driving young people to maintain a level of consistency in the identities that they project online and those that their friends associate with them offline.

In Chapter 2 Brady Robards considers how, given both the longevity and ubiquity of the internet and associated forms of online social networks, many young people today can effectively lay claim to having 'grown up online'. Taking the example of Facebook, which has now been in existence for ten years, Robards looks at how the archival aspects of Facebook provide a basis for young people to look back at themselves and reflect on their process of biographical and personal development since childhood and/or adolescence. As Robards notes, however, such characteristics of Facebook also present young people with some critical issues around aspects of personal privacy. Using Bowker's (2007) concept of digital trace, Robards looks at how young people are developing strategies to effectively manage and account for those aspects of their past lives that live on as digital traces.

In Chapter 3 Siân Lincoln focuses on the ways in which the internet has served to complicate previously held distinctions between private and public space for young people. Focusing on the domestic sphere of the family home, and within this the specific and ostensibly 'private' space of the teenage bedroom, Lincoln examines the impact of the internet and associated digital media in allowing young people to actively reach out beyond that space and to engage online with others in local, trans-local and global contexts. As Lincoln explains, rather than resulting in an anomic situation for youth in which distinctions between private and public space disappear and/or become meaningless, young people are rather empowered by digital media to the extent that they are able to redefine and reinscribe space as private and public in ways that accord with their own tastes and lifestyle preferences.

In Chapter 4, Ian Goodwin, Antonia Lyons, Christine Griffin and Tim McCreanor look at how the internet provides a space of conspicuous display for young people in relation to their drinking practices. As Goodwin et al. observe, while young people, typically those in the 18–30 age range, are more likely to drink to excess than older drinkers, they are at the same time more prone to discuss and exhibit their drinking practices online, typically through online social network sites such as Facebook. According to Goodwin et al., while at one level the portrayal of drinking practices in an online context can be seen as an extension of the tales of drinking excess told in pre-digital contexts, on another level access to online mediums exposes young people to greater risks in terms of personal privacy and potential stigmatisation.

Part 2 of the book focuses on how the internet provides a space for engagement and creativity among young people. In Chapter 5, Kate Douglas and Anna Poletti conceptualise the internet not necessarily as a space in which young people can experiment with and/or deviate from offline identities but rather one in which they can engage in 'life writing', that is to say, in accounts of themselves, their lives, hopes and aspirations in everyday, mundane contexts. As Douglas and Poletti explain, the internet provides an important sense of empowerment for young people, giving them both the resources for the ongoing construction of powerful narratives of the self and an audience of like-minded peers who are willing to engage in discussion and exchange.

In Chapter 6, Carmel L. Vaisman considers how the internet is empowering young girls by providing them with spaces for cultural production within the domestic sphere of the family home. In a similar vein to Lincoln (2012; see also Chapter 3 of this book), Vaisman examines how the internet is serving to blur the lines between private and public space. In this sense, argues Vaisman, the internet allows young girls opportunities to become involved in cultural production without the necessity to enter those male-regulated public spaces in which most cultural production has hitherto taken place. In examining these issues, Vaisman draws on her recent research on Israeli girls' engagement with *Israblog*, currently the largest Hebrew-language blog hosting website.

In Chapter 7, Sun Jung looks at the significance of the internet for music fans across South-East Asia in the discussion and promotion of K-pop. K-pop is a hybrid genre of Korean popular music that draws on various contemporary styles including R&B, rap and dance music. As Jung explains, since its origins in the 2000s, K-pop has rapidly established itself as a highly popular genre across the Asia Pacific. Jung's chapter considers the role of fans in the promotion of K-pop through their work to popularise the genre through various online mediums. According to Jung, the current success of K-pop cannot be disentangled from the role of fans in co-producing a trans-local audience for the genre and clearly demonstrates the increasing dependency of the music industry on its audience and their powers of online taste making.

In Chapter 8, Melissa Avdeeff examines how the internet is giving rise to new forms of eclectic musical taste among young people. Challenging existing criticisms of digital sound-carrying devices, notably mobile phones and iPods, as producing social isolation among youth, Avdeeff suggests that, conversely, such devices are creating new avenues for sociality as young people use them as a medium for discussing and sharing new music they have discovered online with their friends and peers.

In Chapter 9 Raphaël Nowak argues that the emergence of digital music files, despite their fundamental impact on the way in which listeners – and in particular young listeners – access music, must be understood in the context of a broader media landscape where a range of other playback technologies, including analogue technologies, continue to be used. As Nowak observes, among young listeners, different playback technologies are often evaluated in terms of the affordances that they offer. While digital soundfiles are easy to download and to use with mobile technologies such as iPods, analogue playback devices such as vinyl-record decks offer a warmth and are often more conducive to listening to music while at home. Thus, argues Nowak, it is not possible to essentialise internet-based music as having replaced in any holistic sense earlier forms of listening practice. Rather, all forms of listening devices must be considered in a broader context of material engagement.

Part 3 of the book focuses on the significance of the internet in relation to bodies, space and place. In Chapter 10, Adele Pavlidis and Simone Fullagar consider how the internet has offered opportunities for women's involvement in sport in ways that have often not applied to more traditional media forms where a more conservative view of women and sport has often held sway. Focusing on the example of roller derby, Pavlidis and Fullagar note how the recent re-emergence of the sport and the discourses that present and construct it as a women-only sport are largely down to the online spaces in which such work of representation has occurred.

In Chapter 11, Ann Werner looks at how young people are using YouTube as a way of involving themselves in the co-production of youth culture through appropriating the style, image and dance moves of contemporary popular music artists such as Beyoncé and Lady Gaga. According to Werner, such use of YouTube, a major form of interactive online digital media, by young people can be seen as a development in the trend towards use of stylistic and other popular cultural resources in subversive practice that has long characterised youth culture. According to Werner, central here is the hypertext that creators of these videos use to discuss their practices and to link them to other videos and footage posted on YouTube.

In Chapter 12, Liam Berriman examines the relationship between young people and virtual online worlds through a study of the ways in which they are increasingly being used in the production of such worlds. As Berriman observes, the exponential growth in virtual worlds targeting children and young people in recent years suggests a growing appeal for such online forms of activity among these social groups. The active recruitment of young people to work in a consultative capacity in the production of online worlds, however, is a relatively new step, and one that sheds new light on the role of young people as prosumers in relation to digital technology.

In Chapter 13, Susan Bird looks at the importance of the internet in relation to flash mobs. Flash mobs are short-lived, apparently spontaneous gatherings in public spaces to perform acts of mild subversion. Using the example of Melbourne's 'Zombie Shuffle', an annual flash mob gathering, Bird considers the importance of the internet both as a means of organising flash mobs and for the retrospective sharing of feedback on flash mob gatherings. As Bird explains, through Facebook, short bursts of sociality can be organised that impact in a subversive, carnivalesque fashion on the urban landscape and the anonymity that often pervades there.

References

Bausinger, H (1984) 'Media, Technology and Daily Life', *Media, Culture and Society*, 6: 343–351.
Bennett, A (2004) 'Virtual Subculture? Youth, Identity and the Internet', in A Bennett & K Kahn-Harris (eds) *After Subculture: Critical Studies in Contemporary Youth Culture*. Basingstoke: Palgrave.
Bennett, S, Maton, K & Kervin, L (2008) 'The "Digital Natives" Debate: A Critical Review of the Evidence', *British Journal of Educational Technology*, 39(5): 775–786.
Bowker, GC (2007) 'The Past and the Internet', in J Karaganis (ed.) *Structures of Participation in Digital Culture*. New York: Social Sciences Research Council, 20–36.

Brake, M (1985) *Comparative Youth Culture: The Sociology of Youth Cultures and Youth Subcultures in America, Britain and Canada*. London: Routledge and Kegan Paul.

Hall, S & Jefferson, T (1976) (eds) *Resistance through Rituals: Youth Subcultures in Post-War Britain*. London: Hutchinson.

Hebdige, D (1979) *Subculture: The Meaning of Style*. London: Routledge.

Hodkinson, P (2003) '"Net.Goth": Internet Communication and (Sub)Cultural Boundaries', in D Muggleton & R Weinzierl (eds) *The Post-Subcultures Reader*. Oxford: Berg, 285–298.

Lincoln, S (2012) *Youth Culture and Private Space*. Basingstoke: Palgrave.

Reimer, B (1995) 'The Media in Public and Private Spheres', in J Fornäs & G Bolin (eds) *Youth Culture in Late Modernity*. London: Sage.

Robards, B & Bennett, A (2011) 'MyTribe: Post-Subcultural Manifestations of Belonging on Social Network Sites', *Sociology*, 45(2): 303–317.

Part 1
Online and Offline Identities

In the first part of this book, you will find four chapters that cohere around an investigation of young people's identities, and how these identities – and the cultural practices that, in part, constitute identity – play out when mediated online. Key questions for Part 1 include:

- Are the identities young people perform online distinct from their offline identities, or is this binary between the online and the offline a false one?
- As young people's experiences of transition or 'growing up' are increasingly mediated online, what are the implications of this sustained 'digital trace'?
- What is visible online? What is invisible? How might we understand and control a sense of privacy in an era that appears to be characterised by sharing and visibility?

The internet has undergone many changes since scholars started to investigate the social interactions that are mediated online. The MUDs (multi-user dungeons) in Turkle's (1995) and Dibbell's (1998) work and the 'virtual communities' in Rheingold's (1994) would likely appear very alien to many young people today. No doubt the web will look and be very different in another few decades, too. Even if sites like MySpace, Facebook and Twitter are reinvented to retain users, how different might they be in 20 years? Despite this rapidly changing and evolving terrain, it is critical that we continue to ask questions about how identity works in these spaces. We do this not only so that our enquiries might help us better understand the lived experiences of young people using the internet today but also, as Goodwin et al. (Chapter 4, this collection) conclude, so that we can explore the dynamics that structure

9

the societies in which we all live. The four chapters in the first part of this book, by Davis, Robards, Lincoln and Goodwin et al., work to frame the chapters that follow, setting up a series of themes about control, space, and 'being' online that this collection seeks to better understand.

References

Dibbell, J (1998) *My Tiny Life: Crime and Passion in a Virtual World*. New York: Henry Holt.
Rheingold, H (1994) *The Virtual Community: Surfing the Internet*. London: Minerva.
Turkle, S (1995) *Life on the Screen: Identity in the Age of the Internet*. New York: Touchstone.

1

Youth Identities in a Digital Age: The Anchoring Role of Friends in Young People's Approaches to Online Identity Expression

Katie Davis (University of Washington)

Adolescence has long been viewed in Western cultures as a period of individual self-searching. Newly aware of a world beyond their immediate sphere of experience, youth begin to contemplate what role (or roles) they will assume, how they will be recognised by others, and what contributions they will make to society. In our rapidly changing, interconnected, and technological world, the number of roles open to today's generation of youth has never been greater. Digital media technologies, in particular, have expanded adolescents' range of self-expression, as well as the potential audiences for those expressions.

In light of these changes, it is opportune to ask how today's youth conceive of and approach identity expression in a digital era. Pre-digital accounts of adolescent development held self-consistency and coherence as the ultimate goals of identity development (Erikson, 1968, 1980). Is this conception of identity outmoded in today's ever-changing, networked world? Are multiplicity and fluidity more fitting descriptors of youth's 21st-century identities?

In this chapter, I present classical theories of identity from psychology and sociology and put them in dialogue with research on the nature of youth identity in a digital age. Early internet scholarship emphasised the variety of identities open to youth online, as well as the differences between online and offline identities. More recent scholarship calls this view into question. I engage this tension by drawing on findings from an empirical investigation that examined how youth approach identity expression, both online and offline. Specifically, I explore whether today's adolescents strive for consistency and coherence in their personal identity (both online and offline), or whether they embrace a view of the self that is marked by multiplicity. Because peers are so

11

important to the identity development process during adolescence, I also explore the extent to which consideration of their friends and peer group influences adolescents' conceptions of identity and self-expression in a digital era.

The findings suggest that peers play a central role in youth's mental models of online identity. Specifically, peers serve to anchor adolescents' online self-expressions to a recognised offline identity. Some degree of exploration is permitted, but wholesale identity experimentation is generally regarded by peers with suspicion and disapproval. By placing these findings within a broader context of theory and research relating to adolescent identity, I demonstrate how and why youth seek – and ultimately achieve – a sense of consistency between their online and offline identities.

Study Background

Site

The research discussed in this chapter was conducted with youth attending secondary schools in Bermuda, a self-governing British dependent territory located approximately 650 miles east of Cape Hatteras, North Carolina. Bermuda's economy is driven by international business and tourism, and the World Bank ranks the Island among the world's most affluent countries. With a total area of 21 square miles divided into nine parishes, and a population of roughly 68,000, Bermuda is one of the most densely populated regions in the world. Approximately 60 per cent of the Island's population is Black and the other 40 per cent identifies as White or Other (Government of Bermuda, 2010).

While Bermudian heritage draws from many cultural influences, including traditions from England, Canada, the United States, and the Caribbean, the Island's distinct cultural and socioeconomic characteristics and racial make-up prevent generalising the results from this study to other countries.

Sample

In March and April 2010, I collected survey data from a sample of 2,079 students (57 per cent female) between the ages of 11 and 19 years ($M = 15.4$ years) attending school in Bermuda. With approximately 2,600 students attending senior school in Bermuda, overall, the sample contained roughly 80 per cent of all senior school students on the Island. The survey sample included students from both of the public senior schools on the Island and five of the six private senior schools.

Students were enrolled in grades 8 through 12 in the private schools and grades 9 through 12 in the public schools (the public senior schools begin at grade 9).

From the survey sample, I selected 32 students to participate in follow-up interviews in April–June 2010. These participants ranged in age from 13 to 18 years ($M = 15.5$ years), and represented grades 8 through 12. Twenty-one participants (66 per cent) identified themselves as Black, ten participants (31 per cent) identified as White, and one participant (3 per cent) identified herself as Other.

Data Collection

The survey was completed anonymously at school and included questions about students' digital media ownership, online activities, motivations for going online, their feelings about themselves, their close friends and parents, and selected demographic characteristics.

In line with previous studies of youth's digital media use (e.g. boyd, 2007, 2008; Hodkinson, 2007; Ito et al., 2009; Livingstone, 2008; Robards, 2010; Stern, 2007), I also conducted in-depth interviews with each of the 32 students in the interview sample. An interview gave participants the opportunity to describe what their digital media use meant to them and how it fitted into other aspects of their lives. It also gave them the opportunity to reflect on the nature of their self-expressions in different contexts.

Data Analysis

The current investigation focuses primarily on the interview data, and draws only minimally on basic descriptive statistics calculated from the survey data. The coding scheme used to analyse the interviews included both emic and etic codes (Maxwell, 2005). To create the etic codes, which represent the trained observer's interpretations of participants' experiences, I drew on literature relating to theories of identity as well as adolescents' digital media use and processes of identity formation. Emic codes, which reflect participants' accounts of their phenomenological (subjective) experiences, comprised unanticipated themes that emerged directly from line-by-line readings of the interview transcripts (Strauss & Corbin, 1990).

To ensure that I applied the codes consistently and accurately, I enlisted a graduate student with experience in thematic analysis to code a portion of the transcripts independently. We met to discuss areas of alignment and misalignment until we reached consensus for each observation. Upon completion of coding, I used *Nvivo 9* to examine dominant themes, across participants (Miles & Huberman, 1994).

Identity During Adolescence

Erikson (1950, 1968, 1980) depicted identity as a central concern among adolescents. During this period, as they become aware of the values, norms, and roles of the broader society, adolescents begin to consider who they are and what they believe in. Their primary task is to integrate their childhood identifications and new social roles into an identity that is at once personally satisfying and confirmed by others. According to Erikson, this task is accomplished during a psychosocial moratorium, a period of suspended consequences during which one is free to explore various values and goals before making commitments to any of them.

Those individuals who resolve this stage of development successfully experience identity synthesis, which is marked by a sense of 'self-sameness and inner continuity' (Erikson, 1968: 50). In contrast, those who struggle at this stage experience identity confusion, which is characterised by a failure to craft a coherent and consistent picture of one's self. Erikson's focus on wholeness and continuity bears resemblance to an earlier theorist of the self, William James (1890), who emphasised the synthetic nature of personal identity.

Much of the empirical work conducted in the field of identity research draws on Marcia's (1966) identity status model, an operationalisation of Erikson's (1950, 1968) psychoanalytic views on identity and its development (Meeus, 2011; Schwartz, 2001). The identity status model focuses on the degree to which an individual has committed to a set of goals, values, and beliefs within the domains of occupation, religion, and politics. Each of the four statuses in the model differs along the dimensions of exploration and commitment.

A *diffuse* identity status represents low levels of both exploration and commitment. Someone with a diffuse identity neither spends time reflecting on, nor feels particularly committed to, a particular set of values or beliefs. This identity status parallels Erikson's conception of identity confusion. A *moratorium* identity status represents high levels of exploration and low levels of commitment. The moratorium status resembles Erikson's psychosocial moratorium, during which individuals explore their values and beliefs. An *achieved* identity status represents high levels of commitment that follow on the heels of high levels of exploration. Paralleling Erikson's conception of identity synthesis, an achieved identity is attained after a period of deliberate reflection. Lastly, a *foreclosed* identity status represents low levels of exploration and high levels of commitment. Individuals with foreclosed identities hold strong commitments to values and beliefs that they have adopted, usually from their parents or other influential adults, without first exploring possible alternatives. The foreclosed identity status mirrors the muted way in which Erikson believed most young people experience the identity formation process during adolescence (Cote, 2009).

Beyond the Individual: The Social Nature of Identity

Marcia's identity status model has been criticised for its narrow focus and its failure to take into account the social-contextual aspects of identity formation (Cote, 2009; Schwartz, 2001). Subsequent theorists have attempted to address these limitations in their models of identity. For instance, Adams' (Adams & Marshall, 1996) developmental contextual approach to identity formation draws on Bronfenbrenner's (1977) ecological model of development, which posits that development is influenced by a series of embedded and connected environmental systems. In Cote's (1997) identity capital model, the skills, beliefs, and attitudes that form part of one's identity are seen as resources that individuals use to negotiate social resources. In both models, a person's identity is fundamentally tied to his or her social context. Other theories of identity development focus on specific sociocultural dimensions of experience, such as race, ethnicity, and sexuality (see Cross, 1971, 1978; Helms, 1990; Rosenthal, 1992; Tatum, 1992; Waters, 1999).

In contrast to theorists in the psychological tradition, sociologists have generally placed greater emphasis on the social embeddedness of identity. Cooley (1902), Mead (1934), and Goffman (1959) described the self as a product of social interactions. Cooley's 'looking-glass self' and Mead's 'generalized other' underscore the self's reliance on the surrounding social context. In his account of the 'looking-glass self', for example, Cooley explained that our view of ourselves depends in large part on how we imagine that others perceive us. Likewise, Mead used the concept of a 'generalized other' to argue that our sense of self arises when we consider ourselves from the perspective of the particular social system in which we are participating, such as the family or workplace. In a similar manner, in his dramaturgic analysis of social life, Goffman presented the self as a 'collaborative manufacture' between a performer and his or her audience. As such, the self's existence depends on the recognition it receives from an audience. Rather than locating the self within the individual, these sociological accounts of identity place the self at the intersection of the individual and his or her social context.

New Contexts for Identity Development and Friendship Formation

The social contexts of today's adolescents differ markedly from those of their predecessors. Digital media technologies have given rise to many new contexts for adolescents to express and explore their identities, from social network sites, cell phones, and instant messaging platforms, to blogs and vlogs, virtual worlds, and video-sharing sites. These platforms and technologies present new opportunities for adolescents to try on various identities that may bear little resemblance to their offline identity.

Early internet scholarship emphasised the unprecedented opportunities that virtual environments opened up for the expression of fluid, multiple identities. In her classic book, *Life on the Screen*, Sherry Turkle (1995) described how players of multi-user dungeons (MUDs) took advantage of the anonymity and flexibility of online environments to experiment with their identities. She explained:

> The anonymity of MUDs...gives people the chance to express multiple and often unexplored aspects of the self, to play with their identity and to try out new ones. MUDs make possible the creation of an identity so fluid and multiple that it strains the limits of the notion. Identity, after all, refers to the sameness between two qualities, in this case between a person and his or her persona. But in MUDs, one can be many. (Turkle, 1995: 12)

Other scholars from this era similarly emphasised the multiplicity of identity in online environments (see, for example, Plant, 1997; Stone, 1991; Waskul & Douglass, 1997).

'I Am the Same Person Online and Offline'

With the emergence of Web 2.0 platforms, and as more and more people spend increasing amounts of time online, anonymity is no longer a defining experience for many internet users. Indeed, scholarship from the Web 2.0 era shows that individuals' online identities are considerably more intertwined and consistent with their offline identities than earlier accounts of online identity suggested (Davis, 2010, 2012; Robards & Bennett, 2011). Indeed, the majority of interview participants in the present study spoke more about the similarities between their online and offline selves than the differences. Fully 91 per cent of the youth said they feel like the same person online and offline, and all participants described at least one way in which their online self reflects their offline self. Janelle, age 17, echoed the sentiments of most of the youth I interviewed when she said, 'I am the same person online and offline. So, what you get online is what you get offline, and what you get offline is what you can get online, as well. I'm not two different people.'

Despite the technical ease with which one can adopt new identities online, most interview participants rejected the idea that online environments provide opportunities for experimenting with one's identity. Indeed, only four adolescents (13 per cent) stated explicitly that they sometimes try out different ways of expressing themselves online. William, age 16, reflected the views of the other 27 adolescents in the sample when he commented:

> I don't think there is any point in my being any different online than I am in person because, I mean, I don't get as much enjoyment online as I do in person. So, if I was going to try anything new out, I don't see why I shouldn't just do that in person and then adapt my online profile to that.

Evidently, William does not view the internet as a space in which to explore a different identity. This view is mirrored in the survey results, which showed relatively low levels of online identity exploration. On a 7-point scale where 1 represents low levels of online identity exploration and 7 represents high levels, the sample mean was only 3.42.

These results are consistent with earlier findings showing that adolescents tend to present themselves online in a manner that is consistent with their offline identities (Davis, 2010; Subrahmanyam & Šmahel, 2011). In their study of 1,158 Dutch adolescents between the ages of 10 and 17 years, Valkenburg & Peter (2008) found that fully 82 per cent said they never experimented with their identity online. Further, the researchers found no age or gender differences in the percentage of adolescents who engaged in online identity experiments, though other studies have found that younger adolescents are more likely than older adolescents to experiment with their identities online (Schmitt et al., 2008; Valkenburg et al., 2005).

In another study, college students were asked to create personal avatars for one of three different sites: blogging, dating, or gaming (Vasalou & Joinson, 2009). Afterwards, students answered survey and in-person questions about the avatars they had created. The researchers found that study participants tended to construct avatars that, irrespective of the particular online context, reflected their offline identities. With respect to the dating avatars, the hypothesis that students would inflate all of their avatar's attributes was not supported. In fact, only one attribute, physical attractiveness, was inflated consistently. The researchers concluded: '[I]n having equal access to everyday artifacts and fantasy options, participants were inclined to draw on existing self-views rather than grasping the opportunity to explore other personas' (2009: 517).

The Anchoring Role of Friends

Peers play a central role in the identity development process during adolescence (Erikson, 1968; Youniss & Smollar, 1985). By recognising and providing feedback on each other's emerging identities, peers signal to each other which identities are acceptable and which are not. The low proportion of online identity experiments reported by adolescents may thus be unsurprising if one considers the fact that their digital media use is largely embedded in their offline peer networks. In her ethnographic study of teens on MySpace, boyd (2007) found that adolescents' online identities are embedded in their offline peer networks. On sites like MySpace and Facebook, adolescents post pictures of themselves with their friends, leave messages on each other's pages, and list their closest friends on their profiles. Furthermore, groups of friends often adopt a similar tone and style on their respective profiles. Zhao et al. (2008) found similar patterns of identity expression in their study of college students' Facebook profiles. Instead of defining themselves directly in the 'About Me' section of their profile, these students defined themselves indirectly through their friends list, wall-to-wall conversations, and photo albums showcasing their activities with friends. Likewise, in her study of 40 teen blogs, Bortree (2005) observed that teens used their blogs to communicate with offline friends and to document activities they had shared with these friends. Like boyd (2007), Bortree found that friends tended to influence the content of each other's blogs, for instance by adopting similar terms and posting the same internet quizzes.

The anchoring role of peers is evident in the present study, as well. Kyara, age 14, pointed to her friends as the primary reason she doesn't experiment with her identity online. She remarked, 'I don't try to be anybody else online because most of my friends, we have all, like, mostly they are pretty close with me, so they know anyway.' Because Kyara's friends know her well offline, she suggested, they would notice – and disapprove – if she acted differently online. In this way, she is like several other participants who expressed a sense of responsibility to be recognisable to other people online. For instance, 15-year-old Eric noted, 'I wouldn't want to change myself online and then, when someone actually meets me, they notice that I am different.' Similarly, 16-year-old Brandon reflected, 'I try to be, like, one person. I don't want people to think that I am two-faced, or anything. So, I try to remain the same person in school, online, after school.' Like Kyara, both Eric and Brandon feel a sense of responsibility to their peers to maintain consistency between their online and offline selves. This sense of responsibility appears to arise from a belief that self-consistency is synonymous with authenticity. According to Brandon, failure to maintain self-consistency across social contexts places one in jeopardy of being judged 'two-faced'.

Some Room for Exploration

Though friends anchor adolescents' online identities to their offline identities, some tinkering is permissible online. For instance, several adolescents spoke about omitting certain personal details from their Facebook profile in order to present a polished version of themselves. Kyara, age 14, observed, 'Coming to school in the morning, you can see me looking any way, but on Facebook I wouldn't just put, like, a bad looking picture [of myself].' Similarly, Jenni, age 17, reflected:

> You are only putting your highlights online; like, if you had a bad day, you put it online, but if, like, you fail a math test, you are not going to say, oh, I failed a math test. You are going to say, I got a hundred on a math test. People are going to be, like, gee, you are smart. They don't know that that is the only time you have ever gotten a hundred in your life, but – and all of a sudden it seems like, she is a genius because she can do this so well. So, I think you do. I think everything about you kind of seems, like, glammed up. It is kind of, like, the rose-colored glasses, because people aren't going to share about how they got kicked off the soccer team because they were late for every school practice. They are going to share about how their team won, they led their team to victory.

Like Kyara, Jenni is aware that by selecting what she shares about herself on Facebook, she can control the impression that others form of her online. Her offline self, by contrast, is not so easily manipulated. It's not the case, however, that the 'rose-colored glasses' that Jenni wears online transform her into a wholly different person – her friends would call her out if she deviated too far from the Jenni they know; they simply allow her to be a more 'glammed up' version of who she already is offline.

In addition to a polished self-presentation, friends will also grant room for increased expressiveness online. Over half of the interview participants said they feel that it's easier to express certain things about themselves online compared with offline. In explaining their answers, most adolescents pointed to the greater comfort they feel in expressing personal feelings online. This self-disclosure typically occurs when close friends are communicating through private online channels, such as instant messaging, texting, or direct messaging on Facebook. Kyara reflected, 'People are more open on Facebook, like they would say exactly what they are feeling on Facebook, instead of like telling you to your face.' Michaela, age 15, contrasted the shyness she experiences offline to her increased sociability online. She explained, 'I guess sometimes I kind of feel different [online], like more – it's the shy thing again...[I] like, talk more [online]...so I am different in that way.' These youth appear to feel less inhibited online because they don't have to contend with the discomfort of confronting their friends – including their friends' immediate, unfiltered reactions – in person. Peers don't see their greater emotiveness online as a wholesale self-reinvention so much as a freer – but still authentic – expression of who they are offline. For youth like Kyara, Jenni, and Michaela, the online selves they create are neither completely disjunct from nor identical to their offline selves. Rather, they combine elements of who participants know themselves to be with attributes they aspire to embody. In this way, online contexts seem to give individuals an opportunity to transcend the boundaries of offline self-expression.

To make sense of the differences between adolescents' online and offline selves, Valkenburg & Peter (2011) discuss three features of online communication – asynchronicity, anonymity, and accessibility – that influence the way adolescents present themselves online. Each one of these features gives individuals greater control over their online self-presentations than they typically experience when managing their offline identities. For instance, due to the asynchronous nature of most online communication, adolescents are afforded time to plan out what and how they want to communicate. This advanced preparation contrasts with the impromptu nature of most face-to-face conversations. With respect to anonymity, Valkenburg & Peter distinguish between source anonymity, in which a person's identity is dissociated completely from his or her offline identity, and audiovisual anonymity, in which certain nonverbal cues are reduced or lacking entirely online.

The researchers explain that the latter is more common on instant messaging platforms and social network sites, since individuals tend to communicate with people they know from offline contexts. Both types of anonymity can simulate de-individuation effects, which may give adolescents a feeling of greater freedom to express themselves online. Lastly, Valkenburg & Peter argue that adolescents' increased access to a wide variety of audiences online allows them control over which items of information about themselves reach these audiences. At the same time, boyd (2008) observes that adolescents do not always have full control over their online identities due to the fact that their friends may choose to post content about them without permission.

Beyond Friends

Where friends are absent from online contexts, youth experience even greater freedom to explore different identities. For instance, Sierra, age 17, attributed her more outgoing personality online to the fact that 'on the internet...not too many people know me, so they can't judge me'. She was referring specifically to her use of Twitter, where she interacts primarily with people whom she doesn't know offline. There, she can try out different ways of presenting herself. She reflected, 'On Twitter, I try to be joking really, sarcastic, and more serious.' She explained that 'it just makes me interesting'.

The few adolescents who maintained avatars in virtual worlds had the most to say about trying on different identities online. Brandon, age 16, reflected on his experiences playing his character, a human warlock, in the massively multiplayer online role-playing game, *World of Warcraft*. As a human warlock, he explained, 'I have to assume the character, so it is more of a darker type person, I suppose, as the warlocks traditionally are darker.' Brandon said that 'it can be pretty fun' to present himself in a different way in the game world than he is used to presenting himself in offline contexts.

In a similar manner, Keisha, age 17, has maintained an avatar in a virtual world called *Millsberry* since she was in middle school. Keisha uses her avatar – an 'Indian-looking' girl with green eyes and hair that frequently changes style – to try out different ways of expressing herself. She explained that her avatar's appearance is based on 'how I would like to look, and how it would be nice to look something different like that'. This statement by Keisha is reflected in an earlier study of *World of Warcraft* players (Bessière et al., 2007). The players, aged 18–27, were asked to rate their ideal self, *World of Warcraft* character, and actual self for each of the 'Big Five' personality traits (conscientiousness, extraversion, neuroticism, agreeableness, and openness to experience). On average, players rated their gaming character more favourably than their actual self; they also judged their gaming character to be aligned more closely with their ideal self than their actual self, though the character did display aspects of each. Evidently, for youth like Keisha, maintaining an avatar gives them the opportunity to assume an ideal self, one that isn't necessarily open to them offline. Notably for Keisha, none of her offline friends spends time on *Millsberry*. If they did, it's likely that she wouldn't feel the same degree of freedom to explore a different identity that she does now.

Conclusion

The results from this study suggest that, in this rapidly changing, digital world, a sense of self-consistency and coherence are still valued and sought by today's youth. This insight aligns with earlier research indicating that adolescents typically strive for consistency between their online and offline selves (see, for example, Davis, 2010, 2012; Valkenburg & Peter, 2008; Vasalou & Joinson, 2009). For the adolescents I interviewed, their desire for consistency is largely tied to their friends and larger peer group. They feel a responsibility to be recognisable to their friends and want to avoid being labelled as 'two-faced' by their peers. Earlier studies have also found that peers play an instrumental role in shaping adolescents' online identities (see, for example, Bortree, 2005; Zhao et al., 2008). In this way, friends play an anchoring role in adolescent identity development, both online and offline.

In certain instances, friends do permit some leeway for exploring identities online. They recognise the motivation to present a polished image on public sites such as Facebook, and they acknowledge that some people find it easier to express their feelings and opinions through text-based forms of communication rather than face-to-face. However, drastic deviations from one's offline identity don't fall within these parameters. Those youth who do adopt different identities online tend to do so on sites that their friends don't frequent. In short, peer norms appear to be stronger than technical affordances when it comes to adolescents' conceptions of and approaches to identity expression in a digital era.

These findings add insight into the processes of adolescent identity development in a digital era by uncovering the dynamics that underpin youth's efforts to convey consistency between their online and offline selves. As the results suggest, this underpinning pivots on the fact that, for most youth, online contexts are synonymous with peer contexts. Thus, peers play a central role in understanding the contrast between earlier internet research emphasising the multiplicity of online identities and newer research emphasising consistency between online and offline identities.

The research discussed in this chapter points to at least two important sets of questions to guide future investigations. First, to what extent do young people's statements about the relationship between their online and offline selves correspond to how they actually express themselves online and offline? If there proves to be a discrepancy between what they say and what they do, what accounts for this discrepancy? A second line of inquiry pertains to identifying the optimal balance between multiplicity and consistency online. Is it wise to reinforce youth's inclination towards consistency, or would it be better to encourage more youth to find online spaces where they experience freedom to explore different identities? Under what circumstances is such online exploration helpful or harmful to the development of a personally satisfying and meaningful identity during adolescence? Empirical investigations designed around such questions would provide valuable insights into the most promising ways to support youth development in a digital age.

References

Adams, GR & Marshall, SK (1996) 'A Developmental Social Psychology of Identity: Understanding the Person-in-Context', *Journal of Adolescence*, 19(5): 429–442.

Bessière, K, Seay, AF & Kiesler, S (2007) 'The Ideal Elf: Identity Exploration in World of Warcraft', *CyberPsychology & Behavior*, 10(4): 530–535.

Bortree, DS (2005) 'Presentation of Self on the Web: An Ethnographic Study of Teenage Girls' Weblogs', *Education, Communication & Information*, 5: 25–39.

boyd, d (2007) 'Why Youth (Heart) Social Network Sites: The Role of Networked Publics in Teenage Social Life', in D Buckingham (ed.) *Youth, Identity, and Digital Media*. Cambridge, MA: MIT Press, 119–142.

boyd, d (2008) 'Taken Out of Context: American Teen Sociality in Networked Publics'. Unpublished dissertation: http://www.danah.org/papers/TakenOutOf Context.pdf (retrieved 18 January 2009).

Bronfenbrenner, U (1977) 'Toward an Experimental Ecology of Human Development', *American Psychologist*, 32(7): 513–531.

Cooley, CH (1902) *Human Nature and the Social Order*. New York: Scribner's.

Cote, JE (1997) 'An Empirical Test of the Identity Capital Model', *Journal of Adolescence*, 20: 577–597.

Cote, JE (2009) 'Identity Formation and Self-Development in Adolescence', in RM Lerner & LD Steinberg (eds) *Handbook of Adolescent Psychology* (3rd ed.). Hoboken, NJ: John Wiley & Sons, Inc., 266–304.

Cross, WEJ (1971) 'The Negro-to-Black Conversion Experience', *Black World*, 20(9): 13–27.

Cross, WE (1978) 'The Thomas and Cross Models of Psychological Nigrescence: A Review', *Journal of Black Psychology*, 5(1): 13–31.

Davis, K (2010) 'Coming of Age Online: The Developmental Underpinnings of Girls' Blogs', *Journal of Adolescent Research*, 25(1): 145–171.

Davis, K (2012) 'Tensions of Identity in a Networked Era: Young People's Perspectives on the Risks and Rewards of Online Self-Expression', *New Media & Society*, 14(4): 634–651.

Erikson, EH (1950) *Childhood and Society*. New York: Norton.

Erikson, EH (1968) *Identity, Youth, and Crisis*. New York: Norton.

Erikson, EH (1980) *Identity and the Life Cycle*. New York: Norton.

Goffman, E (1959) *The Presentation of Self in Everyday Life*. New York: Doubleday.

Government of Bermuda (2010) *2010 Census: Population and Housing Report*. Bermuda: Department of Statistics. Available at: http://www.govsubportal.com/census/2010-census

Helms, JE (1990) *Black and White Racial Identity: Theory, Research, and Practice*. New York: Greenwood Press.

Hodkinson, P (2007) 'Interactive Online Journals and Individualisation'. *New Media & Society*, 7(3): 79–104.

Ito, M, Baumer, S, Bittanti, M, boyd, d, Cody, R, Herr-Stephenson, B, et al. (2009) *Hanging Out, Messing Around, and Geeking Out: Kids Living and Learning with New Media*. Cambridge, MA: MIT Press.

James, W (1890) *The Principles of Psychology*. New York: H. Holt.

Livingstone, S (2008) 'Taking Risky Opportunities in Youthful Content Creation: Teenagers' Use of Social Networking Sites for Intimacy, Privacy and Self-Expression', *New Media & Society*, 10(3), 393–411.

Marcia, JE (1966) 'Development and Validation of Ego-Identity Status', *Journal of Personality and Social Psychology*, 3(5): 551–558.

Maxwell, JA (2005) *Qualitative Research Design: An Interactive Approach* (2nd ed.). Thousand Oaks, CA: Sage.

Mead, GH (1934) *Mind, Self & Society: From the Standpoint of a Social Behaviorist*. Chicago, IL: The University of Chicago Press.

Meeus, W (2011) 'The Study of Adolescent Identity Formation 2000–2010: A Review of Longitudinal Research', *Journal of Research on Adolescence*, 21(1): 75–94.

Miles, MB & Huberman, AM (1994) *Qualitative Data Analysis: An Expanded Sourcebook* (2nd ed.). Thousand Oaks, CA: Sage.

Plant, S (1997) *Zeros + Ones: Digital Women and the New Technoculture* (1st ed.). New York: Doubleday.

Robards, B (2010) 'Randoms in My Bedroom: Negotiating Privacy and Unsolicited Contact on Social Network Sites', *Prism*, 7(3). Available at: http://www.prismjournal.org/fileadmin/Social_media/Robards.pdf

Robards, B & Bennett, A (2011) 'MyTribe: Post-Subcultural Manifestations of Belonging on Social Network Sites', *Sociology*, 45: 303–317.

Rosenthal, D (1992) 'Ethnic Identity in Adolescence: Process, Context, and Outcome', in GR Adam, TP Gullotta & R Montemayor (eds) *Adolescent Identity Formation*. Thousand Oaks, CA: Sage, 145–172.

Schmitt, KL, Dayanim, S & Matthias, S (2008) 'Personal Homepage Construction as an Expression of Social Development', *Developmental Psychology*, 44(2): 496–506.

Schwartz, SJ (2001) 'The Evolution of Eriksonian and Neo-Eriksonian Identity Theory and Research: A Review and Integration', *Identity*, 1(1): 7–58.

Stern, S (2007) 'Producing Sites, Exploring Identities: Youth Online Authorship', in D Buckingham (ed.) *Youth, Identity, and Digital Media*. Cambridge, MA: MIT Press, 95–117.

Stone, AR (1991) 'Will the Real Body Please Stand Up? Boundary Stories about Virtual Cultures', in M Benedikt (ed.) *Cyberspace: First Steps*. Cambridge, MA: MIT Press, 81–118.

Strauss, AL & Corbin, JM (1990) *Basics of Qualitative Research: Grounded Theory Procedures and Techniques*. Newbury Park, CA: Sage Publications.

Subrahmanyam, K & Šmahel, D (2011) *Digital Youth: The Role of Media in Development*. New York: Springer.

Tatum, BD (1992) 'African-American Identity Development, Academic Achievement, and Missing History', *Social Education*, 56(6): 331–334.

Turkle, S (1995) *Life on the Screen: Identity in the Age of the Internet*. New York: Simon & Schuster.

Valkenburg, PM & Peter, J (2008) 'Adolescents' Identity Experiments on the Internet: Consequences for Social Competence and Self-Concept Unity', *Communication Research*, 35(2): 208–231.

Valkenburg, PM & Peter, J (2011) 'Online Communication Among Adolescents: An Integrated Model of Its Attraction, Opportunities, and Risks', *Journal of Adolescent Health*, 48(2): 121–127.

Valkenburg, PM, Schouten, AP & Peter, J (2005) 'Adolescents' Identity Experiments on the Internet', *New Media & Society*, 7: 383–402.

Vasalou, A & Joinson, AN (2009) 'Me, Myself and I: The Role of Interactional Context on Self-Presentation through Avatars', *Computers in Human Behavior*, 25(2): 510–520.

Waskul, D & Douglass, M (1997) 'Cyberself: The Emergence of Self in On-line Chat', *The Information Society*, 13(4): 375–396.

Waters, M (1999) *Black Identities*. Cambridge, MA: Harvard University Press.

Youniss, J & Smollar, J (1985) *Adolescent Relations with Mothers, Fathers, and Friends*. Chicago, IL: University of Chicago Press.

Zhao, S, Grasmuck, S & Martin, J (2008) 'Identity Construction on Facebook: Digital Empowerment in Anchored Relationships', *Computers in Human Behavior*, 24(5): 1816–1836.

2

Mediating Experiences of 'Growing Up' on Facebook's Timeline: Privacy, Ephemerality and the Reflexive Project of Self

Brady Robards (University of Tasmania)

In 2014, Facebook will have existed for a decade. The site has become embedded into everyday life for many users, and for some young users, significant parts of their social lives have been played out on social network sites. As spaces in which social exchanges, identities and systems of belonging are articulated and made visible, these sites also act as archives of transition for young people, effectively capturing 'growing up' stories through a chronicle of mediated, transitional experiences. Through the timeline format (the most recent iteration of the profile at the time of writing), Facebook has begun to draw attention to and capitalise on the archival nature of the site. By emphasising its role in mediating these social exchanges and recalling status updates made or images uploaded years earlier, Facebook becomes both the site upon which narratives of transition are played out and organised, and also the site through which these variously public and private disclosures are recalled and reflected upon.

This chapter addresses the role of social network sites in both mediating transitional experiences for young people and acting as archives of transitional 'growing up' stories. In doing so, it makes use of Bowker's (2007) notion of the 'digital trace', or that which is left behind when the internet is used and thus produced. I frame this discussion of the digital trace through concerns around privacy, with a particular focus on drawing attention to the many strategies and social conventions young people are developing and deploying to manage a sense of their own digital trace. Although this chapter is not based on empirical findings as such, I will draw briefly from qualitative research conducted with young people (mid-teens to late twenties) on Australia's Gold Coast from 2007 to 2010, contextualised by a broader review of the international and quickly growing literature concerning young people and their use of social network sites.

The Reflexive Project of the Self: Online and Offline?

Giddens argues that identity formation is a reflexive process. Individuals frequently (if not constantly) undergo what he describes as a 'psychic reorganisation' (1993: 304) of their identity, negotiating the influence of large impersonal organisations that characterise late modernity. Giddens defines the 'stable individual' as someone with a 'feeling of biographical continuity which she is able to grasp reflexively and, to a greater or lesser degree, communicate to others' (1991: 54). The social aspect of identity – the act of communicating a reflexive story about self – is central to stability for Giddens. Importantly, he argues against assumptions that we reinvent ourselves only at crisis moments in our lives, instead contending that individuals are actively and endlessly negotiating and constructing self-identity, even amidst the mundane experiences of the everyday. Giddens describes this approach as the reflexive project of self, 'the process whereby self identity is constituted by the reflexive ordering of self narratives' (1991: 244). (See also Chapter 4 of this collection for more on Giddens' reflexive project of self in relation to mediated drinking cultures.)

As Thomson (2007) explains, 'storytelling (to ourselves and others) is central to the...reflexive project of self. As we rework existing narratives and forge new ones, we invent and reinvent who it is possible to be' (2007: 80). Thomson considers the personal website, which, she argues, figures into the reflexive project of self, requiring a specific ordering of narratives. In the years since Thomson's re-framing of Giddens' work in relation to young people's transition narratives, the personal website may continue to operate as a useful 'professional' tool (in the construction of a 'self brand' related to employment) but has of course been dwarfed by the mass adoption of social network sites, with Facebook being the most prominent and widely used (Robards, 2012). Rather than engagement here being entirely optional, it is my argument that having and maintaining a profile on a social network site has become mandatory for many, where not participating can mean being left off invitation lists for parties, not seeing photos of newborn babies or weddings, and appearing 'unavailable' to friends, along with other forms of 'self-exclusion'. Thus, using social network sites has become part of late modern life for many, not in addition to things like employment, a personal life, and a sense of community, but as a medium through which these forms of participation in the social world are mediated.

Relatedly, it is also clear that perceived boundaries between online and offline social spaces are continuously blurring. Jurgenson argues that the binary between the online and the offline is regularly discursively reproduced, while simultaneously being destabilised in everyday practice. He describes the IRL (In Real Life) 'fetish', a 'fervor around the supposed corresponding loss of logged-off real life' (2012). Digital detox weekends, celebrations of 'switching off', and calls for people to disconnect are all manifestations of this IRL fetish, whereby people who are 'online' are seemingly also disconnected from the 'offline'. This is what he describes as a 'zero sum game', ignoring the reality that people can of course be both on- and offline at the same time, and that offline, in-person sociality can be enabled by, enhanced, extended and reflected upon by sociality mediated online.

The problem that Jurgenson points to here is that various discursive frameworks (and language itself) create a distinction between the online and the offline. This distinction, this 'digital dualism', is a false one. In my own research, my participants also seem to reproduce this dualism. Camilla (24), for instance, was very proud to proclaim at the end of our interview where she spoke at length about how she used Facebook that she was, in fact, 'anti-Facebook'. She described it as a distraction from what 'really mattered', from the important happenings of 'real life': 'Obviously I still use it,' she said, 'but if I was committed, I'd just cut it. And I have thought about it.' Opting out, in order to pay more attention to the 'real' world, is a fundamental component of this fetish of the real, and presents a significant problem for the way in which technology use is being discursively framed:

> If we can fix this false separation and view the digital and physical as enmeshed, we will understand that what we do while connected is inseparable from what we do when disconnected. That is, disconnection from the smartphone and social media isn't really disconnection at all: The logic of social media follows us long after we log out. There was and is no offline; it is a lusted-after fetish object that some claim special ability to attain, and it has always been a phantom. (Jurgenson, 2012)

As internet use and participation on social network sites like Facebook become integrated into everyday practices – especially for young people who have been identified here as the 'vanguard' (Livingstone, 2008: 394) and as 'early adopters' (Notley, 2009: 1222) of these newly mediated forms of belonging – the offline and the online constantly overlap; they are enmeshed. Often, especially in popular discourse, the central purpose for an offline/online dichotomy is to relegate all things 'online' to a position of obscurity and in-authenticity; to de-value systems of belonging that are mediated through the web. In this chapter, it is my goal to resist this tendency towards 'digital dualism', and to instead attend to the ways in which the profiles that constitute social network sites can, in relation to Giddens' reflexive project of self, be understood through two different, overlapping frames: first, as a tool that can be used in the process of reflexive self-making, and second, as an object (or a product) of that project.

Through the first frame, the initial construction of a profile and the subsequent social interactions mediated on the site can be understood as labour involved in the ordering of self-narratives. For instance, the user is prompted (but isn't required) to enter employment and education details, to list favourite books, films, music and television shows, to identify favourite quotes, religious and political views, and state their sex and a subsequent 'interested in' field, signalling gender and sexual identity. Thus, filling out the initial profile is similar in some ways to the specific ordering of self-narratives required in the writing of a curriculum vitae in which Thomson (2007) was interested. Interestingly, what I have found in my own research, at least on Facebook, was that these autobiographical narratives were not at the core of the site's functionality. In the words of one of my participants, who I called Melissa (20 years old at the time of the interview in 2010), 'meet me and ask me, don't see that I'm a person on Facebook'. Although Melissa logged into Facebook at least three times per day, sometimes more, she had not updated her basic biographical information for several years. Instead, it is the social exchanges – commenting on and posting pictures, status updates, wall posts, and events; exchanging private inbox messages and participating in IM (Instant Messenger) conversations; and the subsequent (what Hogan, 2010 describes as) 'curation' of this content (untagging, deleting, editing) – that constitute the everyday engagement with the site, and indeed these activities also represent reflexive ordering and reordering of narratives of self.

The second frame, then, is the product of this labour, of the interactions and disclosures undertaken on Facebook, on which the individual can reflect. In this sense, the profile operates as an archive of the reflexive project of self. I borrow here from Axel Bruns' (2006) notion of the 'produser' – a blending of producer and user, where use of a social network site, for instance, actually constitutes production. Through this lens, it also becomes clear that Facebook's users are not its customers, but rather its products. Facebook sells the content produced by users to advertisers by way of probably the most sophisticated form of targeted marketing research in operation. Produsers of social network sites can look back on their lives in a convenient (and, at times, confronting) format: past relationships, distant parties, previous employment, past education, even news items posted to a network, memorialising a tragedy like the Queensland floods or celebrating a political achievement like the passing of (and subsequent roll-back of) same-sex civil unions legislation. All of these experiences figure into that narrative, whether mundane or critical. Thus, through this second frame, the variously public and personal conversations of self with others (and self with self) discussed by Thomson (2007) can be articulated and archived in a single place. In this sense, social network sites 'are both the object and process of self-formation' (Kim, 2010: 109).

Telling the 'Growing Up' Story on Facebook's Timeline

The process of 'becoming adult' is highly contested, multiple, non-linear, and varied, wrought by social and geographical positions. There are sometimes institutional or legal frames that pin down points of transition based on age, such as when an individual can vote, drive a car, legally consume alcohol, consent to sex, access lower insurance premiums, and enter into formalised partnerships like civil unions or marriages (where these rights exist). There are also cultural celebrations to mark out 'rites of passage', such as graduations and birthdays. The 21st birthday, for example, includes a specific script: drinking alcohol, speeches from parents and best friends, and embarrassing childhood photos or videos (see Neighbors et al., 2005 on the tradition of alcohol consumption at 21st birthdays). These events serve both as points at which to reflect on the experiences of transition, and to mark out the beginning of new chapters. As Wyn & White (1997: 95) argue, however, there is often no 'definite point of arrival' in transition narratives, despite the cultural significance assigned to various rites of passage. It is also clear that the deregulation of labour markets and the shift from industrial to post-industrial economies, along with the shift towards a universal post-secondary education system, has meant that more than ever, young people are experiencing transition in varied, complex ways (White & Wyn, 2013: 8). For these reasons, the phenomena of the 'stay-at-home young adult' and the 'boomerang young adult' (White & Wyn,

2008: 130), who leaves the family home and then later returns, appear to be increasingly common. Amidst these flexible, reversible, non-linear and complex experiences of 'growing up', the Facebook timeline operates as a perhaps misleadingly simple life record.

The Facebook timeline is the most recent iteration of the profile page, serving as a linear, singular manifestation of a personal history. When a user visits another user's profile, or their own profile, they are presented with a record of what I am describing here as 'disclosures' (following Stutzman et al., 2012) but which Facebook describes more broadly as 'activity'. These disclosures, made by both the individual and by their Friends, constitute that user's presence or 'performance of self' (Hogan, 2010; Mendelson & Papacharissi, 2011; Pearson, 2009; Peeters, 2007; Pinch, 2010; Sessions, 2009) on Facebook.

Prior to the introduction of the timeline iteration of the profile in late 2011/early 2012, although content (images, status updates, comments, likes, videos, notes, inbox messages, and so on) was persistent by default (boyd, 2011: 46), it was more difficult to recall. Photos and wall posts, for instance, would slide into relative obscurity on the old profile, and could be recalled only by way of what Dubrofsky (2011: 123) describes as 'the unwieldy process of scrolling back'. That is, users would have to 'scroll back' through someone's wall to find old posts. The timeline iteration, however, allows Facebook users to avoid this labour and access the 'past-as-mediated-on-Facebook' (both their own past, and the past of their Friends) more easily.

Users can skip to a specific year by way of a menu to the right of the profile. At the top of the menu is a link to the default 'recent' posts, followed by a link for each year of activity on Facebook. Users can also retrospectively generate activity (retrospective disclosures) even for years where they were not using Facebook, by nominating their year of birth, identifying younger siblings (whose birthdays will register on the timeline), adding education graduation points, and so on. If a user enters 1985 as their year of birth, for example, 1985 (birth) will be the first entry on the timeline from which all other activities follow. While recent activity still appears first by default, the critical change in the way activity was organised was that older activity could be accessed much more readily, without the 'unwieldy' and thus prohibitive scrolling back through the profile. This allows users to reflect on their own digital traces, and to access the traces of others, with relative ease, and signals a fundamental addition to the function of Facebook as an archive of the digital trace, rather than just as the site upon which interaction takes place.

Having established these parameters, the remainder of this chapter focuses specifically on the Facebook timeline through the two frames developed earlier: as both a site upon which reflexive identity-work takes place, and as a record or archive of that identity-work. Sam Lessin, a product manager at Facebook at the time of the timeline rollout in late 2011 and early 2012, explains the timeline as follows:

> Back in the early days of Facebook, your profile was pretty basic – just your name, a photo, where you went to school…stuff you'd cover in the first five minutes you met someone. Over time, your profile evolved to better reflect how you actually communicate with your friends. Now you can share photos of what you did last weekend, and updates about how you feel today. But since the focus is on the most recent things you posted, more important stuff slips off the page. The photos of your graduation get replaced by updates about what you had for breakfast. Say you're catching up with an old friend – would you rather find out that they had eggs this morning, or hear about their new dream job? The way your profile works today, 99% of the stories you share vanish. The only way to find the posts that matter is to click 'Older Posts' at the bottom of the page. Again. And again. Imagine if there was an easy way to rediscover the things you shared, and collect all your best moments in a single place... If important parts of your story aren't included on your timeline, you can go back to when they happened and add them. Or go to your private activity log. This is where you'll find everything you shared since you joined Facebook. Click on any post to feature it on your timeline so your friends can see it, too... Now, you and your friends will finally be able to tell all the different parts of your story – from the small things you do each day to your biggest moments. What will you create? We can't wait to find out. (Lessin, 2011)

I cite this extract from Lessin's blog post in detail, as there are three elements of the timeline rollout to which I will attend. The first is the changing notion of labour involved in recalling the past ('Click "Older Posts"... Again. And again'). There are important privacy implications for this change, reversing the 'digital ephemerality' afforded by the scroll-back labour. In other words, before the timeline changes, it took some effort to dredge up the past. Second, I will align Lessin's distinction between 'small' and 'big' moments with my earlier discussion of fateful/critical moments and mundane/everyday moments in young people's experiences of transition. Third, I will consider broad recognition that as Facebook has developed and become enmeshed into the everyday life of many of its users, it has become not just a place to stay in touch with Friends, but has also come to serve as an archive of the individual's 'story'. I will explore this third element of Lessin's rollout statement both through a discussion of the implications for future research and through the chapter conclusion.

Privacy, Ephemerality and the Digital Trace

Recently, concerns over how Facebook makes use of and passes on information about users have been renewed. In June 2013, Edward Snowden, a contractor for the United States National Security Agency (NSA), revealed a mass surveillance program (known as Prism) which 'allows officials to collect material including search history, the content of emails, file transfers and live chats' (Greenwald & MacAskill, 2013). At the time of writing, this is the most recent (and perhaps most troubling) example of how the digital trace (or at least metadata associated with this trace) can be used outside the intentions of the user.

In a study of twenty-something Facebook users in Toronto, Raynes-Goldie (2010: 2) argues that engaging with new media in the 'age of Facebook' comes at a cost: 'In the same way many people give away some of their personal information in exchange for the perks of an Air Miles card, users of Facebook benefit from their use of the site at the cost of their privacy.' Raynes-Goldie goes on to argue that while the young people in her study were clearly concerned about privacy, they were concerned about a particular form of privacy: 'social privacy' rather than 'institutional privacy'. That is, her participants were more concerned about controlling access to personal information (social privacy) rather than how Facebook itself, as a corporate entity (or indeed, the NSA) used that information (institutional privacy). The implications for social privacy, then, revolve around what photos one's ex-partner can access (as per Raynes-Goldie's example) or what a future employer can access, or, as was common amongst my own participants and also those in the study by West et al. (2009), what one's parents can access.

In my own research, while there was some sensitivity to issues of institutional privacy, participants also actively described a much stronger focus on 'social privacy', expressing concerns over what family, friends, co-workers and other people in their lives could access rather than how Facebook as an institutional entity accessed and made sense of their private disclosures. One of my participants, who I called Brad (20), explained his embarrassment when he realised he had failed to properly conceptualise his own 'social privacy', when his workmates were able to access an intimate conversation he had with a girl on Facebook:

> The boys at work give me a lot of shtick. We're all best mates as well as on Facebook... I remember I was having a conversation with a girl [on Facebook], and y'know, she was dropping the 'I love yous' and stuff like that, so my boss proceeded to print out my comments page and y'know, do like a little role-play re-enactment when I walked in [to work] the next day. So um, it was quite embarrassing, but y'know... you just have to laugh... I suppose when it's happening you don't really think that everyone can read what you're saying. (Brad, 20)

This embarrassing scenario described by Brad is a particularly useful example of how interactions on Facebook trouble conceptualisations of space, in terms of 'public-ness' and 'private-ness', and also in terms of how this troubling relates to strategies of impression management. Brad describes how easy it was to sometimes 'forget' about his actual (compared to his imagined) audience on Facebook, and how slippages like this one work to shape his strategies of impression management. Later in the interview, Brad explained that after this incident he was particularly cautious when it came to personal conversations on Facebook, ensuring they took place through a one-on-one IM conversation or via an inbox thread, visible only to the participants in the conversation rather than the broader network of Friends. This audience segregation failure also made Brad consider what was appropriate for the quasi-public space of 'the wall', for which there was a controlled audience (Friends only), but where, up until this incident, there was no regular *imagining* of that audience. In other words, Brad previously didn't consider exactly who had access to his profile – and the wall specifically – each time he posted to that wall or read a message posted there by one of his Friends. Embarrassing incidents like this one – embarrassing precisely because there was a failure in impression management – worked to shape Brad's future strategies for impression management, and made him rethink his usage of the 'devices' of identity available to him on Facebook. Despite this focus on what Raynes-Goldie describes as 'social privacy', ongoing research is needed here to determine whether or not the recent 2013 NSA revelations described above, which received global news coverage, have increased awareness of 'institutional privacy' concerns.

In their study of undergraduate students in the US, Stutzman et al. (2012) found that Facebook users are increasingly conscious of their social privacy, and that public disclosures, accessible to anyone with a Facebook account who visits the user's profile, are decreasing, whereas private disclosures to a closed group of Friends, managed through the friending and de-friending process, are increasing. Stutzman et al. argue that Facebook regularly undertakes 'system changes' (such as changing the profile to the timeline) to increase disclosures. Whether public or private, these disclosures (status updates, uploaded images, location tagging, friending, and so on) are all, of course, visible at Raynes-Goldie's (2010) institutional level (by Facebook), but a stronger sense of control over social privacy, through the ability to disclose only to specific subsets of Friends, appears to increase in-network, or 'private', disclosure.

When the timeline was introduced, Lessin (2011) actually encouraged users to go back and fill in gaps or important events that were not captured previously: 'If important parts of your story aren't included on your timeline, you can go back to when they happened and add them.' The sharing interface categorises these as 'life events' with five categories, in this order: 1) work and education, 2) family and relationships, 3) home and living, 4) health and wellbeing, and finally 5) travel and the rather nebulous 'experiences'. I would align these categories with my earlier framing of critical moments. Within each category are a series of sub-categories. In work and education (apparently the first and most important domain of life events), for instance, the user is prompted to add new jobs, retirement, new schools, study abroad, volunteer work, and military service. In the family and relationships category, sub-categories include new relationships, engagements, marriages, new children, new pets, the end of relationships, the death of loved ones, and so on. Other Facebook users can be tagged here, and a geo-location and a date can also be added, along with a 'story', crafting an extended narrative around the life event.

The ability to tag other users in these life events, which I am conceptualising here as critical moments in transition narratives, and also in the more everyday or mundane moments (images, status updates, trips to the cinema and so on), allows users to construct a narrative, or a performance of identity, not just about themselves but about other users. While Facebook does allow users to enable a setting whereby they must 'approve' disclosures in which they are tagged before they appear on that user's timeline, this is not the default setting. Thus, the digital trace that is crafted around an individual is also subject to disclosures made by others, which can subsequently be linked to yet more others, further complicating the extent to which individuals have control over their own narrative on Facebook. Even on earlier social network sites like Friendster and MySpace, 'testimonials' or comments from Friends were always part of the profile dynamic (boyd, 2006), but Facebook's timeline anchors these disclosures and ties them to users more directly through tagging.

If previous social network sites and past iterations of the Facebook profile were imbued with a quasi-ephemeral quality as disclosures slipped into obscurity over the years, falling further and further into the profile's history, the Facebook timeline interrupts that ephemerality. The timeline also complicates and obfuscates privacy concerns. The ability to move back through the timeline easily, with disclosures (both critical and mundane) laden with metadata on location and linked to other users, means that the digital trace that manifests on Facebook becomes complicated and connected in ways that individual users cannot fully perceive or contextualise. At the institutional level, both in terms of how Facebook makes use of the disclosures that constitute the site for advertising and other purposes, and in terms of how private disclosures are surveilled by governments, the terrain is unclear, and will likely continue to be so. What is clear thus far, however, is that individual users are more concerned with what Raynes-Goldie (2010) describes as social privacy rather than institutional privacy; that is, privacy from other users and people in their everyday lives rather than from abstract institutions. At the level of social privacy, then, the focus is on the everyday interactions and disclosures that constitute social network sites, both critical and mundane.

The Mundane and the Fateful; the Visible and the Invisible

The process of transition or growing up is punctuated and shaped by 'critical moments' (Thomson et al., 2002) such as moving out of home, starting employment, entering into a relationship, and beginning tertiary study. In Giddens' terms, the 'fateful moment' (from which Thomson et al. borrow in conceptualising the critical moment) is 'highly consequential for a person's destiny' (1991: 121), and should be understood as distinct from but certainly affecting the inconsequential goings-on of daily life. When these moments are articulated and made visible on social network sites, and then subsequently archived by way of the persistent nature of these spaces, they become key markers in a mediated growing-up story for young people. Although the narratives made visible on Facebook are limited, they can potentially represent various perspectives and voices while marking out a complex, detailed personal history. I would argue that the question of whether or not these narratives represent 'real' or 'authentic' accounts of growing up is the wrong kind of question. Even if presented in a particularly optimistic or 'air brushed' way, unless entirely fabricated and fictional, these are lived accounts of life. Sharing, discussing and remembering critical moments become important activities on social network sites, punctuating – as with offline experiences of growing up – the more mundane, everyday experiences of life that often attract criticism and derision when mediated online, like sharing what one has for lunch, or posting an update about feeding the cat.

In addition to the 'life events' identified by Facebook as critical moments, and the more mundane moments that attract the most derision, there are also invisible critical moments that are nonetheless potentially attached in some way to the use of social network sites. For one of my participants, who I called Silvia (15), shifting from MySpace to Facebook was actually motivated by a tragedy in her life and a subsequent need to focus more on family rather than her friends who hung out on MySpace:

> *Int.*: And what stopped you recently from using it [MySpace] 'religiously' like you said?
>
> *Silvia*: I don't know … things just changed. My dad passed away… I got my boyfriend and everything, who I'm still with. And I sort of just became more family oriented. I moved on to Facebook where they all were. I don't live with most of my sisters.

Losing her father was obviously a critical moment for Silvia, and prompted a reordering of narratives and priorities. After the death of her father, and the subsequent focus on family and the intensification of her relationship with her boyfriend, Silvia's patterns of engagement with social network sites began to change. Thomson (2007: 103) explains that bereavement can be 'an opportunity for reflection and growth' for young people, while also serving to draw the attention of the researcher towards 'how and why certain events are perceived as critical'. That the loss of Silvia's father prompted her to disinvest in MySpace and engage with family through Facebook is therefore significant, even though the death of her father may or may not be made visible online (perhaps through supportive wall posts from friends, for instance). Regardless, her use of social network sites can be mapped onto a time of change and upheaval for Silvia, where her priorities shifted especially towards her boyfriend and her sisters.

This example further develops my earlier argument around the enmeshed relationship between the online and the offline, if any such distinction is now even useful. Silvia did not announce on Facebook that her father had died, although it should be noted that the timeline interface does invite these kinds of disclosures around critical moments. However, the death of her father did change her motivations for using social network sites, and through the interview scenario, this link became clear.

Conclusion and Implications for Research

McLeod (2000) points out that the 'in process' nature of identity – especially for young people – makes studying identity particularly difficult. McLeod suggests that longitudinal research provides scholars with the most 'substantial body of evidence for interpreting processes of identity formation and identity practices' (2000: 49), while also being one of the most notoriously difficult forms of research to sustain. McLeod invokes the metaphor of 'the self as a magic writing pad', that consists of two layers: 'a soft wax slate and over it a thin, transparent leaf of paper [...that] all the time receives new inscriptions upon it without having the old ones erased' (Nielsen in McLeod, 2000: 51). McLeod goes on to argue that this metaphor is a useful way of thinking about the formation of identity, especially for longitudinal researchers, who are more interested in that deeper understanding of identity as a long-term project. I would argue that Facebook's timeline represents a digital version of this 'magic writing pad', where Facebook users are already tracing and archiving their experiences of transition, recording and making visible critical moments which punctuate their more mundane, everyday lives.

Conceptualising the profiles that constitute social network sites as transition texts, as manifestations of Giddens' (1993) 'reflexive project of self', gives researchers a rich terrain of content to explore. However, there are clear methodological and ethical complications and limitations, especially around consent and access to these spaces and reliance on self-reports of transition experiences (see Robards, 2013 for a detailed reflection on the challenges I encountered in my own empirical research into how young Australians use and produce social network sites).

From a broader sociological perspective, these profiles are truly significant, detailed records of transition experiences that could potentially help youth researchers better understand reflexive identity-work and the challenges of growing up. However, as Silvia's example makes clear, conceptualising these profiles as a digital trace of transition is only effective when coupled with more traditional modes of sociological inquiry, like interviews, to give the narratives mediated online some context, and to provide opportunities for the invisible critical moments – fateful moments that are not articulated and made visible online, either publicly or privately – to be identified and included in the participant's narrative. Most importantly, beneath the broader sociological potential here should be a recognition that Facebook profiles can both represent and also actually constitute important and sometimes deeply personal experiences, memories and moments. Researchers, corporations, governments and users should treat them as such.

Acknowledgements

I thank Prof. Andy Bennett for his constructive feedback on versions of this chapter, and my research participants for their time and insights.

References

Bowker, GC (2007) 'The Past and the Internet', in J Karaganis (ed.) *Structures of Participation in Digital Culture*. New York: Social Sciences Research Council, 20–36.

boyd, d (2006) 'Friends, Friendsters and MySpace Top 8: Writing Community into Being on Social Network Sites', *First Monday*, 11(12): http://firstmonday.org/htbin/cgiwrap/bin/ojs/index.php/fm/article/view/1418/1336

boyd, d (2011) 'Social Network Sites as Networked Publics: Affordances, Dynamics, and Implications', in Z Papacharissi (ed.) *A Networked Self: Identity, Community, and Culture on Social Network Sites*. New York: Routledge, 39–58.

Bruns, A (2006) 'Towards Produsage: Futures for User-Led Content Production', in F Sudweeks, H Hrachovec & C Ess (eds) *Proceedings from the Cultural Attitudes Towards Communication and Technology Conference*. Tartu, Estonia.

Dubrofsky, RE (2011) 'Surveillance on Reality Television and Facebook: From Authenticity to Flowing Data', *Communication Theory*, 21(2): 111–129.

Giddens, A (1991) *Modernity and Self-Identity: Self and Society in the Late Modern Age*. Stanford, CA: Stanford University Press.

Giddens, A (1993) *The Giddens Reader*. London: Macmillan.

Greenwald, G & MacAskill, E (2013) 'NSA Prism Program taps in to User Data of Apple, Google and Others', *The Guardian*, Friday 7 June: http://www.theguardian.com/world/2013/jun/06/us-tech-giants-nsa-data

Hogan, B (2010) 'The Presentation of Self in the Age of Social Media: Distinguishing Performances and Exhibitions Online', *Bulletin of Science, Technology & Society*, 30(6): 377–386.

Jurgenson, N (2012) 'The IRL Fetish', *The New Enquiry*: http://thenewinquiry.com/essays/the-irl-fetish (accessed 20 July 2012).

Kim, Y (2010) 'Service of Control?: A Critical Thought of the "Social" in Social Network Services', *Communications & Convergence Review*, 2(2): 104–112.

Lessin, SW (2011) 'Tell Your Story with Timeline', *Facebook Blog*, Friday 23 September: https://www.facebook.com/blog/blog.php?post=101502896 12087131 (accessed 8 May 2013).

Livingstone, S (2008) 'Taking Risky Opportunities in Youthful Content Creation: Teenagers' Use of Social Networking Sites for Intimacy, Privacy and Self-Expression', *New Media & Society*, 10(3): 393–411.

McLeod, J (2000) 'Metaphors of the Self: Searching for Young People's Identity through Interviews', in J McLeod & K Malone (eds) *Researching Youth*. Hobart: Australian Clearinghouse for Youth Studies, 45–58.

Mendelson, AL & Papacharissi, Z (2011) 'Look at Us: Collective Narcissism in College Students Facebook Photo Galleries', in Z Papacharissi (ed.) *A Networked Self: Identity, Community, and Culture on Social Network Sites*. New York: Routledge, 251–273.

Neighbors, C, Spieker, CJ, Oster-Aaland, L, Lewis, MA & Berstrom, RL (2005) 'Celebration Intoxication: An Evaluation of 21st Birthday Alcohol Consumption', *Journal of American College Health*, 54(2): 76–80.

Notley, T (2009) 'Young People, Online Networks, and Social Inclusion', *Journal of Computer-Mediated Communication*, 14: 1208–1227.

Pearson, E (2009) 'All the World Wide Web's a Stage: The Performance of Identity in Online Social Networks', *First Monday*, 14(3): http://firstmonday.org/htbin/cgiwrap/bin/ojs/index.php/fm/article/view/2162/2127

Peeters, H (2007) 'The Networked Self: Autofiction on MySpace', *Image & Narrative*, 19: http://www.imageandnarrative.be/inarchive/autofiction/peeters.htm

Pinch, T (2010) 'The Invisible Technologies of Goffman's Sociology from the Merry-Go-Round to the Internet', *Technology and Culture*, 51(2): 409–424.

Raynes-Goldie, K (2010) 'Aliases, Creeping and Wall Cleaning: Understanding Privacy in the Age of Facebook', *First Monday*, 15(1): http://firstmonday.org/htbin/cgiwrap/bin/ojs/index.php/fm/article/view/2775/2432

Robards, B (2012) 'Leaving MySpace, Joining Facebook: "Growing Up" on Social Network Sites', *Continuum: Journal of Media and Cultural Studies*, 26(3): 385–398.

Robards, B (2013) 'Friending Participants: Managing the Researcher–Participant Relationship on Social Network Sites', *Young: Journal of Nordic Youth Research*, 21(3): 217–235.

Sessions, L (2009) '"You Looked Better on MySpace": Deception and Authenticity on Web 2.0', *First Monday*, 14(7): http://firstmonday.org/htbin/cgiwrap/bin/ojs/index.php/fm/article/view/2539/2242

Stutzman, F, Gross, R & Acquisti, A (2012) 'Silent Listeners: The Evolution of Privacy and Disclosure on Facebook', *Journal of Privacy and Confidentiality*, 4(2): 7–41.

Thomson, R (2007) 'A Biographical Perspective', in MJ Kehily (ed.) *Understanding Youth: Perspectives, Identities and Practices*. London: Sage.

Thomson, R, Bell, R, Holland, J, Henderson, S, McGrellis, S & Sharpe, S (2002) 'Critical Moments: Choice, Chance and Opportunity in Young People's Narratives of Transition', *Sociology*, 36(2): 335–354.

West, A, Lewis, J & Currie, P (2009) 'Students' Facebook "Friends": Public and Private Spheres', *Journal of Youth Studies*, 12(6): 615–627.

White, R & Wyn, J (2008) *Youth & Society: Exploring the Social Dynamics of Youth Experience* (2nd ed.). Melbourne: Oxford University Press.

White, R & Wyn, J (2013) *Youth and Society* (3rd ed.). Melbourne: Oxford University Press.

Wyn, J & White, R (1997) 'Youth Transitions', in *Rethinking Youth*. Sydney: Allen & Unwin, 94–119.

3
Young People and Mediated Private Space

Siân Lincoln (Liverpool John Moores University)

The role of private space in youth cultures has been little explored in youth cultural studies, yet it can be argued that for many young people private spaces such as their bedrooms play a central role in providing a context within which they can engage with the media as part of their everyday youth cultural practices. In this chapter I explore the ways in which young people use the realm of 'the private' as part of their everyday youth experiences and the role of the media in their navigation of both the public and private spheres between which they are constantly moving.[1] I argue that the media are a key resource for young people and their emerging adult identities, and that young people use the media as a resource through which they constantly reconfigure public and private space, marking out their identities. In this sense, I explore young people's use of 'private' spaces such as their bedrooms and social network sites (e.g. Facebook) using the concept of 'zoning' (Lincoln, 2004, 2005, 2012) to examine how young people navigate the blurred boundaries of public and private space and how they make those spaces meaningful to them. In this respect, I argue that private spaces of youth culture are inherently mediated and that this mediation is part of the complex series of online and offline interactions in which young people in contemporary society engage.

Looking back on some of the very early work on teenage girls and 'bedroom culture' (e.g. McRobbie & Garber, 1975) the media clearly play an important role in its construction. Reading magazines and listening to music were key activities in the cultural worlds of teenage girls, and engaging in these activities primarily took place within the confines of their bedrooms. Importantly too, this early work made reference to the interplay between public and private space (although these spheres were mostly isolated from one another). For example,

McRobbie & Garber (1975) document music as being primarily enjoyed by teenage girls through their active engagement in 'teeny bopper culture', a culture that was primarily shaped around the 'pop idol'. Along with record buying and record playing, the pop idol was adored and idolised through posters put up on the teenage girls' bedroom walls, as well as worshipped through the multiple articles, features and images found in the pages of their favourite teen magazines, such as *Jackie*. The pop idol provided teenage girls with a fantasy figure that played a starring role in their personal fantasy worlds of love and romance accessed through the medium of magazines, but enjoyed within the confines of the home.

While studies of teenage bedroom culture have been relatively scarce until fairly recently, those studies that do explore this domain also acknowledge and examine the role of media in young people's private spaces. Larson (1995), for example, argues that bedrooms provide a crucial site for young people, especially those experiencing their teenage years, because having a private domain within which they can shut themselves away from family, peers and so on means, they are able to engage in what Larson refers to as a more 'authentic' media experience. Further, Larson argues that 'it is in their solitary bedroom lives where media has some of its most significant functions' (p. 536). For example, the privacy the space affords young people allows them to listen to music that may be different from that of their peers and to explore and experiment with their own personal music tastes. In their bedrooms, young people can display, change and move around their musical tastes and preferences through posters and other related paraphernalia. Music, as well as film, television, literature and so on, provides young people with a range of resources from which identities are drawn, and music specifically is identified by Larson as a key resource for young people in the search for their 'real' identities – or what Larson refers to as the 'authentic' personal self (p. 536). However, while it may be argued that bedrooms can provide a private space for authentic representations of personal self – for example, using music as a resource – the 'politics' of bedrooms, which are situated in the family home, can be complex. For example, bedrooms might be shared with other siblings, entered regularly by adults (parents) when the occupant is or isn't around, or used as a space to hang out with friends. These scenarios will inevitably influence what identity 'markers' a young person will or will not make visible, for example a packet of cigarettes or a porn magazine may be hidden out of sight of parents, or an 'embarrassing' CD or DVD hidden out of view of friends. The 'basics' found in a bedroom, such as carpets, furniture, wallpaper and so on, may be chosen and paid for by a parent. Even if such items are selected in consultation, the young occupants still have to work on the representation of their 'authentic' selves in their bedrooms within what are already specified parameters (e.g. a particular colour carpet or style of furniture). Therefore, the extent to which the bedroom can be understood as a real or 'authentic' identity space for young people is up for debate.

Steele & Brown (1995), writing in the same year as Larson, were similarly interested in mediated bedroom experiences. Much like Larson, they were interested in the ways young people use the media to inform their identities and to construct their social worlds. Their research highlights the many ways in which the media have become embedded into the everyday, ordinary lives of young people. Importantly, in their study, young people's use of the media is documented as ongoing, never static, and the ways in which they draw on it in the construction of their identities is circuitous and governed by young people's lived experiences, both inside and outside the home (p. 557). This means that as young people encounter different social and cultural experiences, their media practices shift and change accordingly. In reference to young people's bedrooms specifically, Steele & Brown argue that the media practices in which young people engage in these private spaces are often complex and are characterised by a continual process of selection, interaction and application. As components in the process of making a bedroom, 'selection' refers to the ways in which young people choose which media to engage in from an ever-changing selection (p. 558), 'interaction' refers to 'the cognitive, affective, and behavioural engagement with media' and the cultural meanings that are produced from this interaction (p. 558), and 'application' refers to 'the "concrete ways" in which young people use the media in their everyday lives' (p. 559), how they become an established part of their daily lives and routines (p. 551).

More recent studies on teenage bedroom culture have also attempted to grapple with the complexities of teenage private space and the role that the media play in these constructions. Elsewhere, I have argued that a medium such as music is often at the core of how young people feel about, relate to and make sense of their own personal space and identity (Lincoln, 2004, 2005). In re-assessing the significance of 'bedroom culture' in the lives of ordinary 'everyday' young people in contemporary Western society I put forward the concept of 'zoning' as a framework through which to capture the contemporary nature of bedroom culture and to understand how 'bedroom culture' can be a mediated experience for those who occupy those spaces. The chapter will discuss the concept of 'zoning' later, but here I offer a way to explore how young people manage their personal space and identity, both as individuals and collectively with friends and peers, and how music, among other media forms, provides an important 'mediator' in the context of the often complex negotiations that young people find themselves working through.

For Kearney (2007) and others (e.g. Bloustien & Peters, 2011; Harris, 2001), recent developments in new media technologies, including accessibility, affordability and usability, have led to an increase in 'domestic cultural productivity' (p. 127) and the 'circulation of media texts' (p. 127) beyond the boundaries of the domestic sphere. The PC is noted particularly by Kearney as a significant piece of technology that has transformed the cultural lives of young people, alongside access to the internet. In addition, the increasing portability of information technology hardware – for example, through the development of laptops, tablets, netbooks and so on – has meant that young people's use of technology is not necessarily dictated by the shared family space such as the living room, office or dining room in which the technology is located and where, in the early days, such a piece of technology, much like a TV set, was likely to be placed. In shared locations such as this, a young person's use of a PC or the internet would potentially be under the watchful eye of other family members and time-restricted given its shared usage. The portability of media technologies such as a laptop means that the spaces of use can potentially be decided by the user and thus there is no longer the limitation of a fixed, shared space. For Bloustien & Peters (2011), location, and particularly private spaces such as bedrooms, is paramount in the lives of young people who make and produce music, providing them with a context in which their musical activities can be 'practiced, rehearsed and improved' (p. 135); in some cases where young people had their own bedrooms, they were able to turn them into a kind of 'pseudo-recording' studio (p. 135) where they could write and perform. Access to the internet within bedrooms opened up 'other' musical spaces for them in that the music made in their bedrooms could essentially be played, recorded, edited, marketed and heard – all from one's bedroom. Further, the ability to plug in headphones and to ensure that noise is contained means that potentially the bedroom can be a music-production space that is always open; something no doubt of great appeal to an 'ever-on' generation.

While the example of the bedroom studio is a very specific one of a media-rich space in which young people are engaging with a particular medium, it is fair to say that media technologies of varying kinds in the contemporary Western world infiltrate many ordinary, everyday young people's lives and, as a part of that, they also infiltrate private space. Televisions, DVD players, music playback technology, iPods and other mobile listening devices, mobile phones and so on are commonly part of contemporary teenage culture and, almost by default, of teenage bedroom spaces too. Indeed, such technologies, and the access to culture that they afford, have contributed significantly to the blurring, even collapsing, of public and private boundaries whereby we now see young people through media technologies opening and closing a variety of different cultural spaces and 'zones' (Lincoln, 2004), which reflects the 'flitting' nature of their cultural and social interactions (Bennett, 1999). The image of the teenager moving from technology to technology in an attempt to keep up with and be engaged in their social networks is indeed a common sight, both inside and outside the home.

Private Space Beyond the Bedroom

It is worth focusing on young people's 'flitting' interactions as part of their youth cultural practices in a little more depth here. This 'flitting' is by no means superficial, as the word might suggest, but in fact demonstrates the constant re-articulations of space, culture and identity that young people engage in as they live out their youth cultural lives in both the public and private realm. Further, and as highlighted in much of the literature on young people and bedroom culture to date, the media are a key resource in the construction of young people's identities, and their use of the media is an ongoing, never static, part of their everyday experiences and social interactions. Young people continue to engage with 'old' as well as 'new' media in the space of their bedrooms (Lincoln, 2012), and the bedroom continues to act as a 'hub' of media activity whereby we see 'in action' a continual interplay of the public and private sphere through an array of media technologies, the 'zones' of which are opening and closing all the time. But perhaps one of the most significant developments in recent years is the rise of social media or, more specifically, social network sites that have very much become an integral part of the experiences of growing up in the Western world, significantly changing the ways in which young people are using and negotiating different spaces in articulating their youth cultural affiliations, cultures and identities.

In many ways the ubiquity of social network sites in contemporary youth cultures has (re)ignited discussions around notions such as 'space' and 'the private' and their significance in contemporary youth cultures.

Traditionally such notions have been used to describe youth cultural activities in the domestic sphere or more specifically within young people's bedrooms, but the onset of social media that has effectively opened up another 'private' domain in which young people are living out their lives – and the fact that many 'private' interactions take place in the public domain of social networks such as Facebook – have brought the meaning of 'the private' in youth cultures into question (boyd, 2008a; boyd & Hargittai, 2010). However, there is now a growing body of scholarly work that is particularly interested in how notions of 'space' and 'privacy' (as well as other notions such as identity, community, individualisation and so on) are being re-articulated in the context of youth culture, particularly through social network media (boyd, 2006, 2008b; boyd & Ellison, 2007; Hodkinson, 2007; Livingstone, 2009; Pearson, 2009; Sessions, 2009). In addition to this, there is also a growing body of work that is more specially focused on exploring the extent to which we might understand social network sites as an extension of a young person's bedroom and use a 'bedroom metaphor' to explain young people's online social networks and interactions (Hodkinson & Lincoln, 2008; Lincoln, 2012; Mallan, 2009; Robards, 2010, Robards & Bennett, 2011).

The use of spatial metaphors is not particularly new in thinking about young people's uses of the internet and internet communication historically, however. Brown et al. (1994), Chandler & Roberts-Young (1998), Reid-Walsh & Mitchell (2004) and Walker (2000), while mainly concerned with individual web pages, examined the ways in which these pages were decorated and personalised by their 'owners' and how they came to represent almost a virtual extension of their bedrooms, for example in terms of the choice of 'wallpaper' used to decorate their virtual and physical personal space. Similarly, Hodkinson (2007) and Hodkinson & Lincoln (2008) were concerned with weblogs or online journals. They (and later Lincoln, 2012) argue that the 'bedroom' metaphor provides a useful theoretical framework for revealing the multiplicities of youth cultural lives: how young people use particular spaces, their identities, 'performances', interconnections and communications. The 'virtual bedroom' metaphor allows one to make sense of young people's use of online spaces as a 'virtual version' or extension of their actual bedroom, a personal space that they can 'mark out' as their own or a private 'social space' where they can 'hang out' with a group of selected friends (Hodkinson & Lincoln, 2008). For example, in the case of Hodkinson & Lincoln, users of online sites such as LiveJournal, a diary-like application in which users reflect 'upon their everyday experiences, thoughts and emotions' (p. 27), would often talk about such spaces as sites of ownership and control using the analogy of their bedroom. In describing her LiveJournal page, Kate said that 'It's like being given a room – and you can furnish it the way you want and paint it the way you want – and you make it your room' (p. 34). Kate draws on the analogy of a room to explain how her LiveJournal page starts out as a simple and generic format and layout, and is personalised and made unique through its 'furnishing': its decoration through, for example, 'a range of images, symbols and background designs symbolic of different facets of [her] identity' (p. 35), much as a generic, four-walled bedroom space would be.

More recently, and in considering the use of social network sites specifically, Pearson applies the 'glass bedroom' metaphor, that helpfully captures the tenuous nature of private space in such domains as negotiated by users and the partiality of the boundaries between public and private space:

> The metaphor can take a number of forms, but at its core it describes a bedroom with walls made of glass. Inside the bedroom, private conversations and intimate exchanges occur, each with varying awareness of distant friends and strangers moving past transparent walls that separate groups from more deliberate and constructed 'outside' displays. The glass bedroom itself is not an entirely private space...it is a bridge that is partially private and public, constructed online through signs and language. (Pearson, 2009)

The 'glass bedroom' metaphor offers a way to explore multiple and shifting subjectivities of young people using social network sites such as MySpace and Facebook. In Pearson's metaphor, the walls of the bedroom are made of glass. Inside the four glass walls, she suggests, 'conversations and intimate exchanges' take place, and those who are inside the glass bedroom will be aware that there are friends, acquaintances, etc., passing by the bedroom walls in some way all of the time (afforded entrance through 'friending', as boyd (2008a) and Robards (2010) would argue). The walls, despite being made of glass, give some sense of the separation from the outside world and an additional sense that, theoretically, with the metaphorical bedroom door shut, the conversations taking place within the bedroom cannot be heard by those outside it. However, the glass walls afford some level of visibility, which may be outside the control of the occupant, unless they were to draw a metaphorical curtain over the glass walls which would privilege complete invisibility or privacy (for instance, through modifying the settings on Facebook). Nonetheless, the glass material used to construct the walls does not assure complete privacy over the space. As Pearson says, there is a blurring of the front and back stage; of public and private.

The 'bedroom metaphor', then, is argued to be useful in a number of ways for thinking about how young people use 'personal' and 'private' domains, such as their bedrooms and social network sites, and the integration of the public, private and virtual domains that make up their everyday social and cultural interactions. It is also a useful metaphor for thinking about how notions such as 'personal' and 'private' are reconfigured in 'private space' within this new media context. So how do young people negotiate the complexities of using multiple personal and private spaces online and offline as well as manage their ever-shifting subjectivities that adapt and change in accordance with the context of each space?

In exploring this multi-functionality and the intricacies of young people's re-articulations of their private online and offline space, I engage with the concept of 'zoning' (Lincoln, 2004, 2012) as a framework through which one may document and understand some of the complex uses of such private spaces by young people as integral to their youth cultural lives. 'Zoning' works on a number of levels to capture young people's experiences of growing up and 'becoming' adult. As the classic youth cultures literature attests, the notion of 'not quite fitting in' is part and parcel of the youth experience and, indeed, youth cultural practices are deemed one of the key ways in which young people try to make sense of their place in the world and their emerging identities within it (see, for example, Erikson, 1968; also France, 2007; Furlong & Cartmel, 2006; Griffin, 1993). 'Zoning' is one way in which we can make sense of the ways in which young people use personal and private spaces such as bedrooms and social network sites as they try to work out and negotiate their own personal 'fitting in'. As a theoretical framework, 'zoning' enables the researcher to explore how young people negotiate their way through the 'blurring' between different spheres, through the cultural choices they make and the contexts in which they make them. Additionally, 'zoning' can capture the ways in which young people negotiate their relationship to the public sphere, their social relations, the tensions and struggles between their individualised media use and broader commercial interests, and the regulation of their personal private spaces, not just within the context of the family but also in relation to wider media cultures.

In considering this idea further, I draw on Sonia Livingstone's work on the mediatisation of young people's cultural spaces, particularly in the domestic sphere. In this work, which considers the mediated experiences of young people in contemporary society, Livingstone calls for a 'revalorisation' of the private (2005: 12) as a binary opposite to the 'public', noting particularly that these two spheres, especially in the context of youth culture, cannot be considered as separate domains of influence. This is because, with the ubiquity of new media technologies, discourses around the blurring of public and private boundaries (and virtual boundaries can be added here too) have become synonymous with the contemporary youth experience.

Livingstone suggests that such blurring is characteristic of contemporary new media cultures and that the nature of this blurring needs to be understood in more sophisticated ways. In her revalorisation, she proposes that the blurring of public and private boundaries for young people can be understood in a more constructive manner as a series of 'intersections' between the personal sphere and the public sphere (the participation of young people in common culture and social relations), the economy (the penetration of youth cultures by commercial interests perpetuated by cultures of commercialism and individualisation) and the state (governing and regulating the media and young people's uses of them). In this context, then, young people are not only finding themselves drifting in and out of the 'blur' between the public and private sphere, but are also suspended within the complex 'web' of these intersections. On the one hand, they seek their individuality and, on the other, they seek commonality with their peers. The media play a key role in young people's lives as tools through which to navigate many of these complexities, albeit without an awareness of how young people's cultural choices are legitimated by the media and enmeshed within them. The concept of 'zoning', then, is an attempt to offer a framework, in the context of Livingstone's call for the revalorisation of 'the private', for understanding the role and significance of 'bedroom' spaces online and offline in the lives of contemporary youth as they work through these various intersections.

In the discussion that follows I draw on ethnographic data from a project entitled 'Youth Culture and Private Space' (Lincoln, 2012) to explore how 'zones' in young people's bedrooms and social network sites do not exist in isolation but rather overlap and interweave all the time, and are indeed an extension of one another. They are both visible and invisible, incorporating the material elements of bedroom space with the invisible flows of communication and information, which suggests that the bedroom is both a container of meaning *and* a portal of communication with varying levels of permanency.

Navigating the Public and Private: Zoning in Action

As noted earlier, young people in contemporary Western society are living out their daily lives through multiple spheres and are constantly involved in a series of negotiations with friends, peers and siblings as well as negotiating the boundaries between public, private, virtual, physical spaces. As Livingstone (2005) notes, young people often find themselves at the intersection of these spheres of influence, negotiating a different type of 'fitting in', depending on the sphere. Private space, whether in a physical bedroom or in a virtual realm, plays a key role in providing a site within which these negotiations can be worked through and, as explored above, the boundaries between 'private' virtual and physical spaces appear to be becoming increasingly blurred.

Discussions with a number of my participants revealed that young people themselves are by no means oblivious to this complex series of negotiations and in some cases demonstrated a real awareness of this constant shifting between the public and the private, particularly when thinking about how their uses of social network sites might in some way be considered an extension of their 'physical' bedroom space. Although MySpace is practically redundant today in comparison to Facebook and Twitter, references were frequently made to the site by my participants, who had used it in their earlier teenage years before eventually moving onto Facebook (Lincoln, 2012; Robards, 2012). The example below illustrates how young people work within the confines of the site (its technological affordances, for instance) to make the space meaningful to them, much as they would when 'zoning' their bedroom in particular ways to personalise it, make it meaningful and their own.

> *SL*: Did you kind of see them [social network sites] as an extension of your personal space?
>
> *Charlotte*: MySpace was more like that, 'cos you could change the layout and background how you wanted it and put music on it whereas Facebook isn't really like that, everyone has the same layout.
>
> *SL*: What did your MySpace page look like?
>
> *Charlotte*: It had all vintage frames and vintage wallpaper and some songs but I can't remember, I used to change them. But with Facebook you can't. You can change your photos and I do that and my profile picture.

Charlotte, aged 18, talked about MySpace in the past tense, as a site that she engaged with in her early teenage years and before she moved on to using Facebook. The ability to 'copy' the private space of her bedroom into her MySpace page, namely through its decoration and music, was of clear importance to Charlotte. At that time, Charlotte's cultural interests and social activities were emerging and changing all the time; she was continually having new experiences, therefore her online 'virtual bedroom' environment gave her the space to 'play around' with this emerging identity with an immediacy and visibility that she did not have in her 'physical' bedroom in the parental home. Further, as Charlotte got older she became more curious about social life in the public sphere and consequently she and her friends were engaging in a busier social life within the public realm. Social media and social network sites in particular provided her with a 'parallel' context within which these new social networks in the public sphere could be documented and nurtured and in which communication could be maintained outside of those social gatherings in the public realm. To this extent, then, contexts like MySpace provided Charlotte with the space to represent her interests and her identity as well as symbolising an 'opening up' of her social worlds beyond the confines of the bedroom.

What Charlotte reiterates in the discussion above is the importance of being able to change the layout of her MySpace, and subsequently her Facebook page, despite the restrictions that might be set, especially by the latter site. Being able to change the layout, change the songs that one is currently listening to, the photographs and so on is considered of key importance because this means that, much like the constant changes one experiences as a teenager, young people are able to document their emerging identities, new experiences, interactions and so on through social network sites. This is particularly pertinent in an age of social media that asserts a 'Look at me!' philosophy (Mallan, 2009; Orlet, 2007).

The layout of Charlotte's MySpace page described above mimicked the decoration of her bedroom space in which she had a number of vintage-style photo frames of varying shapes and sizes covering one of her bedroom walls. When I asked Charlotte whether this was a conscious 'mapping' of one space to another she replied 'I don't think it was deliberate', recognising that this might not have been a conscious decision but that there were indeed similarities in what the space looked like, and to some extent how it was being used. Charlotte also talked on a number of occasions about using photographs, first on MySpace and then on Facebook, and how she liked to change them and upload new ones, capturing a constant process of updating and upgrading her online identity, while her physical bedroom appeared to be a comparatively more 'static' experience (Hodkinson & Lincoln, 2008). In her bedroom, Charlotte also had a number of photographs of family and friends on display, as well as a number of empty frames in which she had not yet put photographs adorning the walls and bookshelves. Charlotte, as noted above, was very 'into' the vintage look, and a number of different-style photo frames could be found in her room, in collages on the wall or clustered on a bedside table to give that 'vintage', second-hand store look. Yet many of the frames did not contain photos. Charlotte explained that this was because 'I just don't want to put any photo in, I want to save it for a good one and then I'll change them [the old photos in frames to new photos].' Similarly, some of the frames around her bedroom had photos in, which she had not got round to changing or she had left up because she liked the picture.

There is, then, a certain temporality that defines how online and offline 'private' spaces are used by young people. In the space of her bedroom Charlotte has time to reflect upon what the space looks like, how it is arranged and what aspects of her life are represented. There is not this sense of 'immediacy' to change as there is in the context of her 'private' social network sites. When being displayed on her Facebook profile, for example, photographs such as those used for her profile picture have to be updated regularly, as they represent an identity 'currency' that needs to be quickly and regularly changed and exchanged, keeping up with the fast pace of the site itself. The Facebook interface means that uploading a photograph is quick and easy and can even now be done through mobile phones at any time if one has access to the internet. This is in contrast to taking a photograph, printing it off and then putting it into a frame on display in the physical bedroom. The photos she selects for her profile can be taken from an array of photos uploaded to the site which are easily interchangeable.

Lisa, 18 years old, also referred to photographs both in her 'physical' bedroom and on her Facebook page, and her discussion usefully illustrates how the medium of photography is used to 'mediate' different 'public' and 'private' identities across the virtual zone of Facebook and the physical zone of her bedroom (and often photos are uploaded from the bedroom onto Facebook):

SL: And have you got lots of photographs on your Facebook?

Lisa: Yeah, I've got absolutely loads, but if I'm on a night out and I take my camera, no one is allowed to see or delete the photos and they all go on Facebook.

SL: Right, OK.

Lisa: No matter what. You can end up with, one night I ended up with like 200 photos from one night out and they all went on and everyone got tagged in every photo they were in. And there were some attempts to un-tag them but they weren't coming off, and there were some hideous ones of me but they were part of that night, they had to be there kind of thing.

SL: Yes, yeah. So why do you think that's so important to you?

Lisa: I think it's down to my lack of ability to delete things again. Like when I went to America I took 1000 photos, I was there for two weeks and took 1000 photos and videos and I wouldn't delete any of them.

SL: Yeah?

Lisa: I only chose selected ones to get printed, but they're all there on CD, there's like four CDs. But I couldn't delete any of them 'cos they're all; they all meant something, part of that.

Lisa was an avid collector of photographs and her bedroom was covered in collages that included photographs of both family and friends. Lisa considered her bedroom space to be the place within which she 'documents' her ongoing life. As a self-proclaimed 'hoarder', Lisa's hoarding practices in her bedroom are carried into her world of social network sites, which she describes as being heavily populated with all sorts of applications, text and images (much like her bedroom). In the discussion above, Lisa talks about how, on nights out, she documents the whole evening by taking photographs, then she uploads them all onto Facebook. Like the content of her bedroom, Lisa's representation of her night out can be considered 'authentic' because she claims not to edit or cut any of the photographs she has taken: they are all put into an 'album' of that evening out documenting the night as it 'naturally' unfolded, capturing whatever states her and her friends would end up in. Lisa, in addition, was keen for her 'friends' to continue to experience and share the evening's events beyond the public context in which they took place and so she embarks on a process of 'tagging' whereby all of the people featured in the photographs who were captured on camera phone on the night out are named.[2] Nicholls (2009) argues that the role of social network sites as documented by Lisa is now an integral and important part of young people's going out experiences and that, in drinking cultures especially, the 'tagging' that Lisa embarks on is a common practice – for example, 'tagging' friends who are clearly drunk or perhaps getting themselves into embarrassing situations. Additionally, mobile technologies such as smartphones mean that a young person does not need to wait until they get home to upload their photographs. They can do it instantaneously from their phones, to their Facebook pages. This means that the photographs can be viewed in the public leisure space that they are occupying at the time, and then again back home at the end of the night either alone or with friends who have come back to wind down after a night of partying (Lincoln, 2004).

Conclusion

In the scenarios covered in this chapter, we see examples of the ways in which young people are navigating their way through different spaces, within which the boundaries between public and private are invariably blurred. Using the example of photographs used in different 'personal' spaces we are able to see how young people engage in different forms of 'zoning', depending on what identity they wish to display in which space, be it online or offline. In the examples above, photographs have different meanings in different 'personal' spaces and, while this meaning is in no way mutually exclusive (there is, of course, still pressure on young people to represent themselves in a particular kind of way if friends and peers ever enter their bedrooms), it does appear that bedrooms can, at times, provide a more meaning*ful* context for young people as a space of identity than their profiles on social network sites.

However, both domains require careful management of their content and both are, to some extent, 'worked upon' in that each represents a particular presentation of the self on- and offline, elements of which invariably interconnect. Further, as spaces that are 'zoned' by young people in an attempt to make such private spaces meaningful and personal, they can be intercepted by others. In the bedroom this can be by siblings or parents and in the virtual sphere through 'friends' (and perhaps siblings and parents too). As I have demonstrated with Lisa above, actions such as 'tagging' on Facebook mean that 'zoning' can be undertaken by the owner of that page, whereby they can represent their version of a night out and other social events. However, also through 'tagging', that particular representation of a night out is opened up to a much wider audience (friends of friends), subject to privacy settings. In this example, Lisa has extended her personal Facebook 'zone' to encompass other 'friends' and their pages and thus the porous boundaries of their 'private' online identities are exposed.

In many ways, then, a young person's bedroom provides an excellent context within which to explore mediated youth cultures. The cultural practices that take place within the bedroom are invariably informed by the media and indeed the boundaries of private space are pushed beyond the four walls of the bedroom through access to virtual spaces such as social network sites. As I have explored, for many young people, sites such as Facebook are regarded as 'extensions' of their private bedroom space in terms of them being a portal through which to represent a particular identity and to communicate with friends. But this extension of bedroom space beyond physical space also highlights the often complex negotiations that young people can encounter, not only in relation to growing up but in relation to the public and private spaces that they are constantly moving in and out of.

Notes

1. In this chapter I draw on ethnographic data collected for two research projects – my doctoral thesis, titled 'Private Space and Teenage Culture: Age, "Zones" and Identity' (2000–2003), and my monograph, *Youth Culture and Private Space* (Palgrave Macmillan, 2012) – that explore the role and significance of private spaces such as bedrooms in contemporary youth culture. Fifty participants, male and female, aged 12–22 years, from Liverpool and Manchester in the North-West of England, took part in the research. Methods included in-depth interviews (the majority of which took place in the participants' bedrooms, either on their own or with a small number of friends), observations and 'room tours' in which participants showed me around their rooms, photography to capture the highly visual nature of the space, and diaries in which to document what bedrooms were used for.
2. Tagging is a function of Facebook that allows you to 'tag' the faces of people who are your Facebook friends and thus creates a link to their profile that can then be viewed, depending on the privacy settings in operation.

References

Bennett, A (1999) 'Subcultures or Neo-tribes? Rethinking the Relationships between Youth, Style and Musical Taste', *Sociology*, 33(3): 599–617.

Bloustien, G & Peters, M (2011) *Youth, Music and Creative Cultures: Playing for Life.* Basingstoke: Palgrave Macmillan.

boyd, d (2008a) 'Facebook's Privacy Trainwreck: Exposure, Invasion and Social Convergence', *Convergence*, 14(1): 13–20.

boyd, d (2008b) 'Taken Out of Context: American Teen Sociality in Networked Publics'. PhD thesis: http://www.danah.org (accessed 11 October 2009).

boyd, d & Ellison, N (2007) 'Social Network Sites: Definition, History and Scholarship', *Journal of Computer-Mediated Communication*, 13(1): http://jcmc.indiana.edu/vol13/issue1/boyd.ellison.html (accessed 21 September 2010).

boyd, d & Hargittai, E (2010) 'Facebook Privacy Settings: Who Cares?', *First Monday*, 15(8): http://firstmonday.org/htbin/cgiwrap/bin/ojs/index.php/fm/article/view/3086 (accessed 29 January 2012).

Brown, J, Dykers, C, Steele, J, & White, A (1994) 'Teenage Room Culture: Where Media and Identities Intersect', *Communications Research*, 21(6): 813–827.

Chandler, D & Roberts-Young, D (1998) 'The Construction of Identity in the Personal Homepages of Adolescents': http://www.aber.ac.uk/media/documents/short/strasbourg.html (accessed 10 February 2006).

Erikson, EH (1968) *Identity: Youth and Crisis*. New York: Norton.

France, A (2007) *Understanding Youth in Late Modernity*. Maidenhead: Open University Press.

Furlong, A & Cartmel, F (2006) *Young People and Social Change: New Perspectives*. Buckingham: Open University Press.

Griffin, C (1993) *Representations of Youth: The Study of Youth and Adolescence in Britain and America*. Cambridge: Polity Press.

Harris, A (2001) 'Revisiting Bedroom Culture: New Spaces for Young Women's Politics', *Hecate*, 27(1): 128–139.

Hodkinson, P (2007) 'Interactive Online Journals and Individualisation', *New Media & Society*, 9(4): 625–650.

Hodkinson, P & Lincoln, S (2008) 'Online Journals as Virtual Bedrooms: Young People, Identity and Personal Space', *Young: Nordic Journal of Youth Research*, 16(1): 27–46.

Kearney, MC (2007) 'Productive Spaces: Girls' Bedrooms as Sites of Cultural Production', *Journal of Children and Media*, 1(2): 126–141.

Larson, R (1995) 'Secrets in the Bedroom: Adolescents' Private Use of Media', *Journal of Youth and Adolescence*, 24(5): 535–550.

Lincoln, S (2004) 'Teenage Girls' Bedroom Culture: Codes versus Zones', in A Bennett & K Kahn-Harris (eds) *After Subculture: Critical Studies in Contemporary Youth Culture*. Basingstoke: Palgrave Macmillan, 94–106.

Lincoln, S (2005) 'Feeling the Noise: Teenagers, Bedrooms and Music', *Leisure Studies*, 24(4): 399–414.

Lincoln, S (2012) *Youth Culture and Private Space*. Basingstoke: Palgrave Macmillan.

Livingstone, S (2005) 'In Defence of Privacy: Mediating the Public/Private Boundary at Home'. London. LSE Research Online: http://eprints.lse.ac.uk/archive/00000505 (accessed 9 November 2008).

Livingstone, S (2009) *Children and the Internet: Great Expectations, Challenging Realities*. Cambridge: Polity Press.

Mallan, K (2009) 'Look at Me! Look at Me! Self-Representation and Self-Exposure through Online Networks', *Digital Culture and Education*, 1(2): 51–56.

McRobbie, A & Garber, J (1975) 'Girls and Subcultures', in S Hall & T Jefferson (eds) *Resistance through Rituals: Youth Subcultures in Post-War Britain*. London: Hutchinson and Co., 209–223. Reprinted in A McRobbie (ed.) (1991) *Feminism and Youth Culture from Jackie to Just Seventeen*. London: Macmillan, 12–25.

Nicholls, J (2009) 'Young People, Alcohol and the News: Preliminary Findings for The Alcohol Education and Research Council': http://www.aerc.org.uk/insightPages/libraryIns0067.html (accessed 1 November 2009).

Orlet, C (2007) 'The Look at Me Generation', *The American Spectator*: http://spectator.org/archives/2007/03/02/the-look-at-me-generation (accessed 12 October 2010).

Pearson, E (2009) 'All the World Wide Web's a Stage: The Performance of Identity in Online Social Networks', *First Monday*, 14(3): http://firstmonday.org/htbin/cgiwrap/bin/ojs/index.php/fm/article/view/2162/2127 (accessed 30 January 2012).

Reid-Walsh, J & Mitchell, C (2004) 'Girls' Websites: A Virtual "Room of One's Own?"', in A Harris (ed.) *All About the Girl: Culture, Power and Identity*. Oxford: Routledge, 173–182.

Robards, B (2010) 'Randoms in My Bedroom: Negotiating Privacy and Unsolicited Contact on Social Networking Sites', *Prism*, 7(3): http://www.prismjournal.org/fileadmin/Social_media/Robards.pdf (accessed 30 January 2012).

Robards, B (2012) 'Leaving MySpace, Joining Facebook: Growing up on Social Network Sites', *Continuum: Journal of Media and Cultural Studies*, 26(3): 385–398.

Robards, B & Bennett, A (2011) 'MyTribe: Post-Subcultural Manifestations of Belonging on Social Networking Sites', *Sociology*, 45(2): 303–317.

Sessions, LF (2009) '"You Looked Better on MySpace": Deception and Authenticity on Web 2.0', *First Monday*, 14(7): http://firstmonday.org/htbin/cgiwrap/bin/ojs/index.php/fm/article/view/2539/2242 (accessed 30 January 2012).

Steele, JR & Brown, JD (1995) 'Adolescent Room Culture: Studying Media in the Context of Everyday Life', *Journal of Youth and Adolescence*, 24(5): 551–576.

Walker, C (2000) '"It's Difficult to Hide It": The Presentation of Self on Internet Home Pages', *Qualitative Research*, 23(1): 99–120.

4
Ending Up Online: Interrogating Mediated Youth Drinking Cultures

*Ian Goodwin (Massey University), Antonia Lyons
(Massey University), Christine Griffin (University of Bath) &
Tim McCreanor (Massey University)*

Across the Western world many young people are increasingly involved in normalised practices around heavy drinking, which they view as pleasurable, involving fun and being sociable (Lyons & Willot, 2008; McCreanor et al., 2005; Szmigin et al., 2008). Researchers have documented a range of factors that have contributed to this development, including the commodification of pleasure into commercialised packages, linked to a 'night time economy' increasingly central to the wealth of cities, that have been termed 'cultures of intoxication' (Measham, 2004) and 'intoxigenic environments' (McCreanor et al., 2008). The 'unfettered expansion of alcohol marketing' (Casswell, 2012: 483) appears to be a key contextual consideration here. While globally young people generally drink to intoxication more frequently than older drinkers (Babor et al., 2010), this is most likely in countries that have liberalised alcohol policy in ways that enhance access to alcohol (Huckle et al., 2012). Furthermore, although specific drinking practices clearly vary from nation to nation and across sociocultural contexts, the globalisation of alcohol marketing and moves towards increasingly similar legislative and regulatory regimes have contributed to a marked trend towards 'an increasing homogenization of drinking cultures across many [Western] countries' (Gordon et al., 2012: 3). The result is that hedonistic public displays of drinking to excess, while certainly not the norm for all young people or in all national contexts, have become much more mundane, and progressively more common in many young people's lives (Gordon et al., 2012). Drinking heavily as a source of shared pleasure, used to facilitate social interactions and enhance nights out, has become a greater part of youth social practices in a growing range of nations across the globe.

While drinking cultures have traditionally been locally bounded (Chatterton & Hollands, 2002), they are now increasingly mediated through online social networking practices. A burgeoning literature is documenting how young people now regularly share their drinking stories and practices online in words and pictures depicting drinking and drunken behaviour (by themselves and others) on social networking sites (e.g. Egan & Moreno, 2011; Fournier & Clarke, 2011; Ridout et al., 2012). Social networking sites (SNSs) differ from other online environments in that they are primarily utilised to 'articulate and make visible' (boyd & Ellison, 2007: 211) users' previously established social networks. That is, they are most often used as a means for developing online extensions of face-to-face relationships. This makes SNSs a key new arena for young people, one affording a degree of relative autonomy, where they can engage in the formation and enactment of social identities, and maintain valued social relationships with friends and their broader peer-group (boyd, 2007; Livingstone, 2008). At the same time SNSs create a unique hybrid of private and public space (Papacharissi, 2010: 138–144); in other words users' profile pages and intimate social connections on SNSs are mapped out across complex 'networked publics' (boyd, 2007: 124–126). Users are able to *share* their tastes and preferences, and to *display* their social connections in online identity performances. Moreover they can augment their private sphere of personal associations through connections to a wider range of associations, affiliations and interests. Facebook, for example, allows users to join myriad 'groups' dedicated to a wide range of specialist topics and areas of interest. The mediating technologies involved also introduce particular dynamics to social life online. Communication in SNSs leaves persistent and searchable traces of self-expression and social interaction, recorded through software and retrievable by other social actors, and exposes users to a range of 'invisible audiences' so that it becomes 'virtually impossible to ascertain all those who might run across our expressions in networked publics' (boyd, 2007: 126). These 'mediated' factors involved in 'ending up online' hold the potential, we argue, to alter the dynamics and consequences of drinking cultures, and introduce novel benefits and risks for young people.

While systematic research examining the extension of drinking cultures into the online environment is only just beginning, the technological affordances of web applications like Facebook certainly appear to offer many opportunities to extend and enhance the pleasures of heavy social drinking. For example, photos documenting nights out can easily be shared and, rather than simply being posted as abstracted artefacts for 'display', can become discursive resources to be actively drawn upon within friendship networks. That is, they can become the catalyst for social exchanges online. The telling and re-telling of 'good stories', often involving the recounting of supposedly 'negative' events (e.g. vomiting in public) in 'positive' ways, has always been a key factor in the social pleasures associated with drinking cultures. Stories about drinking and drunken behaviour are told and re-told amongst friends, playing a crucial role in identity construction (Lyons & Willot, 2008; McCreanor et al., 2005) and maintaining friendships (Griffin et al., 2009; Sheehan & Ridge, 2001). SNSs, however, offer a new user-led means for such stories to be narrated both via text and visually, to be shared and re-shared both asynchronously and in real time, stored and revisited, and made more or less permanently available to be searched for and drawn upon at will even in the (subsequent) physical absence of one's peers. To date Brown & Gregg have made the best attempt to document these new online pleasures. Taking issue with the 'pedagogy of regret' (2012: 357) that structures the way young women's binge drinking is framed by the dominant discourses of government policy initiatives, they highlight the fundamentally social dimensions that structure heavy drinking and its online display. Focusing on Facebook, they argue that status updates linked to upcoming social events, photo uploading, and the ensuing dissemination of albums the morning after 'reveal the anticipatory pleasures, everyday preparations and retrospective bonding involved in hedonistic and risky alcohol consumption' (Brown & Gregg, 2012: 357).

Despite their pleasures, youth drinking cultures involving heavy alcohol use have always introduced elements of harm and risk to young people. Short-term harms from alcohol use include alcohol poisoning, accidents, violence and absenteeism; longer term problems include liver and brain damage, diabetes, cancers, dementia and addiction (Babor et al., 2010). Globally alcohol accounts for 4.6 per cent of the burden of disease and a third of this falls within the age range 15–29 years (Rehm et al., 2009). The *mediated* nature of SNSs, however, overlays new forms of risk and new elements of potential harm. In blurring the divide between private and public space, between private identities and public personas, SNSs make drinking cultures far more 'visible', and do so in complex, uneven and unpredictable ways that are often difficult for users to control. In celebrating their lifestyles online, young people equally expose their activities to broader audiences that are both anticipated and unanticipated. In the context of drinking cultures, family (particularly parents), employers and the police spring to mind. The consequences of having one's hedonistic displays of excess more broadly depicted to such 'audiences'/'publics' complicate the notion of SNSs as an autonomous place of self-expression and (re)introduce a range of different power dynamics that young people must actively negotiate.

Here the technological affordances of SNSs, particularly the way they leave persistent and searchable traces of self-expression and social inter-action, can work to young people's disadvantage. While some of the 'negative' consequences of drinking (vomiting, passing out, even getting into violent encounters) are actively reworked in drunken narratives amongst friends into 'good stories' that facilitate social bonding (Griffin et al., 2009), when factors like digital photography mediate this process on SNSs there is a potential loss of control over the context in which such 'texts' are read, re-read, and shared (potentially ad infinitum). The meanings subsequently made of such behaviour, possibly years after the fact, can be radically different from those of the user's peer-group, and the potential consequences not always positive. The para-digmatic example, and one that has developed an almost mythic status regardless of the frequency with which it actually occurs, would be the employer refusing the young person a job after doing a Google-inspired 'social CV check'. The threat posed by such forms of 'context collapse' is particularly heightened for youth pursuing online activities that sit outside dominant social norms (see Lim et al., 2012).

While the risk of surveillance from 'unseen audiences' is perhaps most salient in popular culture, and arguably most well developed in the minds of young people themselves, the corporate commercial interests involved in SNSs cannot be overlooked and may well prove to be more fundamentally important to our understandings of mediated youth drinking cultures. The branded nature of life online in SNSs, both in terms of engaging with branded products and services and in terms of the self-as-brand (distinctions we discuss later), cannot easily be pigeonholed as *either* positive *or* negative for young people – that is, as *either* facilitating their ability to engage in self-governing identity formation and sociality *or* as manipulative and risk-producing. Rather it introduces, particularly in the context of drinking cultures, a complex interplay between pleasure, leisure, self-expression, sociality, commer-cial exploitation and possible harm.

Multi-national alcohol corporations have been well ahead of the curve in developing the potential of SNSs for commercial gain, perhaps because their marketing activities have traditionally been subject to intense regulatory scrutiny offline but have – so far at least – largely flown under the radar online (Jernigan, 2012). Nicholls has recently documented the extensive use of 'real-world tie-ins, interactive games, competitions and time-specific suggestions to drink' (2012: 1) in SNS alcohol marketing strategies. If we are to fully appreciate the role of drinking cultures in young people's lives, we must recognise that these sorts of heavily branded initiatives are successful precisely because they are actively appropriated by SNS users in constructing their profiles, in displaying their tastes and developing cultural capital, and in facilitating their social interactions and social lives. SNS games, for example, are valued by users primarily as a means for maintaining and enhancing relationships (Wohn et al., 2011). Nevertheless Nicholls argues that increasingly sophisticated SNS marketing strategies that utilise devices like gaming equally draw on additional technological affordances of SNSs, such as the ability for corporations to 'observe, analyse and direct' (2012: 4) conversations about brands 'in real-time' (p. 4), to thoroughly *normalise* daily alcohol consumption. This undermines policy initiatives and health-promotion campaigns seeking to moderate consumption due to health risks and social harms. Indeed Griffiths & Casswell (2010) found that young people actively drew on and shared alcohol-related branding and marketing on Bebo. They concluded that peer-to-peer transmission of commercial alcohol content created 'intoxigenic digital spaces' (2010: 525) that normalised heavy drinking.

Towards a Conjunctural Analysis of Mediated Drinking Cultures

In sum, the shift of drinking cultures into the online environments provided by SNSs introduces a complex array of novel, and potentially highly significant, social dynamics into the lives of young people, with both positive and negative outcomes. The problem is that such changes are still, despite the nascent literature reviewed above, not particularly well understood. They are also subject to competing models of inter-pretation, from a range of academic disciplines. Depending on one's disciplinary location and orientation, there is a tendency either to defend mediated drinking cultures as sites of empowered self-expression and sociality, or to point out their negative health implications and ties to marketing and corporate capital. The combination of new technol-ogy, drinking, and hedonistic displays of excess that structures young people's drinking cultures also makes the broader public and policy debate particularly prone to a range of moral panics that elide broader societal and structural factors, while locating the issues generationally as *purely* related to 'youth' as a problematic 'other', a factor Brown & Gregg describe as a 'significant ideological achievement' (2012: 365). Our own position is to argue, alongside others such as Robards & Bennett (2011), that despite the novelties of life online in SNSs, much could still be learnt from the past, from decades of sustained research into youth subcultures.

However, rather than engaging with debates over whether or not 'traditional subcultural models' still hold or 'post-subcultural models' ought to be applied (Robards & Bennett, 2011: 314–315), we argue for a return to the original impetus of the youth sub/cultures project as summarised by Hall & Jefferson (2006). We suggest that what is necessary here is to develop a symptomatic reading of mediated youth drinking cultures within the frame of a conjunctural analysis. In effect, this means attempting to develop a 'thick description' (Geertz, 1973, as cited in Hall & Jefferson, 2006: x) of the cultural phenomenon under study while connecting it to a 'general social and cultural historical analysis of the social formation' (2006: viii). The key question a conjunctural approach would ask is, simply, why now? Why has mediated youth drinking culture assumed a particular form, as a prominent and 'spectacular' aspect of global youth culture, at this moment, and how does this relate to the 'political, economic, and sociocultural changes' (2006: xiv) of the current time? Such a project is clearly ambitious, and we do not have the space here to explicate it in detail. Rather, we point to two productive conceptual orientations that a full conjunctural analysis of mediated youth drinking cultures could deploy, as a starting point for investigation. The first is to recognise that these practices can be understood as part of a wider consumer culture, with global reach, that stresses the importance of stylised self-presentations as a 'required' part of self-invention. The second, related, point is to acknowledge that this consumer culture, which has particular resonances for young people, increasingly valorises self-branding and celebrity as the epitome of 'successful' self-invention.

Stylised Self-Presentation as a Compulsory Societal Norm: Drinking Practices, Brands-as-Relationships and SNSs

As Griffin (2011: 255–256) has argued, any attempt to make sense of young people's contemporary social practices, public selves and social relationships should first acknowledge some fundamental shifts in the social order with direct implications for all identity work. It is now commonplace, verging on social scientific orthodoxy, to highlight profound structural and institutional shifts in the social formation within advanced industrial societies that have heralded the erosion of traditional anchors for personal and social identities (Beck, 1992; Giddens, 1991). Here key factors such as changes to traditional family forms and the decline of working class communities associated with weakening manufacturing industries are highlighted, and attention is drawn to the rise of 'consumption as a basis for the construction of identities' (Griffin, 2011: 55). Cut adrift from traditional ties in increasingly complex and dynamic 'late modern' societies, individuals are tasked with creating coherent biographies in a reflexive, ongoing project of self-invention (Giddens, 1991; see also Chapter 2 of this collection for more on Giddens' reflexive project of self). While individuals freely choose their identities, the project of crafting a self-identity becomes an *inescapable* issue:

> What to do? How to act? Who to be? These are focal questions for everyone living in circumstances of late modernity – and ones which, on some level or another, all of us answer, either discursively or through day-to-day social behaviour. (Giddens, 1991: 70)

In this light the nature of drinking cultures needs to be re-thought. For example, the 'good stories' associated with re-living nights out become much more significant, as they are tied to cementing intimate social connections in a context where sociologists (see Allan, 1998) argue that freely chosen friendships are most essential to the process Giddens (1991) describes. That is, they become less transitory and frivolous expressions of youthful self-obsession, and more tied to the *necessity* for social subjects to continually narrate a coherent sense of identity in the face of broader structural changes in society as a whole (changes we *all* must negotiate). Similarly, young people's willingness to continually and reflexively share their lives online becomes tied to the demand now placed upon all individuals to achieve a coherent sense of self. That is, young people's online self displays become a rational response related to recurrent and reflexive identity work, using an 'environment' readily available to them (and highly valued by them), as opposed to being a naïvely risky exercise in self-exposure, heedless of potential 'threats', driven solely by ephemeral or trivial pleasures.

In highlighting a greater freedom for subjects to choose their identity, theorists such as Giddens and Beck tend to offer a reasonably optimistic interpretation of such developments. Other theorists, however, characterise the current moment's concern with the 'free' and possessive individual as a crucial element of a broader neo-liberal conjuncture (Hall, 2011). In this respect, the requirement to produce a coherent biography of the self carries embedded within it powerful new forms of govern-mentality (Rose, 1999). Individuals are 'not merely "free to choose", *but obliged to be free*, to understand and enact their lives in terms of choice' (Rose, 1999: 87, original emphasis). Competent personhood becomes related to dominant discourses of self-expression and authenticity that demand we live our lives *as if* this was part of a biographical project of self-realisation in a social formation that affords free choices to all, choices that are to be realised 'through desire, consumption, and the market' (Rose, 1999: 87). Any failure to perform an authentic or socially acceptable self is reduced to a failure of the individual, with *structural* power relations determined through class, ethnicity and gender obscured or even wholly elided even if such demographic 'distinctions' may be played upon through marketing processes.

Rather than placing social 'civility' and 'self-gratification' in opposition, the requirement to display a distinctive and discerning subjectivity through heavily branded consumption, which offers a comprehensive 'matrix of lifestyle and social activities', effectively carries with it new moral and ethical responsibilities to lead a civil, virtuous life (Rose, 1999: 86). If, in relation to these processes, young people behave or appear in ways that are taken to be excessive, unhealthy, undisciplined or irresponsible, this is constituted as a *moral* failure of the *self* (Croghan et al., 2006; Griffin et al., 2009). This is why young people's 'spectacularly' hedonistic and increasingly mediated drinking cultures, with newly heightened visibilities, attract intense moral panic and become increasingly subject to concerted attention. This regulatory gaze overlooks their ties to more general processes of identity construction, and ignores the fact that heavy drinking is not confined, by any means, to 'youth'. This may also help explain why government policy discourses seeking to limit young people's consumption locate the problem at the level of individual responsibility, promote 'sensible' and 'moderate' drinking, and mobilise a pedagogy of regret with heavy moral overtones (Brown & Gregg, 2012). The gendered nature of the dominant policy discourses Brown & Gregg (2012) describe is also relevant here, as it is young women in particular who become the focus of concern and regulation.

While official policy discourse tends to marginalise the role of drinking cultures in the construction of self-identity and social relationships, the same certainly cannot be said of commercial interests. Indeed the societal changes described by Giddens (1991) and Beck (1992) have been enthusiastically endorsed and catalysed through the increasing importance of branding to the profession of marketing. Brands not only instil commodities with specific cultural meanings subsequently drawn upon in the process of utilising consumption for identity work.

Rather branding, which now permeates the life-world, actively makes use of the 'values, commitments, and forms of community sustained by consumers' (Arvidsson, 2005: 236). Thus a brand no longer simply refers to producers or to commodities, but to a 'propertied form of life to be realised in consumption' (ibid.: 244). A brand thus aims to become more intimately connected to social life in general. This heralds a new age of selling in which relationships and identity are the new mantra, with commerce moving beyond mere niche targeting to direct selling to individuals tailored to their co-created needs (Venkatesh, 1999; Viser, 1999). Such developments are key to understanding alcohol marketing practices that increasingly permeate contemporary media. Young people have become increasingly 'familiar' and 'comfortable' with alcohol brands as a result, and take up and use brands in identity work across both personal and social settings (McCreanor et al., 2005). For example, young people are easily able to name a drink that matches their personality, and in peer-groups alcohol marketing messages are seamlessly reproduced in collaborative, humorous co-constructions of their socialising (McCreanor et al., 2008). Thus, at the same time as dominant policy discourses hold young people individually and morally accountable for their drinking practices, the alcohol industry actively promotes drinking as a key part of building a youthful social identity.

This process has been going on for decades across various sites but is now being accentuated online, for example through the interactive games and competitions identified by Nicholls (2012), which we outlined earlier. These not only normalise alcohol consumption through increasing contact with brands, but develop and strengthen broader notions of branded identity work and the brand-as-relationship in novel and intensive ways. Branded messages (for example Nicholls's (2012) time-specific suggestions to drink) reach SNS users through the same technical mechanisms they use to maintain contact with their friends, for example through News Feed in Facebook, thereby materially instantiating the type of 'relationships' brands now seek to build with consumers in the software code of the system. If the corporations behind the brand know their audience well enough, and SNSs equally facilitate sophisticated mechanisms for them to achieve that goal, such messages will subsequently be taken up by users themselves, and then shared and re-shared, making any distinction between social interactions between friends and social engagement with brands more or less meaningless in the act of engaging with the user interface. Brands, ubiquitous for some time, potentially make even further inroads into the mundane and the everyday through such processes, becoming ever more intimately connected to reflexively forging identities in the quotidian flow of young people's lives. This intensification involves both temporal and spatial aspects.

By exploring the power and pervasiveness of such processes we do not mean to imply that they have uniform or predictable effects. Discourses of the 'possessive individual' constitute a core cultural logic of the current neo-liberal conjuncture (Hall, 2011), a conjuncture creating new forms of governmentality globally. However, such logics can drive differing effects. Neo-liberalism as a mode of politics, as a rationalisation for governing, as a new set of relationships between the governing and the governed, is recognisable as distinct sets of logics yet these become enacted and understood differently in different national contexts (see Ong, 2006 for a thorough analysis). Moreover, the specific contextual and structural factors suppressed or elided through such logics not only need to be recognised. They need to *return* as salient points of analysis in our 'thick descriptions' of mediated drinking cultures, particularly if their ties to broader social structures are to be fully teased out and understood. Specifically, we would argue for a need to ask much more discerning questions relating to ethnicity, gender, sexuality and social class; and argue for exploring how such factors influence young people's drinking practices, social lives and social identities despite them being interpellated as 'individuals with free choice' through dominant cultural logics. We already know, for example, that African-American youth are exposed to a disproportionately high amount of alcohol advertising in mainstream mediums such as television, magazines and radio in the USA (Center on Alcohol Marketing and Youth, 2012). How, then, do such discrepancies play out online and in relation to other national contexts and other ethnicities? Indeed the entire relationship between neo-liberalism and (post)colonialism (see Venn, 2009) really ought to be more fully considered in relation to mediated youth drinking cultures in different national contexts around the world. However, we end this chapter by pointing to another aspect of the current conjuncture that cuts across specific contexts, one that can be read as the culmination of the individualised logics of neo-liberalism we have so far described: the increasing pressure on young people to successfully perform a 'branded self', or the self-as-brand, and its ties to celebrity culture.

The Branded Self, SNSs, Drinking and Celebrity Culture

The requirement for highly stylised self-constructions in late modern societies involves, as we have outlined, an increasing investment in consumption as the locus of identity, and has been accompanied by the rise of a corporate branded culture that draws value from people's personal investments in this process. Brands seek to actively make use of consumers' social and identity work, to become brands-as-relationships. Identity work therefore becomes, under the conditions of a globalised neo-liberal consumer society, a form of unpaid 'immaterial labour' (Arvidsson, 2005: 239) that adds value to capitalist enterprise – thereby blurring distinctions between social and economic life, between production and consumption. Corporations attempt to exert control over branding through the active management of such 'free labour' so that it 'comes to produce desirable and valuable outcomes' (2005: 235) for capital accumulation. We have already discussed how such developments are instantiated materially within the software code of SNSs, and their broader relationship to mediated youth drinking cultures. In this final section we briefly point to the ongoing progression of branded culture and its implications for further *encouraging* the performance of the self online in increasingly 'public', or 'visible', ways. Young people, in particular, are often accused of being self-absorbed narcissists, uninterested in 'real' civic virtues or in 'public life' as they engage in increasingly reflexive and intensive forms of self display (see, for example, Bauerlein, 2008). In contrast we argue that, within the current conjuncture, such displays constitute 'successful' self-creation, and that this has implications for understanding young people's willingness to share the intimate details of their lives online, even if the *management* of this process is complicated through mediated youth drinking cultures. This logic unfolds in relation to the rise of the 'branded self', well summarised in the work of Hearn (2008).

Hearn (2008) argues that the developments in corporate branding outlined above have been accompanied by a concomitant rise in a culture of self-promotion that exhorts subjects to be increasingly self-reliant, 'flexible', and willing to meet change and 'risk' as they deal with the consequences of living productive working lives under a flexible, post-Fordist, globalised and unpredictable form of corporate capitalism. Continual reflexive work on the self is required to be able to 'compete' in society. Thus, observes Hearn,

> success is dependent, not upon specific skills or motivation, but on the glossy packaging of the self and the unrelenting pursuit of attention... The most important work *is* work on the self. (Hearn, 2008: 205, emphasis in original)

Such 'work' constitutes a form of 'personal branding' that is ongoing and involves a whole way of life so that 'those in quest of a personal brand are encouraged to expose their braggables in every avenue available to them' (2008: 205). What is most important here is expertise in the strategic crafting of a 'potent *image* of autonomous subjectivity' (2008: 206, original emphasis). Drawing on economist Ernest Steinberg (2001, cited in Hearn, 2008) Hearn argues that the ability to command attention, even if it comes in the form of notoriety, serves as a 'proxy indicator' (2008: 208) of personal ability. While Hearn points out that the resources available to 'compete' in building a personal brand are unevenly distributed across the social formation, especially in terms of class, she argues that the impetus to publicly project a personally branded image of autonomous subjectivity forms a more *general* governmental imperative in the current conjuncture, one increasingly linked to economic success even as it includes the entirety of cultural and social life within its purview.

This dominant imperative acts as an important contextual consideration in (re)assessing young people's often intensive engagement with SNSs, which clearly offer a readily available means for gaining visibility. Rather than being pathological, their willingness to repeatedly post personal photos, to invest inordinate amounts of time in crafting their online identities, and to publicly display their personal social connections is, once again, tied to their broader position in a social structure that they must constantly negotiate – a structure where one of the greatest risks (for *everyone*) is to become 'invisible', to *not* be seen at all, which is rarely acknowledged in public debates over 'youth', drinking and SNSs. This adds an additional layer of complexity to the analysis of mediated drinking cultures, which can be seen as sites where the range of factors we have discussed throughout this chapter come together. 'Ending up online' in mediated displays of drunkenness involves new forms of self-expression and intimate sociality tied to the *necessity* for reflexively crafting a self in a late modern age. It involves complex new engagements with brands-as-relationships that are actively encouraged through marketing practices, and indeed becomes a site for the construction of the self-as-brand. Here notoriety/visibility constitutes an asset *at the same time* as it exposes young people to surveillance and moral judgement by unseen audiences. The line between crafting an authentic and autonomous online subjectivity, and of losing control of the management of the self entirely, becomes very thin indeed. The extent to which this potential for loss of control over self-representation online actually matters to young people themselves, especially given the importance of visibility to the current conjuncture, remains a matter for further research.

While we do not have the space available to unpack it in the detail it deserves, there are obvious parallels here between the creation of branded selves and the broader endorsement of a culture of celebrity that permeates contemporary media and society. Indeed, Hearn argues it is within celebrity culture that we can 'trace the roots of self-branding as a cultural practice' (2008: 208). Celebrity not only constitutes an important additional resource, similar to brands, for individuals to draw upon in order to construct their own identities – that is, another 'matrix of lifestyle and social activities' (Rose, 1999: 86) to be selectively accessed in crafting the self. Rather, celebrity 'becomes a generalizable model of profitable self-production for all individuals' (ibid.: 208). 'Celebrity brands' represent, in many ways, the apex of the economic productivity now accorded to immaterial labour. A celebrity's key asset is the *attention* they garner as they engage in the ephemera of conducting a publicly visible (and heavily branded) 'everyday' life, rather than their inherent skill set or their employment through a traditional workplace. The parallels become even more compelling when one considers drinking cultures and mediated hedonistic displays of drunken excess, of 'partying hard' in the right places with the right people, of conspicuous consumption, that increasingly constitute key sites of celebrity publicity both online and offline (the innumerable references to celebrity excess in tabloid newspaper and magazine culture serve as illustrative examples here). It is against this kind of more critical background that the salient question of a conjunctural analysis of young people's own mediated drinking cultures – *why now?* – needs to be posed.

Conclusion: Interrogating Contemporary Mediated Youth Drinking Cultures

Mediated youth drinking cultures are increasingly attracting attention, both within and outside the academy. In this chapter we have argued that they do indeed deserve close scrutiny, and have suggested that they be 'read' symptomatically as part of a conjunctural analysis. The two conceptual themes we have highlighted by no means exhaust the possible avenues for a conjunctural analysis to pursue, and we have only indicated the general directions we argue analysis should take, rather than producing a conjunctural analysis per se. These directions suggest a need to move beyond dualistic framings of mediated youth drinking cultures as *either* sites of autonomy and empowerment *or* as linked to negative health outcomes and the commodification of culture. Both of these aspects are important. Yet a conjunctural analysis highlights a requirement to explore the complex interactions between these processes that are undoubtedly at play, to hold them *both* in tension and in focus. Perhaps more importantly, it allows us to read young people's online drinking cultures in a way that does not segregate 'youth' as a problematic other, but rather sees in these increasingly visible sites of youth culture an opportunity to explore the power dynamics that structure the societies within which we *all* must live.

Acknowledgements

This chapter is derived from research supported by the Marsden Fund Council from Government funding, administered by the Royal Society of New Zealand (contract MAU0911). The authors would like to acknowledge the contributions of our fellow researchers on this project: Dr Helen Moewaka Barnes, Dr Fiona Hutton, Dr Kerry-Ellen Vroman, Trish Niland, Lina Samu and Dee O'Carroll.

References

Allan, G (1998) 'Friendship, Sociology and Social Structure', *Journal of Social and Personal Relationships*, 15(5): 685–702.

Arvidsson, A (2005) 'Brands: A Critical Perspective', *Journal of Consumer Culture*, 5(2): 235–258.

Babor, T, Caetano, R, Casswell, S, et al. (2010) *Alcohol: No Ordinary Commodity: Research and Public Policy* (2nd ed.). Oxford: Oxford University Press.

Bauerlein, M (2008) *The Dumbest Generation: How the Digital Age Stupefies Young Americans and Jeopardizes Our Future*. London: Penguin.

Beck, U (1992) *Risk Society: Towards a New Modernity*. London: Macmillan.

boyd, d (2007) 'Why Youth (Heart) Social Network Sites: The Role of Networked Publics in Teenage Social Life', in D Buckingham (ed.) *McArthur Foundation Series on Digital Learning: Youth, Identity, and Digital Media Volume*. Cambridge, MA: MIT Press, 119–142.

boyd, d & Ellison, N (2007) 'Social Network Sites: Definition, History and Scholarship', *Journal of Computer-Mediated Communication*, 13(1): article 1.

Brown, R & Gregg, M (2012) 'The Pedagogy of Regret: Facebook, Binge Drinking and Young Women', *Continuum: Journal of Media and Cultural Studies*, 26(3): 357–369.

Casswell, S (2012) 'Current Status of Alcohol Marketing Policy – An Urgent Challenge for Global Governance', *Addiction*, 107: 478–485.

Center on Alcohol Marketing and Youth (2012) *Exposure of African-American Youth to Alcohol Advertising, 2008 and 2009*. Baltimore, MD: Johns Hopkins Bloomberg School of Public Health.

Chatterton, P & Hollands, R (2002) 'Theorising Urban Landscapes: Producing, Regulating and Consuming Youthful Nightlife in City Space', *Urban Studies*, 39(1): 95–116.

Croghan, R, Griffin, C, Hunter, J, et al. (2006) 'Style Failure: Consumption, Identity and Social Exclusion', *Journal of Youth Studies*, 9(4): 463–478.

Egan, KG & Moreno, MA (2011) 'Alcohol References on Undergraduate Males' Facebook Profiles', *American Journal of Men's Health*, 5(5): 413–420.

Fournier, AK & Clarke, SW (2011) 'Do College Students Use Facebook to Communicate About Alcohol? An Analysis of Student Profile Pages', *Cyberpsychology*, 5(2): article 2.

Giddens, A (1991) *Modernity and Self-Identity: Self and Society in the Late Modern Age*. Cambridge: Polity Press.

Gordon, R, Hiem, D & MacAskill, S (2012) 'Rethinking Drinking Cultures: A Review of Drinking Cultures and a Reconstructed Dimensional Approach', *Public Health*, 126: 3–11.

Griffin, C (2011) 'The Trouble with Class: Researching Youth, Class and Culture beyond the "Birmingham School"', *Journal of Youth Culture*, 14(3): 245–259.

Griffin, C, Bengry-Howell, A, Hackley, W, et al. (2009) '"Everytime I Do It I Absolutely Annihilate Myself": Loss of (Self-)Consciousness and Loss of Memory in Young People's Drinking Narratives', *Sociology*, 43(3): 457–467.

Griffiths, R & Casswell, S (2010) 'Intoxigenic Digital Spaces? Youth, Social Networking Sites and Alcohol Marketing', *Drug and Alcohol Review*, 29 (September): 525–530.

Hall, S (2011) 'The Neo-Liberal Revolution', *Cultural Studies*, 25(6): 705–728.

Hall, S & Jefferson, T (2006) 'Once More Around "Resistance through Rituals"', in S Hall & T Jefferson (eds) *Resistance through Rituals: Youth Subcultures in Post-War Britain* (2nd ed.). London: Routledge, vii–xxxv.

Hearn, A (2008) 'Meat, Mask, Burden: Probing the Contours of the Branded "Self"', *Journal of Consumer Culture*, 8(2): 197–217.

Huckle, T, Pledger, M & Casswell, S (2012) 'Increases in Typical Quantities Consumed and Alcohol-Related Problems During a Decade of Liberalising Alcohol Policy', *Journal of Studies on Alcohol and Drugs*, 73(1): 53–62.

Jernigan, DH (2012) 'Who is Minding the Virtual Alcohol Store?', *Archives of Paediatric and Adolescent Medicine*, 166(9): 866–867.

Lim, SS, Vadrevu, S, Chan, YH & Basnyat, I (2012) 'Facework on Facebook: The Online Publicness of Juvenile Delinquents and Youths-at-Risk', *Journal of Broadcasting and Electronic Media*, 56(3): 346–361.

Livingstone, S (2008) 'Taking Risky Opportunities in Youthful Content Creation: Teenagers' Use of Social Networking Sites for Intimacy, Privacy and Self-Expression', *New Media & Society*, 10(3): 393–411.

Lyons, AC & Willot, S (2008) 'Alcohol Consumption, Gender Identities and Women's Changing Social Positions', *Sex Roles*, 59: 694–712.

McCreanor, T, Moewaka Barnes, H, Gregory, A, et al. (2005) 'Consuming Identities: Alcohol Marketing and the Commodification of Youth Experience', *Addiction Research and Theory*, 13(6): 579–590.

McCreanor, T, Moewaka Barnes, H, Gregory, M, et al. (2008) 'Marketing Alcohol to Young People in Aotearoa New Zealand: Creating and Maintaining Intoxigenic Environments', *Social Science and Medicine*, 67(6): 938–946.

Measham, F (2004) 'The Decline of Ecstasy, the Rise of "Binge" Drinking and the Persistence of Pleasure', *Probation Journal*, 5(4): 309–326.

Nicholls, J (2012) 'Everyday, Everywhere: Alcohol Marketing and Social Media – Current Trends', *Alcohol and Alcoholism*, Online First article 23 April, doi:10.1093/alcalc/ags043.

Ong, A (2006) *Neoliberalism as Exception.* Durham, NC: Duke University Press.

Papacharissi, Z (2010) *A Private Sphere: Democracy in a Digital Age.* New York: Polity Press.

Rehm, J, Mathers, C, Popova, S, et al. (2009) 'Global Burden of Disease and Injury and Economic Cost Attributable to Alcohol Use and Alcohol-Use Disorders', *Lancet*, 373(9682): 2223–2233.

Ridout, B, Campbell, A & Ellis, L (2012) '"Off Your Face(book)": Alcohol in Online Social Identity Construction and Its Relation to Problem Drinking in University Students', *Drug and Alcohol Review*, 31(1): 20–26.

Robards, B & Bennett, A (2011) 'MyTribe: Post-Subcultural Manifestations of Belonging on Social Network Sites', *Sociology*, 45(2): 303–317.

Rose, N (1999) *Powers of Freedom: Reframing Political Thought.* Cambridge: Cambridge University Press.

Sheehan, M & Ridge, D (2001) "You Become Really Close…You Talk About the Silly Things You Did, and We Laugh": The Role of Binge Drinking in Female Secondary Students' Lives', *Substance and Misuse*, 36: 347–372.

Szmigin, I, Griffin, C, Mistral, W, et al. (2008) 'Reframing "Binge Drinking" as Calculated Hedonism: Empirical Evidence for the UK', *International Journal of Drug Policy*, 19(5): 359–366.

Venn, C (2009) 'Neoliberal Political Economy, Biopolitics and Colonialism: A Transcolonial Genealogy of Inequality', *Theory, Culture and Society*, 26(6): 206–233.

Venkatesh, A (1999) 'Postmodernism Perspectives for Macromarketing: An Inquiry into the Global Information and Sign Economy', *Journal of Macromarketing*, 19(2): 153–169.

Viser, V (1999) 'Geist for Sale: A Neoconsciousness Turn through Advertising in Contemporary Consumer Culture', *Dialectical Anthropology*, 24(1): 107–124.

Wohn, DY, Lampe, C, Wash, R, et al. (2011) 'The "s" in Social Network Games: Initiating, Maintaining, and Enhancing Social Relationships', *Proceedings of the Annual Hawaii International Conference on System Sciences*, 4–7 January 2011, Koloa, Kauai, HI, USA, art. no. 5718722.

Part 2
Engagement and Creativity

Moving deeper into our explorations of mediated youth cultures, the second part of this collection is concerned with how young people produce the social web. From zines to graphic designs to the 'prosumption' (Ritzer & Jurgenson, 2010) of music, the five chapters that make up Part 2 are concerned with young people as active creators of culture. Key questions for Part 2 include:

- How do young people produce culture – as consumers, as creators – and how does this culture circulate?
- What forms of culture does the internet enable young people to participate in as prosumers, and how might this figure into questions of voice and power?
- What can we learn about place and power from mediated youth cultures that allow knowledges and narratives to flow across borders and persist through time?
- Do youth cultures that are mediated online reconfigure the ways we experience materiality?

This part considers the importance of digital media in facilitating young people's engagement in forms of creative cultural practice, from the production of personal text and narrative, through to access to, and the ability to share, music online. Drawing in places on the threads developed in Part 1, the chapters in Part 2, by Douglas & Poletti, Vaisman, Jung, Avdeeff and Nowak, work to broaden out the focus of this collection. By making enquiries into the circulation of various texts and voices in youth culture, we can also learn about how culture more broadly plays out in everyday life.

Reference

Ritzer, G & Jurgenson, N (2010) 'Production, Consumption, Prosumption: The Nature of Capitalism in the Age of the Digital "Prosumer"', *Journal of Consumer Culture*, 10(1): 13–36.

5
Rethinking 'Virtual' Youth: Young People and Life Writing

Kate Douglas (Flinders University) & Anna Poletti (Monash University)

Youth is widely thought of as 'a time of experimentation with different styles of communicating and articulating identity' (Stern, 2007: 2). However, traditionally, stories about young people's lives, like young people's literature and culture, have been 'written by adults, illustrated by adults, edited by adults, marketed by adults, purchased by adults, and often read by adults' (Jenkins, 1998: 23). And within culture more broadly, as Giroux contends, experiences of youth are rarely narrated by the young. He writes:

> Prohibited from speaking as moral and political agents, youth becomes an empty category inhabited by the desires, fantasies and interests of the adult world. This is not to suggest that youth don't speak; they are simply restricted from speaking in those spheres where public conversation shapes social policy and refused the power to make knowledge consequential. (Giroux, 1998: 24)

However, self-representation is something that most humans have an 'underlying, even unconscious narrative urge' to do (Eakin, 1999: 139). And so, as a consequence, in some visible and some less visible domains, in public and in private spheres, young people have been engaged in life writing practices for centuries. Life writing – the act of representing one's own life or the life of someone else – involves an engagement with the past and a reflection on identity in the present (Smith & Watson, 2010: 1). In this chapter we consider life writing as a practice that has, historically, mediated the representation of youth in adult culture, and that continues to play an important role – in the form of an enabling discourse – in contemporary mediated youth cultures in the case of zines, and crowdsourced online projects. We are also describing life writing as a discourse that structures the representation of identity, life and self in different media – diaries, zines and websites. In thinking this way about life writing, we follow Couldry's suggestion that

> any process of mediation (or perhaps 'mediazation') of an area of culture or social life is always at least two-way: 'media' work, and must work, not merely by transmitting discrete textual units for discrete moments of reception, but through a process of environmental transformation which, in turn, transforms the conditions under which any future media can be produced and understood. In other words, 'mediation' is a non-linear process. (Couldry, 2008: 380)

In this sense, we argue that young people's life narrative has played a role in establishing 'youth' as a distinctive speaking position.[1] We examine three distinct spaces in which young writers and artists construct and circulate autobiographical narratives: private written forms; public literary forms; and multimedia texts, which blur the boundaries between private and public. We locate and historicise the online life narrative practices that have come to define contemporary youth life narrative (blogs, status updates/micromemoirs, photosharing) within a longer tradition of the mediation of youth identity and life.

Private Written Forms

When people think of young people's life writing prior to the internet, they think of the diary. Indeed, the adolescent diary has itself become a re-mediated site of self-representation through projects such as *Mortified!* where people read from their teenage diaries, usually for comic effect. As we shall discuss further below, the diary remains a powerful medium for the representation and mediation of youth in online contexts. As an ostensibly 'private' written form taken up by young people, the diary has a deep and complex history related to the development of education, and the formation of gendered identity in a number of cultures, particularly British, French and American.

   In the interests of brevity we will discuss the case in France, as recent scholarship by leading researchers of French life writing – Lejeune and, more recently, Wilson – has made available primary texts for consideration and provided important analysis of the role of life writing in the formation and mediation of the identity of the 'jeune fille' (young girl) (Lejeune, 2009; Wilson, 2010).

In 19th-century France, diary-keeping was an important means through which young women (of certain classes) became subjects. The practice of reflective self writing was an organised and mediated response to the hail of the discourse of education. As Lejeune asserts, it was, for a period, literally a mandated activity for the development of an identity. However, keeping a diary and reading from it was also, in some cases, a means of connecting to peers – who may also be keeping diaries – and other members of a girl's social circle. A young woman may read aloud from her diary to both entertain select friends and family and conform to surveillance of the formation of her identity (Lejeune, 2009: 136; Wilson, 2010: 1). In this sense, diaries were often 'coaxed' by members of a girl's social network.[2] Wilson's (2010) study of the diary of Marie Bashkirtseff provides a compelling example of the complex social and personal uses of the diary by a young woman between the ages of 15 and 25 during this period. Wilson examines the importance of the diary to Bashkirtseff educating herself in the practices of self-display (dress, behaviour and physical poise) required of a young woman on the periphery of polite society (Wilson, 2010: 86–87). The work on the use of the diary by the 'jeune fille' in France provides vital historical detail that evidences the long history of young people's use of self-life-writing as a means of producing and sharing self-representational texts that demonstrate their proximity to social norms of behaviour. Wilson's work in particular explores the important and complex role of mediation, particularly textual strategies, in that process.[3] Wilson's analysis of Bashkirtseff's diary is an exemplary study in the use of the technique of the narrating 'I' of the adolescent diary to produce the appearance of honesty, and is a representation of identity formed to satisfy the reader of the 'private' nature of the writing.[4] This seemingly paradoxical character of the diary demonstrates how mediation contributes to the formulation of identity itself *as* private, and the writer as self-knowing. It is the very ability to master this technique, mapped in the diary itself, that allows the young life writer to present themselves as engaging in a process of development towards adult identity.

Public Literary Forms

The practice of public self-representation by young people in the 21st century might seem novel, but young writers have been engaged in public literary forms of life writing for centuries. The corpus of texts is expansive and foundational to self-representation in the online sphere; we offer some notable examples in this section.

Historically, much of the life writing by young people has been assumed to belong to other prominent genres – for instance, poetry – and not labelled as autobiography. This is perhaps a reflection on life writing's position within the literature cultures of these times. Nineteenth-century French poet Arthur Rimbaud, the Romantic poet John Keats, and World War I poets Ivor Gurney and Wilfred Owen each penned some of their more notable works during their youth. Many of these works were written to negotiate life experiences – asserting particular styles, subjects and perspectives. For example, Wilfred Owen's often quoted 'Anthem for a Doomed Youth' was written when he was just 24. Employing sombre, graphic realism, Owen reflects on the unceremonious end to the life of those young soldiers who died on the battlefields of World War I. Owen had witnessed this at first hand and the poem reflects his intention to advocate, through his poetry, for the young who died.

War has provided a distinct subject and a space for young life writers in the last two centuries. Arguably the most famous of all young life writers is Anne Frank, who penned her Holocaust memoir from age 13. *Diary of a Young Girl* came into public circulation in 1947 and is still widely read. Since then, a plethora of (young) World War II diarists have been discovered and their diaries published (whether in their entirety or anthologised, or both).[5] These narratives, which were often published many years after the fact, have a social justice agenda: adding to historical records.

Such World War II diaries fuse the private and public: like the 'jeune fille' before them, many of these young authors anticipate a reader beyond their immediate family and friends – as if predicting their future role as historian, or perhaps just dreaming that they might become famous writers. Mary Berg (Poland), Eva Heyman (Hungary), Hannah Senesh (Hungary), Janine Phillips (Poland), Tamarah Lazerson (Lithuania) and Yitshok Rudashevki (Lithuania) recount experiences of living in European cities during the war, tales of exile, radicalism and protest, and, of course, life in work and death camps. These texts offer a poetics for representing trauma, and an aesthetic for writing about resistance. They also satisfy a cultural hunger for traumatic stories about childhood and youth. As these original narratives travel through their various mediations – from embodied, first-person narratives by adolescent witnesses, to the original material diary, to discovery (preservation and archival), through to translation, publication and anthology – they are inevitably mediated by adult gatekeepers such as editors and publishers.

This legacy continues to propel the production and reception in the 21st century of war diaries and memoirs by young writers. In the early 2000s twentysomething bloggers Salam Pax and Riverbend gained notoriety (and book contracts) through their insider's view of the invasion of Iraq. And Ishmael Beah, former child soldier in Sierra Leone, achieved infamy (and visibility) for young people's testimonies of civil wars in Africa.[6]

In the public literary forms of young people's life writing (i.e. in published books), as Douglas (2010) contends, it has been narratives of extremity that have been of most interest to publishers and, in turn, readers. Another subgenre that exemplifies this is the plethora of narratives published in the 2000s of exceptional or 'borderline' girlhoods (to use Elizabeth Marshall's (2006) term). Such texts form part of a contemporary tradition – following on from the likes of Mary Karr, Susanna Kaysen, Lauren Slater and Elizabeth Wurtzel from the 1990s – and covering territory such as illness, addiction and sexuality. These are narratives of extremity and conversion via creativity. They have been, and continue to be, highly visible modes for young female life writers at this cultural moment. This is most likely because they often confirm prevalent ideas about girlhood; some deal explicitly with adolescence (e.g. Koren Zailckas's *Smashed: Memoir of a Drunken Girlhood* (2005) or Abigail Vona's *Bad Girl* (2004)), others with the 'quarter-life crisis' (e.g. Diablo Cody's *Candy Girl: A Year in the Life of an Unlikely Stripper* (2006) and Brianna Karp's *The Girl's Guide to Homelessness* (2011)). Of course, this interest in, and stereotype of, youth-in-crisis extends beyond literature to alternative media and online spaces where such conceptions of youth are up for debate.

Multimedia Texts

While public literary forms are often mediated by gatekeepers of the publishing industry, young people have also self-published texts as part of their subcultural or creative activities. In the next section we will examine two case studies of communities of young autobiographers constituted by self-published multimedia texts. The use of multimedia forms is often influenced by DIY discourse,[7] bypassing mainstream cultural outlets and focusing on the creation of communities of taste beyond mainstream, commercial culture.

Zines: An Analogue Network

Prior to the internet, zines were probably the best example of a globalised mediated youth culture. Self-published texts, ranging in length from one to 30 pages, zines (pronounced 'zeens') are produced in small editions, usually using the photocopier. They are sold and traded through mail order distributors, in temporary physical spaces such as at markets or fairs, and in independent record and bookstores. Since the explosion of the internet, zines have remained a dynamic international network of publishing and reading, where the handmade text has gained importance in juxtaposition to the ease of online 'push button' publishing.[8]

The topics covered in zine culture are diverse, from recipes to music, 'how to' guides to sustainable living, fiction, journalism, politics and comics.[9] However, a dominant genre over the last 20 years has been the personal zine – or 'perzine' – an autobiographical mode that takes the author's life or experiences as the focus. This trend in youth self-publishing mirrors the larger shift towards autobiographical discourse in English-speaking cultures, epitomised by the 'memoir boom', the confessional talkshow genre and, in US political culture in particular, the increasingly significant role played by affect and identification in the conceptualisation of US citizenship. Poletti's (2008) large-scale study of autobiography in Australian zine culture found that young people use the 'underground' medium to speak to each other about a range of issues in their lives, including current political issues (such as Australia's involvement in the invasion of Iraq), negotiating government services such as Centrelink (which administers student and unemployment payments), travelling, sexuality, identity, and experiences with mental health. In what follows we examine how the zine functions as a unique form of mediation of life narrative, and how it retains its status as a sequestered site of reading and writing through eschewing the pressure to publicness that comes with other mediated forms, particularly those online.

Materiality and Mediation: Reading Zine Culture as a Public

While some booklet publishing software exists online,[10] the vast majority of zines are handmade by their authors. This is an important threshold for participation in the culture; participants must learn how to physically make a zine by mastering basic skills in layout, including pagination, photocopying, collation and binding. These activities require access to particular resources: paper, a photocopier, and adequate physical space in which to undertake collation.[11] The complexity and quality of zines can vary widely, from basic black and white photocopying, to the use of a range of materials such as coloured papers and clear plastic overhead sheets used to create complex relations between words and images.

The extent to which self-publishing is a political critique of the mass media's control of dominant narratives by each individual zine maker is debatable, and Poletti has argued that attempts to synthesise zine culture into a political movement run into significant problems by overemphasising the resistant political commitments of authors and participants (2008: 18–32). Rather, we suggest that the importance of zines is better understood as serving aesthetic and communicative ends – particularly in the case of personal zines – rather than (narrowly defined) resistant political ones. This is not to suggest that zines are not political. It is precisely the opportunity to engage in mediation – through life writing and textual production – that attracts many young people to zine culture, and makes zines an important site of youth self-representation. We follow Rak's framing of autobiography as a discourse, rather than a genre, which encourages us to recognise how life narrative texts that circulate outside institutionalised media – such as book culture and broadcast media – make marginalised subjectivities visible:

> Autobiography must be thought of as a discourse rather than as a genre, and as discourse that is sustained by the trappings of identification that have underwritten what the self is and how it has been seen in much of the Western world. When autobiographical discourse is used by writers or speakers who do not have access to the privileges of autobiographical identity – such as print literacy, a sense of one's 'place' in history that others will recognize, or the leisure time to write a book – then that discourse changes as it is used, even as it brings certain advantages. (Rak, 2004: ix)

As a non-fiction discourse, life writing is the practice of mediating a life to have it recognised by a community. To do this, each text purports to speak the truth about the self and about a life. Makers of personal zines – like all life writers – work to establish a relationship with their reader that confirms that they write about their life 'in a spirit of truth' (Miller, 2007: 538), and they use both material and textual strategies to do this.[12] The handmade nature of zines is key to maintaining and regulating the size of the audience because they are both difficult to access – circulated in comparatively small print runs and sold in non-commercial and out of the way spaces – and require considerable time to produce and distribute.

As a mediated youth culture, zines are an excellent example of Warner's theory of the public as the product of self-organising discourse

(Warner, 2002). Young people's use of autobiographical discourse in zine culture is a means of engaging in cultural practices for self- and world-making. Producing autobiographical texts for a limited and self-selecting public gives young people access to the discourse of autobiography in order to explore, construct and communicate identity. Unlike other sites where young people are 'incited to [autobiographical] discourse',[13] zine culture remains largely resistant to attempts to commercialise or control it. Indeed, zine makers create a public *of* autobiographical discourse through specific practices of mediation, and in doing so retain control over the circulation of zines by writing for 'known' strangers (Warner, 2002: 54–55).

Thinking of zines as an autobiographical public helps us understand their importance as a mediated youth culture because publics, Warner suggests, are a means of imagining and making a world of like-minded others. He describes the importance of strangers to the formation of publics and their ability to enable hope:

> The unknown element in the addressee enables a hope of transformation; the known, a scene of practical possibility. Writing to a public helps to make a world, insofar as the object of address is brought into being partly by postulating and characterizing it. (Warner, 2002: 64)

In zines, material strategies are often used to postulate and characterise the reader as known and intimate. These include the use of envelopes as covers, the inclusion of handwriting on covers and inside the zines, colour and collaged covers that mark each individual zine as being handmade, and the practice of editioning each copy. At the level of the written text, it is in the opening pages of the zine that the work of imagining an unknown addressee often occurs. For example, in the Australian personal zine *Ampersand and Ampersand #3*, the narrator (Amanda) describes her doubt about the value of narrating her experiences of her recent diagnosis with polycystic ovarian syndrome and the risks communication entails:

> I have never been able to just casually talk about my emotions and those who have been in conversations with me when I've tried to open up and overcome my own walls will recognise how silly I often look – I lose my voice, my mouth opens and closes like a guppy, I fidget uncontrollably and I generally appear constipated.

The risks of sharing experience in person and in speech are described here as manifesting in bodily evidence of embarrassment and discomfort, and a suspicion that the addressee (in person) will notice these bodily clues to Amanda's resistance to speak about her feelings and see them as 'silly', rather than empathetically respond to her struggle for articulation. On the next page, this risk of looking 'silly' is presented as being compounded by the threat of miscommunication:

> I can't help but feel that revealing anything of myself to others is to set myself up for the inevitable disappointment of miscommunication. There is a certain inelegance to putting emotions into words and saying them out loud – seeing them leave you, twisting and turning and changing shape as they do, inevitably becoming something that you don't recognize.

Again it is the bodily presence of the speaker and the addressee that symbolises the dangers of communicating feelings: Amanda characterises the process of putting emotions into words as inelegant, and involving clumsiness or imprecision of expression. This risk is compounded by the problem of interpretation: once achieved, the meaning of verbal expression is unfixed, 'twisting and turning and changing shape... inevitably becoming something that you don't recognize'. In Amanda's formulation, speaker and addressee confront bodily and semiotic barriers to communication and recognition. It is the act of mediation – the zine – that is posited as the solution to these problems:

> This is why I keep coming back to zines. The words are still mine, but in a zine they are somehow separate from the neuroticism and trust issues that make it so hard to open to those close to me. In a zine I can write what is important to me without fear because I will never have to see if you react with indifference, boredom or judgment. (Amanda u.p., 2010)[14]

These descriptions of the problems associated with face-to-face communication establish the idealised addressee of the zine, and mark out the importance of a mediated site of communication as the solution to problems of autobiographical communication. Here, then, is an example of the world-making Warner describes in publics: the imagining of a solution to problems of talking face-to-face by positing an idealised addressee and a narrating self who is unhindered by the bodily habits that undermine Amanda's ability to talk about 'so many important things'.

Evidencing a World Online: The 'We Make Zines' Ning

Warner qualifies his suggestion regarding the world-making potential of publics by stating that 'This performative ability depends, however, on that object's being not entirely fictitious – not postulated merely, but recognised *as a real path for the circulation* of discourse. That path is then treated as a social entity' (Warner, 2002: 64, emphasis added). While the zines themselves materialise the path for the circulation of youth auto-biography in their modes of distribution, online spaces have recently opened up which extend zine culture online precisely to evidence, but not replace, the social entity that is imagined by zine narrators. The relatively new development of online networks for zine makers extends the physically mediated culture in the online environment in order to affirm zine culture's status as a public, and to increase access to it. The We Make Zines 'ning'[15] is one example of how zine culture has extended online in a way that supports and validates the practice of handmade text production and distribution, and solidifies its importance as a pub-lic of autobiographical discourse. Krissy, the Portland, Oregon-based zinester who began the ning, describes the aim on the home page:

> We Make Zines is an online community for zine makers and readers. Although there are many social networking sites out there, there is little that focuses on zines. We all have our facebooks or blogs, but those accounts are filled with friends from work, from the third grade, people who don't know what a zine is and some who probably don't care. This space creates a place that focuses on the zines. I want this place to be less about personality and friends and more about the zines – what we produce and read.

Like Amanda, Krissy confirms the unique addressee posited by the zine maker: someone different from the 'usual' members of one's social life and network. Importantly, sites such as these give zine culture a fixed online presence – evidencing the social entity to which zines are addressed – without replacing the homemade texts, their ephemeral nature or the relationships the material object of the zine makes pos-sible. The handmade and the ephemeral nature of zines, so central to their appeal as a site of youth autobiographical practice, is not impacted by the creation of social networking spaces. Rather, these sites have been developed to increase access to the world-making public of zine culture, thus strengthening its status as a legitimate space of cultural activity, while maintaining the thresholds to participation outlined above. This online presence, and distinct culture of youth life-writing, sits alongside more recent practices of life narrative taken up by young people online, to which we now turn.

Creative Crowdsourcing, Community Art as Life Narrative

In the 1990s and 2000s, life narrative has thrived on the web, and young people have taken on a leadership role. For example, Kearney summarises young women's activity in making-media thus:

> [F]emale youth became active participants in the digital revolution of the late 1990s, not just through emailing, chat rooms, and instant messaging, but also by engaging in web design, producing their own websites. (Kearney, 2006: 3)

Much of this activity is life storytelling. Through using personal computers and now mobile technologies such as phones and tablets, young people have embraced technologies to tell stories about everyday life and to negotiate adolescent and post-adolescent identities and communities. As Sefton-Green argues, online media have been conducive to the exploration and indeed redefinition of childhood, adolescence and youth identities:

> [T]he digital age is one in which conventional definitions of childhood and adulthood are being redefined through social usage rather than in terms of biological age. If childhood and adulthood are destabilized by these processes, then it almost goes without saying that youth, the theoretical category occupying a hazy liminal space between these two states of being, is further thrown into disarray. (Sefton-Green, 2003: 4)[16]

The use of these online tools is, significantly, a *cultural practice*, like zine making, in which digital modes are trialled and used as mechanisms for communicating experience and finding audiences. So, how do young people share life stories on the internet? As Kathryn C. Montgomery asserts:

> As active creators of a new digital culture, these youth are developing their own Web sites, diaries, and blogs; launching their own

online enterprises; and forging a new set of cultural practices. (Montgomery, 2007: 2)

Sometimes storytelling is as simple as sharing a tweet or Facebook status. In other instances it is through more complex creative practices. For example, young people were the first to seize upon and develop interactive ICT for creative writing, and mechanisms for publishing and distribution (Abbott, 2003: 85). In online spaces, young life writers have been able to bypass traditional modes of publishing and self-publish aspects of their life narrative through photographs and music, for example. Like zine culture, these practices allow young people to exert some control over media production and through this, the production of their own images and life narratives, to authenticate their own life experiences through participation in everyday culture. This is especially pertinent for youth cultures because, as previously mentioned, the societies from which these texts emerge are largely ambivalent about their existence and validity.

Alongside alternative and smaller-scale digital projects, youth life narrative has also been at the forefront of well-known, high-circulation digital art projects, such as *PostSecret* (the community 'mail art' project where visual art and life writing meet to offer short confessions), *Learning to Love You More* (the crowdsourcing community art project; hereafter referred to as *Learning*), and *The Open Book Project* (a creative crowdsourcing site containing adolescent diary extracts). Although not all of the contributors to these sites are young people, a cursory glance at the sites reveals a large proportion of the texts published are explicitly authored by young artists. Site creators, software designers and publishers actively court young cultural producers – appealing to their skills and knowledge, consumption habits and consumer potential. For example, Frank Warren has successfully targeted his community art project *PostSecret* to high school and college-age audiences in the United States, speaking to sell-out crowds at campuses across North America. In 2006 Warren collected secrets by young contributors to the project into a collection titled *My Secret: A PostSecret Book*, which claimed to showcase cards from teenagers and college students (although the age of contributors to the project is unable to be verified given that contributors are anonymous).[17]

Learning is a 'collaborative public art project' created by Miranda July, Harrell Fletcher and Yuri Ono, which ran from 2002 to 2009 (extending to exhibitions and a book). The premise of this online art project was to give prescriptive assignments to everyday people. The written, photographic and video assignments ranged from short and easy to complete – for instance, 'Draw a constellation from someone's freckles' – to more time consuming and complex – for example, 'Make a paper replica of your bed'. The assignments commonly relied upon participants drawing on aspects of life experience. Some assignments presumed participants' creativity – for instance, 'Write your life story in less than a day' – but most were very easy and required little creative skill – for example, 'Take a family portrait of two families'.[18] The ethos of the website (as evident from its name) is a belief in the empowering and/or restorative value of creative pursuits.

Learning was not set up specifically as a space for young people's life narrative. However, many of the contributors are young people. This is perhaps not surprising considering the site is structured around participants completing 'assignments': a very familiar discourse for high school and university students. Looking through hundreds (of the thousands) of submissions, many examples emerge in which a youthful narrator mentions his or her age. For example, one assignment asked contributors to 'Photograph a scar and write about it'.[19] The body, so often invisible in cyberspace, becomes visible in this telling. There is a lot of variety in the different interpretations of the scar theme; recurring narratives include illness and injury, and stories of self-harm. In this assignment, *Learning* offers a confessional space for young people's testimony of trauma. More particularly, it gives trauma an aesthetic through the trauma's location within an artistic space.

The Open Book Project is another example of creative crowdsourcing.[20] It is a project that relies on contributions from the public: in this instance, the site asks for pages from teenage diaries:

> If you've still got your teenage diary, great! Just scan or take a photo of a page and upload it. If not, you can recreate your entry instead. Either way, you'll show teenagers that we all go through the same stuff growing up. (*The Open Book Project*)

Of course, in *The Open Book Project* it is again adults retrospectively choosing which aspects of their youthful self to reveal (and the use of some celebrity diary entries may set a particular tone for the project). There is the potential that this youthful self has been edited and finessed for public consumption. But, as we have suggested earlier, this is a potential criticism of all such online creative projects. What is significant about *The Open Book Project* is that it is a digital archive of young lives: it contains primary textual forms of diaries and the site has a welfare ethos and idealistic socio-political agenda.[21] It employs these life narratives artistically and therapeutically, courting a youthful readership to remind the youth of today that

> they're not alone. By sharing a page of your teenage diary, today's teenagers will know that, no matter where life takes you, there are similar things we all experience when growing up. It's a courageous act that will make a big difference in the lives of Australian teenagers. (*The Open Book Project*)

Reminiscent of the *It Gets Better Project* (in which contributors upload videos to YouTube discussing their sexuality and offer messages of empowerment to those young people struggling to come to terms with their own sexuality), *The Open Book Project* reveals how young people's life narratives so often stem from notions of youth crises.

Of course, it is worth asking here, 'Why would young writers and artists give their energies to crowdsourcing projects such as this?' Surely the producers of the projects have much more to gain than those who contribute their free creative labour? Further, there is an overt therapeutic ethos in the *Learning* 'assignment' format – the promise of healing (which cannot be guaranteed). Perhaps being part of a community art project like *PostSecret*, *Learning* or *The Open Book Project* is a means for transgressing the sorts of stigmas that have affected social networkers and bloggers, because these crowdsourcing projects are framed as art. Further, there is always space to transgress the medium provided and it is at this moment of transgression, where the medium is stretched to its limits, where fascinating examples of youth life narrative can be found.

Conclusion

This review of young people's life-writing practices reveals young writers' long engagement with autobiographical modes of storytelling as a process of mediation focused on subjectivity, identity and community. Young writers tell personal stories as they enter available cultural spaces – attempting to take control of and shape these different subgenres – inevitably (at different times) conforming to and also transgressing sanctioned forms and subject positions.

In attempting this partial historical review, which extends to contemporary examples, we are not attempting to set up 'good text'/'bad text' paradigms for young people's life narrative (depending on evidence of young people's creative agency within the different texts and modes).

Each of these examples tells us something significant about young writers' creative engagement with self-life-writing, revealing insights into constructions of youth identities, communities and creative styles via autobiography as a practice of mediation. These texts, collectively, show youth to be active producers of life narrative and reveal how self-life-writing as a process of mediation offers different kinds of visibility and sanctions for the narratives produced.

However, these texts and sites also remind us of the process of mediation at work in almost all life writing. In many instances, young people's life narratives are mobilised for adult agendas. The 'use' of young people's life narratives on public sites raises ethical questions: for example, do such texts establish therapeutic frameworks only to bypass the ethical responsibilities that stem from them? When young writers engage with established life narrative genres and models, the life writers are asked to 'Put your life narrative here', but there is no infrastructure for assessing the ramifications of such participation. For example, what if the young writer later regrets their youthful creative entry into the public sphere? Young life writers potentially become 'vulnerable subjects', to use Couser's (2003) term. But perhaps we are assuming (unnecessarily) a lack of agency on the part of youthful life narrators here. There's an agency within the participation itself; the imposition of parameters and mediation is inherent within almost all life writing texts. How can we define autonomy and/or autonomous creativity? How do we know when it's evident? It is not productive to underestimate the individual agency and creativity at work in these life narratives.[22] To borrow terms from Holloway & Valentine, it is better to be a 'booster' rather than a 'debunker' of young people's life narrative (2003: 72). The life narrative texts surveyed in this chapter unlock opportunities for creativity: for artistic production and for life stories that offer a very meaningful addition to the corpus of life narrative texts. These texts mark territory for young people's life narrative – an under-theorised life narrative mode – and create a space for the ethical reception of these texts.

Notes

1. We use the term 'youth' in recognition of its unique status as a culturally and socially constructed category. The term is used interchangeably with adolescence to denote the stage between childhood and adulthood. More recently it has been used to encompass young adulthood (adolescence through to early to mid-twenties), responding to social trends such as young people living at home longer, and delaying marriage and full-time employment (see Best, 2007; Giroux, 1998, 2003; Jones, 2009; Savage, 2007).

2. Extending Plummer's work, Smith & Watson use the term 'coaxing' to describe the production of life narrative in response to a person, institution or cultural imperative that requires life story (2001: 50–56).

3. See for example Wilson's chapter on Bashkirtseff's preface to her diary (written shortly before her death from tuberculosis) (2010: 25–45) which analyses Bashkirtseff's complex engagement with dominant discourses around autobiography, the diary, and the 'jeune fille' as a writing subject 'incapable of knowing herself' (Wilson, 2010: 39).

4. The narrated 'I' is 'the protagonist of the narrative, the version of the self that the narrating "I" chooses to constitute through recollection to the reader' (Smith & Watson, 2010: 60).

5. These include Jacob Boas's *We are Witnesses* (2005), Laurel Holliday's *Children in the Holocaust* (1995), and Alexandra Zapruder's *Salvaged Pages* (2002).

6. Ishmael Beah's account of his two years as a child soldier is into its 35th printing and has sold over 600,000 copies worldwide. In *A Long Way Gone*, Beah describes his life during Sierra Leone's civil war in the 1990s. During this civil war, tens of thousands of people were killed. Beah – young, attractive and eloquent – became an ideal spokesperson for the child soldier cause. The narrative presents its reader with a flawed hero – a young man who confesses to having murdered countless people during his drug-fuelled, civil war battles. However, the publication of *A Long Way Gone* marked the beginning of complex drama, revolving around the reception of Beah's text and the veracity of his story. To summarise: Beah's narrative was exposed by *The Australian* newspaper as 'exaggerated' in parts and 'false' in others. Other child soldier memoirs to emerge around this period include Emmanuel Jal, *War Child: A Child Soldier's Story*; Faith J.H. McDonnell and Grace Akelo, *Girl Soldier*; and Benson Deng, Alephonsion Deng and Benjamin Ajak, *They Poured Fire on Us from the Sky*.

7. See Poletti, *Intimate Ephemera*.

8. See Poletti, *Intimate Ephemera* for an extended analysis of the persistent appeal of the handmade zine text in the age of the digital.

9. See for example Microcosm Catalog 'Subjects': http://www.microcosmdistribution.com/catalog/

10. See for example http://bookleteer.com/

11. In both Australia and the US, not-for-profit collectives provide space and resources for zine making to be undertaken. In Portland, the Independent Publishing Resource Center (IPRC) offers photocopying, letterpress, and binding equipment for use. In Australia, the Octapod (in the port city of Newcastle) and the Sticky Institute in Melbourne also provide cheap or free access to resources and space for zine making.

12. See Poletti, *Intimate Ephemera* for an extended analysis of the material strategies used to situate the reader as a known stranger.

13. See Harris (2004).

14. Amanda, *Ampersand after Ampersand #3*. Sydney, 2010.

15. A 'ning' is a social networking platform designed to allow people to create and monetise networks. Originally a free service, a ning is now a subscription-based operation. When the *We Make Zines* ning began, the service was free and it has been successfully maintained by donations. Other examples of websites that extend zine culture to the online domain and in so doing

create the social entity to which zine texts can be addressed are the Zine Wiki (zinewiki.com), and Chip Rowe's website which accompanies his book *The Book of Zines* (http://www.zinebook.com).

16. We are going to leave aside, for the moment, the plethora of debates surrounding young people's use of internet/social media and its potential hazards. Suffice to say that there have been many studies and much scholarship devoted to this issue.

17. Interestingly, *PostSecret* also makes use of handmade texts to authenticate and situate the contributed content as autobiographical; see Poletti (2011).

18. By the end of its run, the project had over 8,000 participants from all over the globe.

19. The precise instructions read: 'Photograph a scar on your body or on someone else's body. Make it a close-up shot so that it shows just the scar. Include a story… about how the scar happened. Please do not send images of wounds that are fresh and have not healed. Only images of scars will be accepted.' There are over 300 responses to this assignment.

20. It is fascinating to note that during the writing of this chapter this seemingly flourishing project has now disappeared from the web. This demonstrates how short-lived such projects can be precisely because they depend upon the contributions of the general public.

21. It is sponsored by The Reach Foundation, a social welfare foundation aimed at 13–18-year-olds.

22. When studying youth life narratives, it is important to look closely and to not underestimate the creativity at work. Kearney points to McRobbie & Garber's work on girls' bedroom culture:

> [B]y continuing to focus primarily on the immaterial leisure activities of girls' bedroom culture, such as listening to records and daydreaming about stars, they ignored its material and productive components, such as letter writing, scrapbook making, and newsletter production. (Kearney, 2006: 23)

References

Abbott, C (2003) 'Making Connections: Young People and the Internet', in J Sefton-Green (ed.) *Digital Diversions: Youth Culture in the Age of Multimedia*. London: Routledge, 84–105.

Beah, I (2007) *A Long Way Gone: Memoirs of a Boy Soldier*. New York: Sarah Creighton.

Best, A (ed.) (2007) *Representing Youth: Methodological Issues in Critical Youth Studies*. New York: New York University Press.

Boas, J (2005) *We are Witnesses: Five Diaries of Teenagers Who Died in the Holocaust*. New York: Henry Holt.

Couldry, N (2008) 'Mediatization or Mediation? Alternative Understandings of the Emergent Space of Digital Storytelling', *New Media & Society*, 10: 373–391.

Couser, GT (2003) *Vulnerable Subjects: Ethics and Life Writing*. Ithaca, NY: Cornell University Press.

Douglas, K (2010) *Contesting Childhood: Autobiography, Trauma and Memory*. New Brunswick: Rutgers University Press.

Eakin, PJ (1999) *How Our Lives Become Stories: Making Lives.* Ithaca, NY: Cornell University Press.

Giroux, HA (1998) *Channel Surfing: Racism, the Media, and the Destruction of Today's Youth.* London: Martin's Press and Macmillan.

Giroux, HA (2003) *The Abandoned Generation: Democracy Beyond the Culture of Fear.* New York: Palgrave.

Harris, A (2004) 'Being Seen and Being Heard: The Incitement to Discourse', in *Future Girl: Young Women in the Twenty-First Century.* New York: Routledge, 125–150.

Holliday, L (1995) *Children in the Holocaust and World War II: Their Secret Diaries.* San Francisco: Washington Square Press.

Holloway, SL & Valentine, G (2003) *Cyberkids: Children in the Information Age.* London: Routledge.

It Gets Better, http://www.itgetsbetter.org (viewed 14 September 2012).

Jenkins, H (ed.) (1998) *The Children's Culture Reader.* New York: NYU Press.

Jones, G (2009) *Youth.* Cambridge: Polity.

Kearney, MC (2006) *Girls Make Media.* New York: Routledge.

Learning to Love You More, http://www.learningtoloveyoumore.com (accessed 14 September 2012).

Lejeune, P (2009) 'The "Journal de Jeune Fille" in Nineteenth-Century France', in K Durnin, J Popkin & J Rak (eds) *On Diary*, trans. Biographical Research Center. Manoa, Hawai'i: University of Hawai'i Press, 129–143.

Marshall, E (2006) 'Borderline Girlhoods: Mental Illness, Adolescence, and Femininity in *Girl, Interrupted*', *The Lion and the Unicorn*, 30(1): 117–133.

Miller, NK (2007) 'The Entangled Self: Genre Bondage in the Age of Memoir', *PMLA*, 132(2): 538.

Montgomery, KC (2007) *Generation Digital: Politics, Commerce, and Childhood in the Age of the Internet.* Cambridge, MA: MIT Press.

The Open Book Project, http://www.theopenbookproject.com (accessed 14 September 2012).

Poletti, A (2008) *Intimate Ephemera: Reading Young Lives in Australian Zine Culture.* Melbourne: Melbourne University Press.

Poletti, A (2011) 'Intimate Economies: *PostSecret* and the Affect of Confession', *Biography*, 34(1): 25–36.

PostSecret, http://www.postsecret.com (accessed 14 September 2012).

Rak, J (2004) *Negotiated Memory: Doukhobor Autobiographical Discourse.* Vancouver: University of British Columbia Press, ix.

Savage, J (2007) *Teenage: The Creation of Youth Culture.* New York: Viking Adult.

Sefton-Green, J (ed.) (2003) *Digital Diversions: Youth Culture in the Age of Multimedia.* London: Routledge.

Smith, S & Watson, J (2001) *Reading Autobiography: A Guide for Interpreting Life Narratives.* Minneapolis, MN: University of Minnesota Press.

Stern, ST (2007) *Instant Identity: Adolescent Girls and the World of Instant Messaging.* New York: Peter Lang.

Warner, D (2002) 'Publics and Counterpublics', *Public Culture*, 14(1): 49–90.

Wilson, S (2010) *Personal Effects: Reading the Journal of Marie Bashkirtseff.* London: Legenda.

Zapruder, A (2002) *Salvaged Pages: Young Writers' Diaries of the Holocaust.* New Haven, CT: Yale University Press.

6
The 'Designs Industry': Girls Play with Production and Power on Israeli Blogs

Carmel L. Vaisman (Hebrew University of Jerusalem)

We live in an unprecedented time in human history, in which more girls than ever before have access to the public sphere, and the ability to make their voices heard and to display their creativity online with less filtering or monitoring. Much of the communication, play and exchange between girls nowadays is publicly available on websites, blogs and social networking profiles. These recorded exchanges are an opportunity to identify, document and expose, in real time, the values, concepts and mechanisms involved in shaping identities, communities and ideologies among girls.

While girls and young women receive a lot of attention as consumers, they still receive little as creators of media and culture (Kearney, 2006). McRobbie & Garber (1976) were the first to point out that cultural production is expected to occur in public spaces, but since girls are under tight social control and have limited access to means of production and creation, their participation in culture usually involves practices of consumption and fandom from the safety of their bedrooms. To date, cultural studies have still focused mainly on youth occupying public spaces, while private spaces such as household bedrooms are comparatively under-researched (Lincoln, 2012).

Web spaces, however, blur the boundaries between public and private, turning the bedroom into a portal of communication and extending some of its aspects online (Lincoln, 2012). The opportunity to create a blog – that is, to have a personal online space with no supervision, boundaries, cost or advanced technical knowledge needed – affords girls an equal chance to gain visibility in the public domain without leaving their bedrooms, and allows them access to means of production and creation of texts and images in the public symbolic sphere.

Academic research relating to girls has been based on a tradition of moral panic and a discourse of risk rather than empowerment

(Mazzarella & Pecora, 2007a; Pipher, 1994). In recent years, the paradigm of 'Girls' Studies' (Mazzarella & Pecora, 2007b) has distanced itself from this approach and has instead focused upon the original creative culture of girls, inter alia on the internet. However, the majority of research on girls' online activities concerns practices of consumption, reception, gender discourse and identity performance, while there is little to no research on girls' online production practices (Kearney, 2011).

This study offers an analysis of graphic design production, display, and exchange practices on adolescent girls' blogs, filling this empirical gap by looking into the dynamics of girls' digital production as a peer culture, instead of examining the designed products as content. The study is part of a larger ethnographic project I conducted between August 2004 and December 2007, targeting girls' engagement with blogs as play and display spaces on *Israblog*, the largest Hebrew-language blog-hosting website. The project included multimodal discourse analysis of blogs, as well as offline observations of bloggers' meet-ups and individual interviews.

According to statistics provided by the website each year, as of August 2011, 80 per cent of *Israblog* users were female and 83 per cent were under the age of 21. When creating a blog on *Israblog*, it must be associated with at least one blog category. As many as 4,905 blogs listed themselves under the categories 'graphic design blogs' and 'graphic design and tutorials for blogs', most of them created by girls between the ages of 11 and 16. These are the subjects of this chapter. Although in theory these blogs are publicly available online, in practice they are known only within their peer group on *Israblog* and I have seen no evidence of outsiders or adult interference on these blogs.

Existing research on blogs treats the blog as text characterised by writing practices. This study, in contrast, focuses on graphic design practices that have in fact become the main channel of expression and the most prevalent blogging practice among Israeli girls on the *Israblog* website. *Israblog*'s software supports customised blog themes as well as combining graphic images/icons within the blog frame in place of text to describe links, headings and lists on the blog's side bar. Many girls make use of this option to decorate their side bar with assorted pictures and text-in-pictures that change frequently. They refer to these 'badges' as 'buttons' in Hebrew.

Buttons are usually square icons of various sizes, probably named thus because of their original function: they resemble the buttons that represent links to be clicked on. They usually harmonise with the design theme of the blog and often change more often than the rest of the design as a result of 'game'[1] practices developed by the girls. Girls who identify with the same social groups and subcultures decorate their blogs with similar stylistic elements and often circulate identical buttons.

The described practices are by no means culturally unique and should not be treated as such just because the discourse surrounding them is in a language other than English. Most of the buttons contain images from international popular culture and their accompanied texts are often in English. In addition, the girls admit in their posts and interviews to mimicking and copying many of those practices and contents from girls on MySpace, LiveJournal and other international girls' websites.

Similar practices of graphic design and/or gift exchange have been mentioned on MySpace (boyd, 2008; Dobson, 2012; Lincoln, 2012) and LiveJournal (Pearson, 2007). However, the freedom of blog customisation offered by *Israblog* has facilitated a broader phenomenon involving the circulation of images within a collaborative game of graphic design contests and playful exchanges engaging thousands of blogs and referred to by bloggers as the 'designs industry'.

In recent years researchers have defined the age group of pre-adolescents as 'tweens' and noticed their unique online spaces as well as being worried about their relationships with commercial markets (cf. Martens, 2011; Mitchell & Reid-Walsh, 2005). In this chapter I bring forth a tween space that creates its own make-believe market and examine its rules *vis-à-vis* commercial markets and peer negotiation game spaces. Specifically, I address two key issues that stem from this 'designs industry': the meaning of the industrial and labour discourses framing this gift-economy-based game, and the meaning of 'girl power' within this context, as ownership of or access to the means of production of symbols.

Girls' Peer Cultures Online

Peer cultures are defined as 'a stable set of activities or routines, artifacts, values, and concerns that children produce and share in interaction with peers' (Corsaro & Eder, 1990: 197). The models of socialisation that view young people as passive reproducers of adult culture are gradually being replaced with 'interpretive reproduction' approaches that respect young people's agency and negotiation abilities in taking a variety of stances towards cultural resources, playfully transforming them and sometimes even actively resisting adult models through those transformations (Gaskins et al., 1992). Young people reformulate social categories appropriated from the adult culture in ways that are context sensitive and reflective of their momentary goals (entry into or achieving power) in their peer cultures (Goodwin, 2001; Katriel, 1987).

Young people's peer culture research is usually discourse focused, since the strategies of affiliation, affirmation and ritualisation within peer groups are preformed through speech events (e.g. Cook-Gumperz & Szymanski, 2001). Two of the key discursive strategies for elaboration of norms within peer cultures are conflict talk that reveals the group's social organisation (cf. Goodwin, 1990) and the setting of game rules that provide their own criteria for evaluating participants' performances. For example, in games like hopscotch, girls sanction and hold each other accountable to rules and standards of the peer group (Goodwin, 1998).

When examining young people's peer cultures online it is not always useful to speak of groups and communities but rather helpful to view them as affinity spaces (Gee, 2004), where youth engagement with a technology is often viewed as a means of group belonging and agency. The internet provides a safe platform for young people's play and often acts like a cyber-bedroom reflecting some of the material cultures displayed in the actual bedrooms (Mitchell & Reid-Walsh, 2002) and in some aspects reminiscent of girls' bedroom culture (Lincoln, 2012).

The discourse of girlhood in general is marked by two major and contradictory discourses. The first is the discourse of power, often associated with the ambiguous notion of 'girl power'. This concept represents the post-feminist ideal of a young woman who possesses agency and a strong sense of self, yet at the same time it has become a marketing slogan intended to attract the profitable girls' market (Aapola et al., 2005). The second discourse is the discourse of risk, which is concerned with the problems young girls must face: low self-esteem, eating disorders, depression and high-risk behaviour (Mazzarella, 2005). Among other things, this discourse of risk and crisis is based on the concept of loss of voice defined by Brown & Gilligan (1992). According to them, adolescent girls tend to silence themselves in the sense that they do not listen to their own feelings, thoughts and experiences or do not take these seriously.

In the past, girls were seen as the potential victims of the popular media culture surrounding them, such as girls' magazines, romance novels and popular music. Such research linked the consumption of popular media to the findings of studies focusing on girls' decreasing self-esteem, negative body image and average achievements in certain school subjects. Subsequent studies began pointing out girls' success in objecting to cultural messages, though other studies showed girls as active consumers of their cultural products (Mazzarella, 2008) and the studies of girls' practices in the new media point to options for empowerment: negotiation of identity, impression management, self-reflection, civic participation and the creation of a peer network (Mazzarella, 2005; Stern, 2008).

In the last decade there has been a growing interest in girls' creativity and identity performances as reflected on their websites, blogs and social networks (e.g. Kearney, 2011; Mazzarella, 2005; Mitchell & Reid-Walsh, 2005; see also Chapter 5 in this collection). However, as Kearney (2011) elaborates in the introduction to her latest book, there is a need for research looking beyond content, at the practices of girls' online cultural production. Davies (2004) and Willett (2008) have laid some ethnographic grounds for the examination of tween girls' affinity spaces at the level of interaction around the production of media symbols, while Mitchell & Reid-Walsh (2005) have examined the relationships of girls' online peer cultures with material commercial markets.

In Israel, Golan (2006) documented the patterns of socialisation and exchange characteristics of Israeli teenagers, mostly male, defined as 'virtual virtuosos'. Their peer culture was gift economy based and included graphic design of their *Diablo* game forum avatars as a literacy skill in the repertoire of the 'virtual virtuoso'. Golan underplayed the importance of the relationship between these practices and capitalist consumption patterns, emphasising the productivity and creativity of these playful digital practices.

In this chapter I examine the dynamics of graphic design production in an Israeli tween girls' peer culture occurring in the affinity space of *Israblog*. Their collaborative playful exchanges offer a unique opportunity to explore the ways a large affinity group of tween girls organises media production and sociability norms in a peer space free of commercial interventions.

Graphic Design as a Blogging Practice

My first blog was here [on *Israblog*] but it was designed so ugly and I didn't know how to use it so I opened another one on *Tapuz* [another Hebrew website]. But they don't have the functions available here so I decided to come back. I'm opening this new blog, in hopes that I'll figure out how to add background music, design it properly, make a cool designed cursor and well, just use it. ('Ariel' on 8 October 2005)

The perception of blogs as online diaries implies that the constituting practice of blogging is writing. However, Ariel's first blog post reveals an important difference in the way Israeli tween girls perceive blogging: the verb 'write' is absent from her post and replaced by 'design', 'add', 'make' and 'use'. Girls like Ariel used to comment on strangers' blogs in search for new audiences with phrases like 'You've got a beautiful blog! You're invited into mine [link]', leaving older bloggers to wonder (as reflected in their posts and comments) how beauty is even relevant to a blog. For Israeli tween girls, blogging is not about writing but about design and customisation and a blog need not be interesting as much as it needs to be beautiful and well kept. Girl bloggers figure out pretty fast that participation in this blogging community requires the expressive language of graphic design as well as the decent level of design skill that allows for meaningful interaction with other bloggers, as blogger 'Nitsi' expresses in the following post:

> It's almost 6am and I've been up all night...doing graphic design. I've taught myself soooo many new things tonight that I think I've aligned myself with the high standards here on *Israblog*. I can design stuff for you if you want now. I like designing. :}}} Look what I've prepared tonight for the design contest. ('Nitsi' on 30 June 2005)

Over a decade ago, Danet (2001) documented online fan cultures collecting fonts, and predicted that various professional interests and skills would become popularised on the web. A few years ago, Lankshear & Knobel (2007) argued that the cropping of images with graphic design software is a basic literacy skill in new media environments. Nitsi's post suggests this bar has already been raised by revealing a rich tween culture engaged in graphic design on blogs and implying that social interaction and social capital in the blogosphere may partially depend upon it.

As mentioned above, in August 2011, as many as 4,905 *Israblog* blogs were opened under the categories 'graphic design and Photoshop blogs' and 'graphic design and tutorials for blogs'. These blogs, solely dedicated to the practice of graphic design, are joined by many other personal blogs of tween girls like Nitsi, that display the designs they circulate and occasionally experiment with their own designs.

The girl bloggers organise whimsical design contests on a daily basis, from thematic buttons to entire blog themes, in order to solicit interaction between designers and supply a platform for gaining visibility and attracting the attention of new potential 'clients'. Since contests that occur on popular blogs are open to all bloggers and the entire process of submission and judgement is visible online, participating in these contests serves as an entry strategy for new bloggers to the 'designs industry' and endorses their reputation through the gifting of various buttons attesting to the winning of or mere participation in those contests, which are displayed on blogs' side bars.

Israeli tween girls who engage in blogging are compelled to accept graphic design as a literacy skill that constitutes the practice of blogging and constantly attempt to improve and test it. Girls who master the skill demonstrate it by sharing their knowledge in the form of tips and tutorials and/or open critique blogs/blog categories writing reviews of other designers. Girls who don't create original designs become 'clients' (or consumers rather than producer-consumers), customising and decorating their blogs with other girls' designs. Therefore, Israeli tween girl bloggers use the blog not only as a text but also as a (display) space and (meticulously decorated) avatar.

The described practices have gained such a visibility on *Israblog* that online graphic design is no longer considered a 'virtual virtue' for boys to pride themselves upon, as it was just a few years back (Golan, 2006). Instead, my ethnographic evidence suggests it has become a gendered practice associated with tween girls. Young male bloggers engaged in graphic design either withdrew from it quickly or had to constantly justify the practice and fight off peer ridicule, with the claim that graphic design is a serious creative and legitimate profession and not a 'girly game'.

Inside the Blogosphere's 'Designs Industry'

A Peer Negotiation Culture without Negotiation

The creative exchange space bloggers to which refer as the 'designs industry' on *Israblog* operates by a set of self-regulated norms that are often expressed as explicit rules varying from blog to blog. Although this inter-blogs interaction is based on a gift economy and best described as a peer negotiation culture, the girls construct and perform it through labour frames and discourses.

Design blogs are maintained as brands and are often playfully named 'Icon Factory', 'Sharon Designs Ltd' or 'Rotem Designs Inc.', while designer-bloggers often refer to themselves as 'blog manager' or 'CEO'. Most bloggers accept new orders solely in the comments section of a dedicated blog post they refer to as 'the factory', and often scold 'clients' who comment on other posts to go and fill in the form and order at the factory properly (see Figure 6.1 for an example of such a form).

Figure 6.1   An order form and rules for design work

TRANSLATION:

Details

Name/nickname:
Blog:
Picture (mandatory):
Text on the picture:
Lists titles (up to 15):
Linking button (100*100):
Graphic dividers:
Signatures (up to 2, simple, with brushes, with part of the title):

Colours (desired colours, restricted colours):
Paintbrushes (without/soft/full):
Other:

Rules

I don't make icons backgrounds and graphic ornaments for lists
You must link to my blog after receiving your order
I don't design for blogs that operate less than 2 months and don't have a
 reasonable number of posts
You can order a new design once a month
If your blog isn't updated for 2 weeks your order is suspended till you
 update

Since this creative playful activity involves thousands of blogs, each blogger potentially engages with a large number of friends as well as strangers and is required to negotiate her position within this activity. Bloggers follow a grassroots norm to set explicit rules for the blog and for interaction with the designer-blogger and articulate it in their blog frame. New or marginal bloggers tend to have few simple rules encouraging interaction, while veteran and/or popular designers tend to have many specific rules limiting interaction. Figure 6.1 is an example of both an order form and blog rules.

Every order form and every set of rules is unique, although inspired by other bloggers. The most 'nasty' rule I have encountered in my corpus reads: 'You don't get to nudge after you ordered. If you ask me even once when's your order ready, and I don't care how long you've waited, your order is automatically cancelled and I will not even bother to update you on that omission, just so you'd know.' The explicit rules of interaction may vary, yet all blogs go through similar steps of ordering designs, a waiting period, display of the designs on the blog, and copying of the design to the recipient's blog after public appreciation has been shown in the form of a comment on the relevant post.

However, the make-believe frames of market and labour that mitigate the interaction with strangers in the blogosphere were broken when designers wanted to give a friendly gift to a blogger. Since the 'design industry' is gift economy based, a 'real' gift for a friend had to be differentiated by another set of rules/rituals: a friendly gift is never requested, only initiated spontaneously by the designer and given right away outside of the waiting list of clients often displayed on busy design blogs. The receiver has no influence on the design and has to receive and display the surprise gift as it is.

I have followed and documented the richness of this peer culture for a little over three years, but only when I left the field and started writing the ethnography did I notice that the most important detail is not in the data but in what's absent from it: the element of negotiation. These types of interactions are called 'peer negotiation cultures' because of the centrality of negotiation processes in exchanges, games and self-regulated spaces. It suddenly struck me that I have never seen negotiations occur on these blogs and the few attempts to negotiate in the comments section were silenced by a reference to the blog rules, or a suggestion to turn to a different design blogger who operates under other rules, or simply ignored.

It appears that the strict rules on each blog are designed to rule out any opportunity for negotiation: the designers demand specificity and raw materials so there is no room for error, and limit the number of changes or refuse to consider them at all after an order is done. Both parties know that there are a thousand more designers and if someone is not happy she can always ask for a new design from someone else the very next day, thus negotiations are rendered obsolete, and as potential conflicts they are being carefully avoided.

This represents a significant departure from commercial producer–client relationships, wherein the client's will is key. In this scenario, the client's request is merely the starting point but then the designer is in final control of the product, as if she plays solo and needs the others only as an excuse or stimulus to trigger her creative process.

Performing Professionalism to Minimise Social Risks

Design blogs are often operated by two or more partners sharing the load of the design work. Although a small number of design blog partnerships were based on offline friendship, the vast majority of partners were strangers chosen as work colleagues, according to their design skills and availability. When seeking another partner, bloggers often ask for the submission of a short formal application that includes details like number of years of experience with Photoshop software and number of hours one can spend on the computer, and requires design samples, as seen in the following example:

> Hi people, I'm leaving you but just for a week, family trip to Bulgaria. But we are looking for another partner that has Photoshop or Paintshop because Dina's license expired and I was the only one doing the designs. If you're interested (you can remain our partner even when I'm back) please write:

Name:
Blog number:
Graphic software:
Attach 3 samples you designed so we can see your style.
How many hours you spend on the computer every day:
Dina and I will choose quickly and will let you know the results as
early as tomorrow.

One would assume such partnerships facilitate friendship yet they often
remain virtual and 'professional'. One blogger who cooperated closely
with a partner for years told me in an interview that they never even
discussed meeting and only met by chance during army service after
they had closed their design blog, but never became friends. On the
other hand, some bloggers admitted that bringing up 'professional'
considerations serves as a good excuse to reject partnerships with real
friends that suggest 'playing' together, without risking conflict.

Although negotiations and conflict with 'clients' were avoided, they
were quite apparent between designers cooperating on the same blog
and often expressed publicly through blog posts in order to solicit
support from other bloggers. In one case, the partnership agreement
appeared in the form of a public contract written with legal performative acts within a blog post. In Figure 6.2 (p. 106) I present unique
evidence of conflict in the form of a direct threat to break the partnership, mitigated through this contract.

Much like the African-American working-class girls' in 'he-said-she-
said' reports (Goodwin, 1990), Moran is artful in her ability to elicit
commitments to courses of action in the future and attempts to transform the dispute into a larger public event. However, despite Moran's
fierce accusations and ultimatum reflected through legal discourse in
this post, she carefully hedges it and leaves room for Ella to continue
the partnership safely and respectfully: the contract is only 'kinda'
broken and school tests are suggested as an acceptable excuse. Moran
simply wants Ella's attention and makes some attempt to avoid conflict within this public challenge. It would seem that the formality was
invoked only after less formal and social attempts were ignored, thus
Moran is softening the social risk of breaking the partnership through
professional labour discourse.

'Girl Power' as Production Power

I found it very surprising that so many girls as young as 11 present
themselves on blogs as a manager with '2 years of experience with

כשהצטרפת לבלוג הזה כשותפה,
את חתמת על חוזה וירטואלי!!
‹קישור לפוסט המקורי›

12.12.07

בחוזה הזה, אני [מורן], מנהלת הבלוג, מצרפת אותך [אלה] לצוות.
בחוזה הזה הינך מאשרת כי:
* את תנהלי ביושר את מפעל הביקורות.
* את תעדכני את הבלוג פעם בשבוע מינימום.
* את מבטיחה לא להתערב בענייני העיצוב בבלוג.
* ואת תעזרי לי לשפר את הבלוג, ולהפוך אותו לבלוג מצליח.

החתימה של אלה: החתימה של מורן:
אלה   **מורן**

החוזה עדיין קיים!
ואת די' הפרת אותו. (למרות ההתחשבות בבגרויות)

תקשיבי אלה.
אם אני לא רואה שום שינוי מצידך עד סוף השבוע הזה,
אני נאלצת להוציא אותך מהבלוג לאלתר.

ממני,
מורן - מנהלת הבלוג.

Figure 6.2   Publicly mediated conflict between designers

TRANSLATION:

When you joined this blog as a partner you signed a virtual contract [link to the original contract].

Contract, 12/12/07: with this contract I, Moran, the blog CEO, hereby adds you, Ella, to the blog team. By this contract you confirm that:

- *You will run the designs critique factory rightfully*
- *You will update the blog at least once a week*
- *You promise not to intervene with design style affairs*
- *You will help me improve the blog and make it successful*

(Signatures)

The contract still exists and you kinda broke it. (Even when considering your high school final exams and all...)

Listen, Ella, if I don't see any change on your part by the end of this week, I shall be forced to release you from this blog immediately.

Yours,

Moran – blog CEO

Photoshop', for example. It does not necessarily mean that in a decade Israel will be overpopulated with graphic designers, but rather, as I argued earlier, that graphic design is becoming a basic skill, a part of new media literacy. The power to create images, perform identities through them and circulate them may be regarded as a literacy resource, symbolic cultural capital, as well as a power of production in the more traditional notion of power as the ownership of and access to the means of production.

Indeed, professional graphic design software used by the girls, like Photoshop, Paintshop and Animationshop, is not common on household computers and is quite costly. Very few girls in my corpus displayed the skill of hacking such software or even downloading a cracked version, and none of them was aware of the existence of alternatives such as free open source design software. Most girls downloaded trial versions and after 30 days would manipulate the software for an extension of the trial: they would download it on a different computer or format the computer so it would be identified as new by the software. As a result, many girls had some experience with different design software, exhausting the options for trial.

Loss of access to the means of image production was a key motivation behind blog partnerships, making sure at least one blogger was able to design, as seen earlier in the quote from the designer who was heading to Bulgaria for a family trip and was seeking a third partner with a 'license to design'. After a while it became easy for me to identify the girls who did not have access, since they would always 'work' harder on the blog to compensate for their loss of power: update more, engage with blog rules and logistics and invest time in finding cool images and icons around the web to serve as giveaways to clients and inspiration to designers. They were clearly the lower class within this 'industry' and always felt the need to justify their position in the game.

Against this backdrop, two 18-year-old girls, who referred to themselves as 'Power Girls', had opened a blog named 'power point' which offered designs that were created with PowerPoint presentation software which is more common on household computers. Graphic design is both a language and a resource and these older girls wanted to make sure younger girls had a voice and were free to express their creativity and earn social capital free of the economic constraints associated with more expensive software like Photoshop. The blog offered tutorials on the possibilities of image design with PowerPoint, empowering tween girls who lacked access to professional software. 'Power Girls' played with the concept of power through word play, juxtaposing PowerPoint with 'girl

Figure 6.3   Power Girls' PowerPoint blog header

power', acknowledging the ability to create images as a form of power. Figure 6.3 shows the header image of their blog.

Discussion and Conclusions

Israblog's 'designs industry' is a make-believe game frame within a tween girls' peer culture in a digital affinity space. As such, it aligns with the discourse of girls' empowerment online, yet the notion of 'girl power' takes on a context-sensitive meaning, collapsing the dimensions of power as aesthetics (the beauty of the blog design as an avatar), as literacy (graphic design skill) and in the traditional sense of ownership of the means of production (access to graphic design software).

Israblog's 'designs industry' indeed functions as an empowering safe space, since it is free of commercial interests, created solely by the girls as a collaborative game between personal blogs, as opposed to participating in cultural products produced for them and creating content on commercial sites where their labour commodifies and brands them (Martens, 2011). The girls' choice to frame their make-believe collaborative game as a labour industry might be interpreted as an internalisation of neoliberal market ideology, which is transforming the values of the game.

Self-branding is primarily a series of marketing strategies applied to the individual. It is both a mindset, a way of thinking about the self as saleable commodity to a potential employer, and a set of practices. In social media, self-branding produces a set of status markers that are related to visibility and attention, reflecting these values through technical status such as blog analytics, number of friends on a social network, and so on (Marwick, 2010). The described practices of Israeli girl bloggers are clearly identified as self-branding aimed at gaining visibility and attention within the blogosphere and attracting 'clients'. Through the designs game, Israeli tween girls learn to commodify their play, literacy and skills, thus configuring the power relations within their peer culture through the adult frame of industry labour.

Lazzarato (1996) argues that we live in an economy of immaterial labour, in which leisure time and working time are increasingly fused, making life inseparable from work. This is an aspect of what Marx called 'real subsumption' – the absorption of capitalist logic and the dictates of surplus value through more and more of everyday life. Cote & Pybus (2007) applied the concept of immaterial labour to MySpace, suggesting that aspects of immaterial labour become the quotidian activities of youth in a place of their own, where entrepreneurial and brand management skills become necessary for forging effective links and achieving popularity:

> The particularity of the commodity produced through immaterial labor consists in the fact that this is not destroyed in the act of consumption, but enlarges, transforms, creates the 'ideological' and cultural environment of the consumer. This does not produce the physical capacity of the workforce, it transforms the person who uses it. Immaterial labour produces first of all a 'social relationship'... Social networks enable an exponential explosion of such social and economic relations. MySpace demonstrates the extent to which this social factory has already become ensconced in youth-specific social relations. (Cote & Pybus, 2007: 95)

In the Israeli blogs 'designs industry', immaterial labour is being framed as labour without the pretensions of fan work and virtual communality, and it produces immaterial goods that organise social relations around this symbolic and cultural capital. In this case, the analysis of the capital as a logic that increasingly flows through more and more social relations, and finds passage in different techniques and practices, gains another interpretive layer from the point of view of peer cultures research.

Since young people reformulate social categories appropriated from the adult culture in ways that are context sensitive and reflective of their momentary goals in their peer group, pretend play provides them with rich affordances to accomplish exclusion through the pretend frame, while minimising their responsibility (Sheldon, 1996). I argue that industry and labour frames are strategically deployed as resources to help girls organise their social worlds: to enter the collaborative game, improve their position within it and avoid conflicts that present social risks.

The professional make-believe frame is based on the appreciation of male-dominant values of success, which are in contrast to the gift-economy feminine-dominant values of sharing and sociability. The professional frame allows the girls to challenge one another while remaining conveniently separated from a social conflict (for example, breaking a 'contract' with a design partner without breaking a friendship). However, becoming a successful designer often means risking social resources and relationships: some girls get caught up in the labour frame and complain about the loads of design work, neglecting the social dimensions of the interactions with 'colleagues' and 'clients'.

This strategy results in confusion between social and professional relationships within the game frame, creating mechanisms of alienation in a space wired for play, sharing and cooperation. Labour rules and contracts are used to regulate what otherwise might have been messy friendships, leaving less room for negotiations and reducing some of the social risks presented in the game. The case study of the Israeli blogs 'designs industry' provides evidence of the bidirectional influence between work and play spaces. As play began to take over work discourse in the digital era and changed the nature of work by decreasing its alienating mechanisms (Fisher, 2010), it seems work discourse has infiltrated digital play, resulting in potential alienation and the dominance of individual professionalism and reputation over friendship and communion.

The strict rules system that girls follow while avoiding negotiations may be interpreted as a gendered practice, resulting from girls' tendency to emphasise sociability and cooperation over competition and challenge (Brown & Gilligan, 1992). However, other ethnographies of girls have shown them negotiate, challenge rules and even fight (Brown, 2003; Goodwin, 1998, 2001).

I argue, therefore, that a lack of negotiation is medium specific, enabled by the mediation of the peer culture game. In face-to-face activities girls cannot avoid negotiations, conflicts and challenges and are dependent on a relatively small number of participants. However, in a mediated space facilitating a game between thousands of strangers, those intrinsic practices could easily be bypassed, although avoiding potential conflicts seems to undermine potential sociability and serve as an alienation mechanism rather than create harmony within a peer group.

Note

1. I refer to the entire set of practices – the contests, the pretend labour frame – as a game. Essentially, the game is graphic design, and any other framework is a make-believe one that the girls themselves assign to it.

References

Aapola, S, Gonick, M & Harris, A (2005) *Young Femininity: Girlhood, Power and Social Change*. New York: Palgrave Macmillan.
boyd, d (2008) 'Taken Out of Context: American Teen Sociality in Networked Publics'. PhD dissertation, University of California-Berkeley, School of Information.
Brown, LM (2003) *Girlfighting: Betrayal and Rejection Among Girls*. New York: New York University Press.
Brown, LM & Gilligan, C (1992) *Meeting at the Crossroads: Women's Psychology and Girls' Development*. Cambridge, MA: Harvard University Press.
Cook-Gumperz, J & Szymanski, M (2001) 'Class Room Families: Cooperating or Competing? Girls' and Boys' Interactional Styles in a Bilingual Classroom', *Research on Language and Social Interaction*, 34: 107–130.
Corsaro, W & Eder, D (1990) 'Children's Peer Cultures', *Annual Review of Sociology*, 16: 197–220.
Cote, M & Pybus, J (2007) 'Learning to Immaterial Labour 2.0: MySpace and Social Networks', *Ephemera: Theory & Politics in Organization*, 7(1): 88–106.
Danet, B (2001) *Cyberpl@y: Communicating Online*. Oxford: Berg.
Davies, J (2004) 'Negotiating Femininities Online', *Gender and Education*, 16(1): 35–49.
Dobson, AS (2012) '"Individuality is Everything": "Autonomous" Femininity in MySpace Mottos and Self-Descriptions', *Continuum: Journal of Media and Cultural Studies*, 26(3): 371–383.
Fisher, E (2010) *Media and New Capitalism in the Digital Age: The Spirit of Networks*. Basingstoke: Palgrave Macmillan.
Gaskins, S, Miller, PJ & Corsaro, WA (1992) 'Theoretical and Methodological Perspectives in the Interpretive Study of Children', in WA Corsaro & PJ Miller (eds) *Interpretive Approaches to Children's Socialization*. New Directions for Child Development Series, No. 58. San Francisco: Jossey-Bass, 5–24.
Gee, J (2004) *Situated Language and Learning: A Critique of Traditional Schooling*. New York: Routledge.
Golan, O (2006) 'Friendship over the Net: The Social Construction of Friendship Among Israeli Youth in Computer Mediated Communication'. PhD dissertation, The Hebrew University of Jerusalem, Department of Sociology and Anthropology.

Goodwin, MH (1990) *He-Said-She-Said: Talk as Social Organization among Black Children*. Bloomington, IN: Indiana University Press.

Goodwin, MH (1998) 'Games of Stance: Conflict and Footing in Hopscotch', in SM Hoyle & CT Adger (eds) *Kids Talk: Strategic Language Use in Later Childhood*. Oxford: Oxford University Press, 23–46.

Goodwin, MH (2001) 'Organizing Participation in Cross-Sex Jump Rope: Situating Gender Differences Within Longitudinal Studies of Activities', *Research on Language and Social Interaction*, 34(1): 75–106.

Katriel, T (1987) '"Bexibudim!" Ritualized Sharing Among Israeli Children', *Language in Society*, 16: 305–320.

Kearney, MC (2006) *Girls Make Media*. New York: Routledge.

Kearney, MC (2011) *Mediated Girlhoods: New Explorations of Girls' Media Culture*. New York: Peter Lang.

Lankshear, C & Knobel, M (2007) 'Sampling "the New" in New Literacies', in M Knobel & C Lankshear (eds) *A New Literacies Sampler*. New York: Peter Lang, 1–24.

Lazzarato, M (1996) 'Immaterial Labour', in P Virno & M Hardt (eds) *Radical Thought in Italy: A Potential Politics*. Minneapolis, MN: University of Minnesota Press, 133–147.

Lincoln, S (2012) *Youth Culture and Public Space*. Basingstoke: Palgrave Macmillan.

Martens, M (2011) 'Transmedia Teens: Affect, Immaterial Labor, and User-Generated Content', *Convergence: The International Journal of Research into New Media Technologies*, 17(1): 49–68.

Marwick, A (2010) 'Status Update: Celebrity, Publicity, and Self-Branding in Web 2.0'. PhD dissertation, New York University, Department of Media, Culture, and Communication.

Mazzarella, SR (ed.) (2005) *Girl Wide Web: Girls, the Internet, and the Negotiation of Identity*. New York: Peter Lang.

Mazzarella, SR (2008) 'Reflecting on Girls' Studies and the Media: Current Trends and Future Directions', *Journal of Children and Media*, 2: 75–76.

Mazzarella, SR & Pecora, N (2007a) 'Girls in Crisis: Newspaper Coverage of Adolescent Girls', *Journal of Communication Inquiry*, 31(1): 6–27.

Mazzarella, SR & Pecora, N (2007b) 'Revisiting Girls' Studies', *Journal of Children and Media*, 1(2): 105–125.

McRobbie, A & Garber, J (1976) 'Girls and Subcultures: An Exploration', in S Hall & T Jefferson (eds) *Resistance through Rituals: Youth Subcultures in Post-War Britain* (1993). London: Routledge, 209–222.

Mitchell, C & Reid-Walsh, J (2002) *Researching Children's Popular Culture: The Cultural Spaces of Childhood*. London: Routledge.

Mitchell, C & Reid-Walsh, J (eds) (2005) *Seven Going on Seventeen: Tween Studies in the Culture of Girlhood*. New York: Peter Lang.

Pearson, E (2007) 'Digital Gifts: Participation and Gift Exchange in LiveJournal Communities', *First Monday*, 12(5): http://firstmonday.org/htbin/cgiwrap/bin/ojs/index.php/fm/article/view/1835/1719 (accessed 8 June 2008).

Pipher, M (1994) *Reviving Ophelia: Saving the Selves of Adolescent Girls*. New York: Putnam.

Sheldon, A (1996). 'You Can Be the Baby Brother But You Aren't Born Yet: Preschool Girls' Negotiation for Power and Access in Pretend Play', *Research on Language and Social Interaction*, 29(1): 57–80.

Stern, S (2008) 'Girls as Internet Producers and Consumers: The Need to Place Girls' Studies in the Public Eye', *Journal of Children and Media*, 2: 85–86.

Willett, R (2008) 'Consumer Citizens Online: Structure, Agency and Gender in Online Participation', in D Buckingham (ed.) *Youth, Identity, and Digital Media.* Cambridge, MA: MIT Press, 49–70.

7
Youth, Social Media and Transnational Cultural Distribution: The Case of Online K-pop Circulation

Sun Jung (Asia Research Institute,
National University of Singapore)

Since the late 1990s, Korean popular culture has circulated broadly across the Asian region and to a lesser degree the global cultural market via a phenomenon commonly known as the Korean Wave or *Hallyu* (Chua & Iwabuchi, 2008). Popular television drama series like *Winter Sonata* (2002), *Dae Jang Geum* (2003–2004), *Full House* (2004) and *Boys over Flower* (2009) have met with great success in many Asian countries including Japan, Singapore, Hong Kong and Thailand. Recently, K-pop (Korean popular music) has been widely circulated via new media technologies such as fan-blogs, peer-to-peer websites, video-sharing websites, micro-blogging and mobile internet.[1] Employing K-pop circulation as its primary case study, this chapter examines how youth social media activities reinforce and construct a new global cultural dissemination model that I identify as social distribution. I use this term to refer to distribution practices enabled by fans' online social networks, which involves distribution across fan bases in different regions of the world, thus allowing for the simultaneous, multidirectional and transnational circulations of creative products. Advanced digital media technologies render the global pop culture market landscape extremely changeable, and through these channels Korean pop products have become visible in a range of online and offline markets globally. As demonstrated by the case of K-pop boy band Super Junior, which topped the Taiwanese music chart KKBox for over 100 weeks (2011–2012), K-pop songs often rank highly on local music charts. K-pop has also risen in visibility in Australia since the late 2000s when it first appeared on radio shows and at club parties, leading to national television station SBS establishing the regular programme *PopAsia* which is dominated by K-pop music videos. In Indonesia, so-called I-pop (or Indo pop) idol band music became one of the most significant socio-cultural phenomena in 2011, largely inspired and influenced by K-pop idol music and its visual styles. However, youth fan group-led online K-pop inflows existed in these various pop markets long before the KKBox chart, SBS *PopAsia* and the I-pop phenomenon. These once-marginalised virtual pop flows have evolved over time into major and in some cases even mainstream phenomena.

These cases demonstrate how creative content can freely cross cultural borders and enter into local mainstream markets via non-commercial online transmission by local youth fans and their activities. The current online K-pop flows signify the deconstruction of a conventional schema of mono-directional cultural flows once predominantly led by media conglomerates (particularly Western ones), and reinforces the construction of a new paradigm of multidirectional creative distribution, which accelerates cultural divergence. Web 2.0-driven participatory youth culture is not only 'subordinate and subversive' (Hall & Jefferson, 1976), but also economically substantial. Within this emerging transnational social distribution paradigm, youth culture is identified not only through the notions of 'youth-as-trouble' and 'youth-as-fun' (Hebdige, 1988), but also through the notion of youth as active agents in the transnational circulation of popular culture products. Recent research has already challenged the simplistic opposition between 'subversive' and 'mainstream' culture (Buckingham, 2008: 5), and everyday youth interactions with digital media reinforce the blurring of boundaries between these oppositional concepts. Buckingham remarks that we need to acknowledge how 'commercial forces both create opportunities and set limits on young people's digital cultures' (2008: 5). Using the empirical case study of K-pop online fandom, this chapter explores how it achieves this kind of blurring in the realm of digital technology-empowered youth culture in order to form a basis for understanding newly arising youth-led media cultural transmissions in the global creative industries.

Youth, Social Media and Asia as the Pop Prosumer

The focus of this chapter is twofold: firstly, it asks how recent developments in youth participation in social media and its interactions with transcultural flows of popular content combine to produce the definition of social distribution applied in this chapter. Secondly, it examines how social distribution is distinguished from the established cultural distribution paradigm, which is predominantly led by global media conglomerates. With the increased emphasis on dynamic user participation, social interaction and collaboration, the current Web 2.0 internet environment enables social distribution. It is thus useful to look at the recent K-pop phenomenon through the conceptual framework of emerging transnational youth culture driven largely by their collective autonomous participation. I use 'transnational' here rather than 'global' as the former more accurately illustrates how cultural products cross national borders through the virtual border-crossing activities of youth groups. It is also crucial to point out how social distribution enhances cultural divergence, while deconstructing earlier understandings of cultural globalisation that are often associated with the notion of cultural imperialism (Crane, 2002; Schiller, 1979; Tomlinson, 1991). According to earlier treatments, cultural globalisation refers mainly to cultural domination by core (predominantly Euro-American) countries over peripheral ones. However, cultural flows are not necessarily one-way but are multidirectional, often flowing from the periphery to the core (Berger, 2002; Crane, 2002). The cultural imperialist theory also fails to acknowledge the significance of local sovereign power upon and resistance to the dominant culture, and ignores processes of negotiation, adaptation and indigenisation of the receiving countries (Lull, 2000; Robertson, 1994). Elsewhere I have argued that this cultural imperialist theory cannot fully explain the current phenomenon of Korean popular culture flows (Jung, 2011a). This is particularly true in the case of online K-pop flows, which are multidirectional and driven largely by the sovereign decision power of youth groups in various – both core and peripheral – local pop markets.

In recent years, an emerging field of scholarship has examined how youth fan community practices are increasingly incorporated within the logics of media industries (Green & Jenkins, 2009; Jenkins, 2006; Johnson, 2007; Murray, 2004; Shefrin, 2004). Youth activities on social media are the key to social distribution as I define it here. So far, only limited research is available about online youth communities on social networking sites, their cultural consumption and distribution practices and their impact on cultural economies. As key users of grassroots media, with the rise of social media technologies youth networks speak to and interact with a vast number of users simultaneously across borders, through which they can easily reproduce and mass-distribute cultural products from various origins. Youth studies scholars have acknowledged the significance of youth and youth cultures in the mobilisation of ideas and goods, and the creation of globalised cultures within transnational contexts (Helve & Holm, 2005; Suárez-Orozco & Qin-Hilliard, 2004). Advanced digital media enhance this mobilisation even further. They are relationally linked via their participation in an online social network that is an exemplar of the radical connectivity of our digital era (Stornaiuolo et al., 2011). Such participation reinforces cultural flows of ideas, artefacts, texts and images across national, cultural, textual and linguistic borders (2011). However, existing research on recent online cultural distribution centred around youth social networking remains marginal to the discipline as a whole. Social media are the newest and most extensively used communication tool among youth (Reich, 2010; Subrahmanyam et al., 2008), encouraging the development of transferable and valuable socio-cultural and technical skills in both formal and informal learning processes (Crook & Harrison, 2008; Ito et al., 2008) and also enabling youth to actively participate in 'networked publics' through producing and circulating cultures and knowledge (Benkler, 2006; Shirky, 2008; Varnelis, 2008). Although there is a field of scholarship around the distribution practices of grassroots media that has acknowledged their increasingly significant role in the Web 2.0 era (Jenkins, 2006), there currently exists no broader conceptual analysis that provides a specific paradigm of youth social networking practices in relation to the global cultural industries. This chapter will address this absence by offering a new way of thinking about the role of online youth practices within the transnational pop distribution paradigm.

East Asia in particular demands special attention with regard to the growth of creative industries and markets and the development of information technology, two essential facets of this new transnational distribution paradigm. The emergence of this new paradigm in the region stems from the development of digital infrastructure and hardware that has been strengthened by the national innovation strategies of each country. In the early 21st century, East Asian companies dominated almost all key aspects of digital equipment manufacture, albeit with stepwise shifts in design and manufacturing from Japan to Korea, Taiwan and most recently China (Holroyd & Coates, 2012: 149). East Asian digital manufacturing provides a strong example of the effectiveness of national innovation strategies. In Taiwan, the government has had a series of multi-year projects in the information technology sector including e-Taiwan (focusing on information technology), m-Taiwan (focusing on mobile technologies), and u-Taiwan (focusing on ubiquitous computing) (Holroyd & Coates, 2012: 155). It is not only physical infrastructures, but also the creative content industries, that these East Asian states have recognised as important. Due to the global economic resurgence in 2010, the size of the global creative markets has increased by 4.6 per cent to US$1.4 trillion, and the growth rate of the Asian market (6.3 per cent) is the second highest after the South American market (12.2 per cent) (Kim & Kim, 2011). According to Kim & Kim's analysis of the regional creative market share (creative industry sales volume) of GDP in 2010, Japan is ranked 5th and Hong Kong is 10th while Korea is second only to the UK. Another analysis reported the total creative industry sales volume of Korea as US$64 billion and its total exports as over US$3.2 billion (KOCCA, 2011). As such, Korea's creative industries are continuously expanding their export market and, along with Japan, Taiwan and Hong Kong, Korea has now become one of the major exporters in the region.

The high penetration of advanced digital technology in the daily lives of consumers across the region is another crucial facet to address. Amongst the top five internet service markets, three are in Asia – Japan (1st), China (3rd) and Korea (4th) (Kim & Kim, 2011). The rapid development of digital technologies and the creative content industry sector reinforces new media network-driven transnational creative distribution in the region. Strong user growth in social media in the region allows instant, simultaneous and multidirectional circulation of pop content. For example, India is the third largest user of Facebook followed by Indonesia (4th) and the Philippines (8th) (Socialbakers, September 2012). In Indonesia, youth aged 18 to 24 constitute the majority of the social media user population – 40.55 per cent (Hui, 2010). According to my previous research on Indonesian youth fandom of K-pop, over 95 per cent of questionnaire participants specified that they mainly use the internet to consume and circulate K-pop, among which almost 91 per cent of them chose social media (Facebook and Twitter) as their first preference (Jung, 2011b). Youth consumers and their increasing online pop consumption practices are behind this transnational social distribution paradigm.

Youth as Social Distributors: The Taiwanese Case

This study is part of an ongoing longitudinal project called 'Social Media and Transnational Cultural Distribution in Asia'. For this project, I have collected fieldwork data from Indonesia, Thailand, Taiwan and Singapore. The ethnographic research of the Taiwanese case study and industry analysis in this chapter expand earlier findings and offer new critical insights into the role of youth as social distributors. Between 2009 and 2012, I conducted archival research on aspects of globalisation, cultural distribution and digital youth culture. I have also conducted online participant observation research on various fan pages and channels on social media websites such as Facebook and YouTube. From May to August 2012, I collected 121 questionnaires from Taiwanese K-pop youth fans, and conducted email and telephone interviews with industry professionals in related fields such as music and social media. The questionnaire participants were aged between 18 and 24, and most were students. Of those who took part in the study, 105 were female and 16 were male (Table 7.1).[2]

Table 7.1 Demographic details of questionnaire respondents (gender)

Gender	Female	Male
No. of respondents (%)	105 (86.78)	16 (13.22)

Today, a large percentage of youth access and consume popular products through online media. In my previous study on Indonesian youth, 91 per cent chose social media such as Facebook and YouTube as their first preference for consuming K-pop online – the three main reasons offered for this were 'easy access, fast update, and low-cost' (Jung, 2011b). Many mentioned how 'connectedness' is another important factor in choosing social media as they can 'keep in touch with' other fans and/or their beloved idols (2011b). Members of this young generation are the so-called 'digital natives' (Prensky, 2001), and their mode of cultural consumption and distribution is already ideally configured to various new media forms including text messaging, blogs, micro-blogs, social networking sites and video-sharing websites. With quickly advancing smartphone technologies, this is rapidly moving to the mobile internet environment. As in the Indonesian case, these Taiwanese youth typify the digital native, and their digital technology-driven lifestyle is evident from the large amount of time they spend on online activities every day (Table 7.2).

Table 7.2 Responses to the question, 'How many hours are you online every day?'

Hours spent online/ day	Less than 1 hour	1–2 hours	3–4 hours	5–6 hours	7–8 hours	More than 8 hours
No. of respondents (%)	1 (0.83)	3 (2.48)	35 (28.93)	28 (23.14)	43 (35.53)	11 (9.09)

Over 96 per cent of the respondents spent more than 3 hours online every day, while over 35 per cent stated that they spent 7–8 hours online. Of those 11 respondents who spent over 8 hours, some expressed that they were online about 12 hours per day, while one mentioned that she spent more than 16 hours online daily. While the rate of youth access to the internet varied from country to country, previous research has indicated that, globally speaking, youth on average spend more time online than older generations. For example, in 2002 market research suggested that online spending by young Americans (18–24) was four times greater than that among older age groups (Pastore cited in Osgerby, 2004: 160).

It is also important to note how much of this online time is spent on K-pop activities such as watching music videos, reading K-pop news articles and chatting with other fans about K-pop. The highest percentage of participants spent 1–2 hours (38.84 per cent) followed by 3–4 hours (27.27 per cent) and 5–6 hours (13.22 per cent). The majority of respondents spent at least 1–8 hours on K-pop activities online, while two respondents spent over 8 hours a day (Table 7.3).

Table 7.3   Responses to the question, 'How many hours do you spend on K-pop activities online?'

Hours spent on K-pop activities online/day	Less than 1 hour	1–2 hours	3–4 hours	5–6 hours	7–8 hours	More than 8 hours
No. of respondents (%)	13 (10.74)	47 (38.84)	33 (27.27)	16 (13.22)	10 (8.26)	2 (1.65)

It is worth considering the notion of the digital native in the Taiwanese context, as it is one of the highest social media-penetrated countries in Asia. As the above figures indicate, Taiwanese users spend a significant amount of time online and many of the Taiwanese young people interviewed for this study mentioned that it was their 'habit' to log into certain web platforms to check the latest news about their favourite artists and related information. For the question 'Which online platforms do you use for K-pop activities?', 107 out of 121 participants chose YouTube while 56 chose PTT, one of the biggest bulletin boards in Taiwan (Table 7.4).[3]

Table 7.4   Responses to the question, 'Which online platforms do you use for K-pop activities? (Choose three)'

Social media platform preferred	YouTube	PTT	Facebook	Twitter	Kpopn	Tudou	Weibo
No. of respondents	107	56	53	22	20	14	10

Significantly, there is a difference in the preferences of Taiwanese and Indonesian youth. The former prefer using the local platform PTT over the Western-origin social media platforms, namely Facebook and Twitter. In the case of Indonesian youth, after YouTube (90), Twitter (77) was the second most preferred channel to consume K-pop content, while only 22 Taiwanese participants chose Twitter.[4] This is because Taiwanese participants have rather diverse options in their own language such as PTT, Kpopn (Chinese-language K-pop news website), Tudou (Chinese-language video-sharing website), and Weibo (Chinese-language micro-blogging website). Such diversity in K-pop consumption channels reflects the long and rich history of Korean pop culture fan networks in Chinese diaspora communities that have been active in different parts of the global pop culture markets. For example, a high proportion of the video content on Tudou and Youku is Korean television programmes. Finally, some minor responses include another micro-blogging service Plurk (7), an English-language K-pop news website allkpop (5), another Chinese-language video-sharing website Youku (4), and some Korean portal websites like Naver and Daum.

Taiwan is renowned for its high smartphone penetration. According to the questionnaire survey result, 79 participants (65.29 per cent) owned smartphones. However, in regard to the overall time online, participants spent comparatively fewer hours on K-pop related activities when on their mobile phones: 45.57 per cent answered that they spent less than 30 minutes, while 21.52 per cent specified that they spent 1 hour every day. Again, among those who participate in K-pop activities on their mobile phones, the majority answered that they listened to music, watched music videos and read K-pop related news.

The Taiwanese research participants specified three main reasons why they chose social media platforms for consuming K-pop: the speed of updates, convenience, and the range of resources available. Like Indonesian youth, Taiwanese youth also mentioned speed as the most important element in terms of using social media for consuming K-pop, with 73 participants (60.3 per cent) indicating it was a key factor. Many emphasised their appreciation of receiving information in close to real time. These participants chose Twitter because they could receive 'first-hand' information 'immediately' and 'directly' from their artists. Comments made included the following:

> The fan pages on Facebook would update latest and immediate information. (TW10, TW15, TW23, TW28, TW33, TW51, TW78, TW110, TW116, TW118)

1. YouTube: to listen to and watch K-pop immediately. 2. PTT: the information on many specific group boards update fast. 3. Twitter: to follow Korean stars' status immediately and directly. (TW104)

K-pop board (on PTT) has immediate video links or links for watching live programs very often, so I usually can receive information simultaneously. (TW99)

Twitter, I can follow people from any country, no matter what latest gossiping information released by any country or official Twitter, could be gained immediately. (TW75)

On Twitter, following the status of artists and friends to gain first-hand message. (TW116)

The second and third top-ranking reasons participants offered to support their choice of social media platform were convenience and the range of resources available, respectively. Many participants highlighted 'plentiful and lots of information' (e.g. TW92, TW108) as an important feature, as well as the 'diversity' of information (e.g. TW45, TW88). Some pointed out how these platforms provide them with 'complete' information.

1. YouTube has abundant videos, it has most users around the world, which is easier to find the videos or music I want. 2. The content in PTT you find is complete...and the information and source are plentiful. 3. kpopn reports the latest information in a way that is adaptive to Taiwanese K-pop information receivers, and also because the information has already been collected and translated, it's convenient to read. And the contents are abundant! (TW4)

As is evident from TW4's comment, for these young Taiwanese users it is also important to consume various forms of information – audio, visual and text – in one place. This aspect therefore unites both the issue of convenience and quantity of material and information available.

Another key reason raised was connectedness. Many mentioned how they 'communicate', 'interact', 'share', 'chat' or 'get in touch' with other fans or with their chosen idols. TW73 stated, '[I use] Twitter because most K-pop stars have their own Twitter account where they would share their daily feelings. The fans would feel they are closer to their stars.' Twitter has become an important way for many fans to follow their idols, and increases a sense of connectedness with them. Twitter is faster and more immediate than other platforms, and gives the impression (although this may not materialise) of possible direct communication. Elsewhere I have discussed how Twitter has influenced dramatic shifts in star–fan dynamics (Jung, 2011b). Twitter has changed these dynamics between stars and fans with different national and language backgrounds, and has greatly diminished the language barrier within transnational fandom. I identify three key aspects in communication between the stars and their overseas fans through Twitter. First, communication tends to be smooth thanks to many translation groups on Twitter who immediately translate K-pop idol stars' tweets as soon as they are uploaded. Second, the photos and videos uploaded by stars do not require written or verbal explanation. Third, the 140-character limit on tweets encourages non-native-English-speaking K-pop stars and fans to post in short English sentences. It appears that more and more K-pop stars are communicating with their overseas fans via Twitter. The emergence of Twitter has not only changed the dynamics of overseas K-pop fandom, but has also created a new paradigm of transnational K-pop distribution (Jung, 2011b).

There are three main differences between the Indonesian and Taiwanese responses: price, issues of translation and issues of quality. Only one Taiwanese participant celebrated the 'cheap cost' of social networking, compared with the Indonesian participants where a majority highlighted this as a crucial factor. Many Taiwanese participants also indicated that they could easily acquire translations via certain online platforms, particularly Kpopn:

> Kpopn: Even though it's not a formal news website, but it gathered a group of fans who love K-entertain, and who usually translate artists' Twitter and Korean first-hand news and information. (TW78)

> Kpopn: It's easy to receive the latest K-pop information, and translated information, which is released by Korean official sites. (TW93)

> On Facebook, the information has been translated by the administrator, I can receive messages in Chinese. (TW1)

The ways in which these Taiwanese youth discuss translation differ from the views of the Indonesian participants, reflecting shifts in their socio-cultural backgrounds. The issue of translation is closely linked to Chinese fan sub groups (subbing or subtitling), which have been active for decades, even predating the online era. These groups can translate a one-hour TV programme and post it on Chinese online video-sharing websites such as Tudou and Youku within hours of its broadcast. Lastly, many respondents mentioned that they use YouTube because of the higher quality and more reliable streaming of videos. TW18 states, 'It's faster, clearer and smoother in watching programs.' It is significant that they consider not only the quantity but also the quality of products. In this sense, both the Taiwanese and Indonesian participants demonstrated both differences and similarities in their responses. This suggests that while there are shifts in the characteristics and inclinations of these youth from different regions stemming from their unique socio-historico-cultural contexts, there are still some areas where they merge. This, in turn, indicates that further in-depth comparative research is required to explore more fully the online pop consumption and distribution habits of each group.

Combination Between the Bottom-Up and Top-Down Models: 'Gangnam Style'

Using Taiwanese youth online practices concerning K-pop fandom as a case study, this chapter has looked at the essential elements of a newly emerging mode of transnational pop distribution. This does not suggest that this newly emerging pattern of youth-led social distribution is completely separated from the existing media industry paradigm. It rather attempts to demonstrate how youth practices have become a crucial part of the pre-existing global pop distribution paradigm, while such practices are still under the strict control of a corporate-led environment. It is crucial to explore how social distribution is constructed through interactions and collaborations between mainstream distribution bodies such as iTunes, major record companies, K-pop entertainment companies, youth networks on YouTube, Facebook and Twitter, and sometimes local entertainment management companies in countries of reception.

The current notable rise in the circulation of K-pop demonstrates how social distribution operates within the new creative industry paradigm. The above-mentioned combination model places the recent phenomenal success of Psy's 'Gangnam Style' as a particularly strong example of this. Since the music video was released on 15 July 2012, it has gone viral online. Within two months, the video had surpassed 200 million views on YouTube and by 29 September 2012 Psy had topped the *Billboard* Social 50 for the fifth week in a row.[5] On 21 September 2012 the *Guinness Book of Records* announced it was the most played YouTube video of all time (Milano, 2012). There are four primary driving forces behind the success of 'Gangnam Style' and its transnational (particularly US) circulation, which while chronological are also to some degree cyclic: social media, mainstream media, management, and online music stores and their associated rankings. Most immediately, social media and online K-pop networks lay at the heart of the song's huge success from the outset. The music video was initially released through Psy's management company YG Entertainment's official YouTube Channel, from where it was circulated among existing K-pop fan networks on YouTube, Facebook and Twitter. As an extremely successful internet meme,[6] it leaked outside these areas into the mainstream through the rise of so-called 'reaction' and parody videos on YouTube (some of which themselves have become YouTube sensations), coverage on popular US celebrity websites like Gawker.com, and even being mentioned on Twitter by famous celebrities like Katy Perry, Tom Cruise, T-Pain and Britney Spears. Additionally, mainstream network television programmes in the US like *Eye Opener* and *Big Morning Buzz* showcased the music video, and included shots of their cast and crew mimicking Psy's signature horse dance in their studios. The role of Psy's management also must not be underestimated. Due to his signing with the influential US talent agent Scooter Braun (manager of teen sensation Justin Bieber) in August 2012, Psy was exposed to a much larger American audience via his appearance on the MTV Video Music Awards on 6 September, which was followed by appearances on major television shows such as *The Ellen Degeneres Show, The Today Show* and *Saturday Night Live*. These appearances again helped in part to propel the phenomenon to even further success, with 'Gangnam Style' ranking at the top of the US iTunes Video charts for over a month, and number one in the Top Song charts in ten countries including the US. Suggesting the cyclic nature of these driving forces, these rankings then continued to see Psy and 'Gangnam Style' rise in their positive coverage on social media.

Corporate media power holds a great influence over grassroots-driven social distribution, and vice versa. As William Gruger observes:

> Psy's Schoolboy Records/Universal Republic partnership announcement, along with the continued soaring popularity of the song, helped Psy to remain secured in the No. 1 spot. A 69% increase in weekly overall fanbase acquisition was fuelled by 92,000 new Facebook fans, 54,000 new Twitter followers and 95,000 new YouTube subscribers. 'Gangnam Style' currently sits above 150 million YouTube views. (Gruger, 2012)

The Psy case study suggests that the combination of a social network-driven bottom-up model with a more recognisable media-led top-down model constitutes the newly emerging social distribution paradigm. It begins with the grassroots practice of youth fans sharing their interests with each other in online social networking groups and then combines with the corporate forces of mainstream media to create substantial cultural flows.

The Korean media often compare Psy's case with The Wonder Girls, a group that spent three years in the United States attempting to break into the US pop market. The Wonder Girls had a huge online fanbase as well (although the main fanbase was in Asia), learned English for three years, worked with US producers and released their singles in English. Overall, however, their attempt is considered a relative failure. Psy broke into the US market and achieved remarkable success within two months. His border-crossing is worth studying further because it signifies the new paradigm of transnational creative distribution empowered by bottom-up grassroots activities on which this chapter has focused. His song is sung in Korean and he did not physically cross a national border (until invited to work with Scooter Braun), so there was no local marketing promotion. On the other hand, under their management company JYP's strategic global market expansion scheme, The Wonder Girls physically crossed the border to the US, recorded their US debut single 'Nobody' in English, followed by the second single 'Two Different Tears', and were distributed through iTunes as well as through offline music stores. In special promotion, their 'Nobody' remix CDs were even sold for just one dollar in Justice Stores, a popular retail fashion chain across the US aimed at teenage girls. Even with such an assertive local promotion and corporate-controlled top-down marketing strategies, their border-crossing music distribution was not successful. The Wonder Girls' three years represents the old distribution model while Psy's two months represents a newly emerging model that this chapter refers to as social distribution.

Conclusion

Social media is now one of the most significant pop culture distribution channels, not only in terms of fan networks, but also as part of the culture industry's marketing strategies. YouTube has become the key marketing tool for any K-pop product attempting to cross cultural borders. All major entertainment companies have their own YouTube channels (e.g. SM, JYP, YG, Cube, Loen Entertainment) and actively promote their products internationally. The total hit counts of the videos of the top three K-pop entertainment companies – SM, YG and JYP – reached 2.3 billion in 2011, almost three times higher than the previous year (Woo, 2012). YouTube is not only a marketing tool but has also become a new revenue model. These K-pop companies signed a 'content partnership' agreement with YouTube: they provide YouTube with K-pop content and they share the revenue (i.e. multinational enterprises' advertising fees), which enables the dynamic online distribution of K-pop music (Jeong, 2012). As such, mutual collaborations between global media corporations, YouTube, K-pop entertainment companies as well as fans' social networks enable the current dynamic transnational flows of K-pop.

By examining these collaborations and interactions, this chapter has developed an analytical framework to better understand the dynamics between grassroots practices on social media and corporate media practices where the boundaries between conventional and alternative cultural distributions are blurred or unclear. Employing the case study of the consumption of K-pop by Taiwanese youth, this chapter is among the first pieces of academic research to address the newly emerging transnational social distribution practices of young pop consumers in the region. This digital generation utilises social media platforms and mobile media predominantly to consume and distribute K-pop. The success of Psy's 'Gangnam Style' demonstrates that this social network-empowered grassroots practice is a crucial part of the pre-existing global pop distribution paradigm within the corporate-led media environment. It is a substantial reciprocal online and offline distribution circle consisting of different media forces that continuously influence each other, and thus constitute the core of the emerging transnational social distribution paradigm.

Notes

1. For instance, there are over 320 million 'K-pop' related websites found on Google (15 September 2012, English only). On Google Trends (search volume index), the search volume for K-pop has exceeded the one for J-pop (Japanese pop music) since late 2009. Before the emergence of K-pop, J-pop had been the most widely recognised Asian popular music genre.
2. Although I am fully aware that the younger demographic group is even more active in terms of such social media-driven pop culture distribution, I did not include it. This is due to the complexity of the ethics (IRB) approval, which would inevitably delay the research process.
3. The participants were advised to choose up to three platforms.
4. Again, multiple selections were allowed.

5. The Social 50 chart ranks the most popular artists on YouTube, Vevo, Facebook, Twitter and MySpace, using a formula that blends weekly additions of friends/fans/followers along with weekly artist page views and weekly song plays.
6. Internet meme refers to a concept, an idea or a style that spreads from person to person via the internet.

References

Benkler, Y (2006) *The Wealth of Networks: How Social Production Transforms Markets and Freedom*. New Haven, CT: Yale University Press.

Berger, P (2002) 'Introduction: The Cultural Dynamics of Globalization', in PL Berger & SP Huntington (eds) *Many Globalizations: Cultural Diversity in the Contemporary World*. Oxford: Oxford University Press, 1–16.

Buckingham, D (2008) 'Introducing Identity', in D Buckingham (ed.) *Youth, Identity, and Digital Media*. Cambridge: MIT Press, 1–22.

Chua, BH & Iwabuchi, K (eds) (2008) *East Asian Pop Culture: Analysing the Korean Wave*. Hong Kong: Hong Kong University Press.

Crane, D (2002) 'Culture and Globalization: Theoretical Models and Emerging Trends', in D Crane, N Kawashima & K Kawasaki (eds) *Global Culture: Media, Arts, Policy, and Globalization*. New York: Routledge, 1–25.

Crook, C & Harrison, C (2008) *Web 2.0 Technologies for Learning at Key Stages 3 and 4*. Coventry: Becta.

Green, J & Jenkins, H (2009) 'The Moral Economy of Web 2.0: Audience Research and Convergence Culture', in J Holt & A Perren (eds) *Media Industries: History, Theory and Methods*. Chichester and Oxford: Wiley.

Gruger, W (2012) 'Psy Still No. 1 on Social 50 Chart, 50 Cent Makes "Sexy" Return', Billboard.biz, 14 September: http://www.billboard.biz/bbbiz/industry/digital-and-mobile/psy-still-no-1-on-social-50-chart-50-cent-1007949682.story

Hall, S & Jefferson, T (eds) (1976) *Resistance through Rituals: Youth Subcultures in Post-War Britain*. London: Hutchinson.

Hebdige, D (1988) *Hiding in the Light*. New York and London: Routledge.

Helve, H & Holm, G (eds) (2005) *Contemporary Youth Research: Local Expressions and Global Connections*. Burlington, VT: Ashgate.

Holroyd, C & Coates, K (2012) 'East Asia in the Digital Age: National Innovation Strategies of Japan, Taiwan, South Korea, and China', in Z Zhu (ed.) *New Dynamics in East Asian Politics: Security, Political Economy, and Society*. New York: Continuum, 148–169.

Hui, L (2010) 'Facebook in Asia: Total Users and Age Groups', *Grey Review*, 2 March: http://www.greyreview.com/2010/03/02/facebook-in-asia-total-users-and-age-groups-latest-stats

Ito, M, et al. (2008) *Living and Learning with New Media: Summary of Findings from the Digital Youth Project*. Chicago: John D. and Catherine T. MacArthur Foundation.

Jenkins, H (2006) *Fans, Bloggers, and Gamers: Exploring Participatory Culture*. New York: New York University Press.

Jeong, J (2012) Phone Interview. Google Korea, 19 June.

Johnson, D (2007) 'Inviting Audiences In: The Spatial Reorganization of Production and Consumption in "TVIII"', *New Review of Film and Television Studies*, 5(1): 61–80.

Jung, S (2011a) *Korean Masculinities and Transcultural Consumption*. Hong Kong: Hong Kong University Press.

Jung, S (2011b) 'K-pop, Indonesian Fandom, and Social Media', *Transformative Works and Cultures*, 8: http://journal.transformativeworks.org/index.php/twc/article/view/289/219#itnote1

Kim, Young-Soo & Kim, Eun-Jeong (2011) *Creative Entertainment and Media Industry Analysis and Future Perspectives*. Seoul: Korea Creative Content Agency.

KOCCA (2011) *Creative Industry Statistics 2011*. Seoul: Korea Creative Content Agency.

Lull, J (2000) *Media, Communication, Culture: A Global Approach*. Cambridge: Polity Press.

Milano, D (2012) '"Gangnam Style" Video Breaks Guinness World Record', abcnews.com, 21 September: http://abcnews.go.com/blogs/technology/2012/09/gangham-style-video-breaks-guinness-world-record/

Murray, S (2004) '"Celebrating the Story in Way It Is": Cultural Studies, Corporate Media and the Contested Utility of Fandom', *Continuum: Journal of Media and Cultural Studies*, 1(18): 7–25.

Osgerby, B (2004) *Youth Media*. London: Routledge.

Prensky, M (2001) 'Digital Natives, Digital Immigrants', *On the Horizon*, 9(5): 1–6.

Reich, SM (2010) 'Adolescents' Sense of Community on MySpace and Facebook: A Mixed-Methods Approach', *Journal of Community Psychology*, 38(6): 688–705.

Robertson, R (1994) 'Globalization or Glocalization?', *The Journal of International Communication*, 1(1): 33–52.

Schiller, H (1979) 'Transnational Media and National Development', in K Nordenstreng & HI Schiller (eds) *National Sovereignty and International Communication*. Norwood, NJ: Ablex, 21–32.

Shefrin, E (2004) '*Lord of the Rings, Star Wars*, and Participatory Fandom: Mapping New Congruences Between the Internet and Media Entertainment Culture', *Critical Studies in Media Communication*, 21(3): 261–281.

Shirky, C (2008) *Here Comes Everybody: The Power of Organizing without Organizations*. New York: Penguin.

Stornaiuolo, A, Hull, G & Sahni, U (2011) 'Cosmopolitan Imaginings of Self and Other: Youth and Social Networking in a Global World', in J Fisherkeller (ed.) *International Perspectives on Youth Media: Cultures of Production and Education*. New York: Peter Lang, 263–280.

Suárez-Orozco, M & Qin-Hilliard, DB (eds) (2004) *Globalization: Culture and Education in the New Millennium*. Berkeley, CA: University of California Press.

Subrahmanyam, K, Reich, SM, Waechter, N & Espinoza, G (2008) 'Online and Offline Social Networks: Use of Social Networking Sites by Emerging Adults', *Journal of Applied Developmental Psychology*, 29(6): 420–433.

Tomlinson, J (1991) *Cultural Imperialism: A Critical Introduction*. Baltimore, MD: Johns Hopkins University Press.

Varnelis, L (ed.) (2008). *Networked Publics*. Cambridge, MA: MIT Press.

Woo, S (2012) Email Interview. YouTube Korea, 24 May.

8

Young People's Musical Engagement and Technologies of Taste

Melissa Avdeeff (Independent Scholar)

The relationship between youth and music, as mediated through technology, has been evolving since the advent of transistor technology and the production of portable music players. With the ability to take music into personal spaces, such as the bedroom, youth's relationship with music began to alter dramatically. Today, smartphones, MP3 players and iPods, complete with ear buds and built-in speakers, dominate the technological landscape. The ways in which these technologies are incorporated into social relationships reshape not only how youth listen to and find meaning in music, but also how they define their musical tastes and, to a large extent, their behaviour in social situations. Through the results of a large-scale, empirical study, this chapter explores how taste and sociability are highly intertwined, with boundaries becoming increasingly blurred between people and technology, music and genre definitions, and artist and fan. Throughout, youth are categorised as those under 30, and while having only two broad demographics can be seen as problematic, the dataset showed statistically significant differences in mobile music device use and behaviours between those over and under the age of 30.

The following discussion is guided by the results of an empirical study that took place in 2007–2008. A total of 2,143 surveys and 216 interviews were collected.[1] While 44 countries were represented, 89 per cent of respondents were located in Canada (28.2 per cent), the United Kingdom (25.7 per cent) and the United States (34.7 per cent). As such, the results yielded a predominantly Western, or Developed World, perspective. Ages of the survey respondents ranged from 13 to 82, with a median of 26, and a balance of genders, with 52 per cent reporting as male and 48 per cent as female (Avdeeff, 2011).

The results demonstrated stark differences in technological engagement between those under and over the age of 30, or between youth and adult respondents. Building on previous research by Tapscott (2009) and Palfrey & Gasser (2008), who also utilised the age of 30 as an indication of generational differences, this chapter explores how those under the age of 30 are demonstrated as engaging with mobile music media technologies in significantly different ways from their older counterparts. Throughout, I refer to the younger respondents as youth, whereas Don Tapscott refers to this cohort as the Net Generation, and Jon Palfrey and Urs Gasser prefer the term digital natives. Creating distinctions based on age group remains problematic, but the evidence uncovered from this empirical study suggests that behaviour-based distinctions are forming, as defined by different groups' relationship to music playback technologies. The vast majority of music encountered in our daily lives is recorded, and then disseminated through playback devices.

Conducting an ANOVA test between youth and adult respondents reveals that youth are statistically more likely to listen to music on their computers (Sig. = 1.6E-17), iPod/MP3 player (Sig. = 7.0E-05), or phone (Sig. = 3.0E-07), while older respondents showed a significant preference for more traditional media sources, such as buying CDs (Sig. = 0.00257) and listening to music on a CD player (Sig. = 1.2E-06) or radio (Sig. = 1.2E-09) (Avdeeff, 2011). With youth, we can observe significantly more involvement with digital music playback devices, arguably to the point where they can be defined as 'generationally' different from older respondents.

Typically, generational differences are often marked by a collective relationship with a particular traumatic event, such as war, but today it is to a particular set of technologies. David Buckingham (2006) explored these questions. He argues that, while the issue needs further academic investigation, the ways in which youth use and interact with technology are fundamentally different from older members of society. He remains sceptical about adopting a technological determinist standpoint concerning the influence of media use on generational differences, but acknowledges that there do appear to be age-related differences in how people interact with new technologies. Buckingham encourages us to recognise the banality of media technologies. Youth may be highly involved with digital technologies, but not in a spectacular way; rather, it is the invisibility, or indispensability, of the technology that defines their relationship to it. This is not to say that variations in technological engagement do not occur within demographic groups, just that the overall experience that youth have with digital technologies differs from that of adults (Grimley & Allan, 2010). Technology affects everyone, but the effects tend to be generationally specific. This invisibility of technology was noted by a large proportion of youth interview respondents. When asked how long they spent on the internet per day, most respondents indicated that they were unsure of the time spent, as it was often included in other multi-tasking activities. In regard to multi-tasking, answers included:

> *Female/15*: Sometimes when I get home, and then in the evening after I'm done homework, or after dinner, just kinda off and on when I have nothing else to do.

> *Female/13*: I just go on all my favourite sites, and listen to music at the same time. And talk to friends online. It's pretty fun.

> *Male/15*: Just talking to people, like, MSN. Like, watching videos and that.

Returning to the advent of mobile musical playback devices, as they became increasingly miniaturised, their role in youth culture expanded exponentially. Controlling their musical environment, or soundscape, has become a way in which youth can define the boundaries between their public and private life, as well as parental influence and personal exploration. In the late 1950s and early 1960s, being able to listen to records in your own room was akin to the contemporary youth ritual of inserting a set of ear buds, or donning a pair of Beats By Dre headphones, while escaping into a private world of sound that is personally chosen to reflect mood and desires, or to conjure and create memories. In this sense, the youth of today and those of the 1950s and 1960s have much in common. Where they differ, however, is in how newer digital technologies command a higher level of social interaction. It is no longer 'good enough' to just listen to your favourite artist, as youth expect a certain level of intimacy and engagement with the artist, whether through Twitter, Facebook, YouTube or various other emerging social media sites, while also laying bare their own musical tastes online, via Facebook and Twitter. Because of the immense quantity of music available online, artists must make a concentrated effort to reach out to fans on a personal level. This competition for fans is now rated in Twitter followings and YouTube hits, as opposed to album sales and record charts.

The blurring of boundaries between artist and fan is reflected in the ways in which playback technology devices are used by youth. The sight of someone wearing ear buds or headphones is no longer a symbol of desired social isolation. As will be shown, for youth, it is often seen as a way to invite conversation, to share musical tastes, or to engage in general social interaction. The control that one had regarding personalised playback has partially been given over to social media. Through perpetual contact (Katz, 2006; Katz & Aakhus, 2002), our future is increasingly focused on the concept of the social (Keen, 2012), with music occupying an interesting space in this development.

Moreover, having access to an immense quantity of online music is promoting changes in how music is classified, with it becoming less bound by genre and replaced by new systems, such as folksonomies, which will be discussed below. This movement away from rigidly defining musical taste by genre distinctions is favouring a culture of eclecticism.

Music and Technologies of the Self

A body of research exists that examines the way in which society affects musical taste, beginning with Pierre Bourdieu's 1960s seminal study of cultural taste in France (Bourdieu, 1984). For Bourdieu, it is the habitus that determines our tastes, including musical taste. Habitus can be described as a lens through which we encounter the world, our social makeup, position in society and predispositions. Our habitus influences how we interpret the world around us and, in turn, the media with which we interact. As such, our musical tastes are socially constructed, based upon a variety of influences, including age, gender, education, socio-economic status and familial influences.

While habitus, on the whole, remains an integral aspect of how we interact with the world from a social perspective, the technological aspect of our habitus – the technology that we use to mediate our relationship with the world – is increasingly altering the way in which we define our relationships with each other, the media we consume, and our musical tastes. It could be argued that a much-needed redefinition of the term would include which technologies we use and how they alter our behaviours and perceptions of society, such as how contemporary youth use seemingly socially isolating technologies, such as headphones, in social ways. On the flip side, social media sites, such as Facebook and Twitter, restrict the way in which people can communicate with each other: Twitter, for example, is confined to 140-character messages, and Facebook (c. 2000–2009) encouraged users to update their status in the third person, ultimately affecting the way in which people organise their thoughts before updating.

Research focusing on the consequences of technology has a complicated past. Historically, technology studies have sought to examine how technology and society coexist and whether one impacts the other, or whether it is a symbiotic relationship. Technological determinism, a perspective where technology affects societal norms and structures, has largely fallen out of favour, as theorists have sought to downplay the role technology itself had on society, while social constructivist theories have risen to the forefront. In particular, the SCOT (Social Construction of Technology) theory remains the most utilised and relevant in regard to an understanding of technology and society. The principal scholars, Wiebe Bijker, John Law and Trevor Pinch (Bijker, 1995; Bijker & Law, 1992; Bijker et al., 1987), primarily developed this theory as a reaction to technological determinism. They, along with their followers, wanted to acknowledge the social in technologies, as well as how technologies themselves mirror society – an approach that inspires exploration. Instead of taking the technologies we use on a daily basis for granted, it encourages us to look deeper and open the 'black box' of technology, to examine its creation and function, in order to ultimately tell us more about ourselves (Winner, 1993). However, as noted by Bijker & Law (1992), it is unnatural for the general public to question everyday technologies and their development, for it would occupy too much time and thought. Technologies work best when they are seamlessly integrated into society and everyday use.

Although a description of other theories is outside the scope of this chapter, what is useful to note is that scholars have since explored individualised theories of technology. Essentially, one creates a theoretical framework to examine a particular technology. This method allows for a more well-rounded, and device-focused, sociological analysis. Perhaps most applicable to this discussion is Marc Katz's (2006) apparatgeist theory. Although Katz does not explicitly define apparatgeist theory as a theoretical approach, it can nevertheless be used as a lens through which to examine technology. It is a combination of 'apparatus', or mechanism, and 'geist', meaning spirit. Katz notes that the term is not intended to imply that technologies have spirits, but rather, that they can represent the spirit of the times. For example, Katz argues that the mobile phone captures the spirit of the late 20th and early 21st centuries. Today, we could say that smartphones capture that spirit, with iPods occupying the space between mobile phones and smartphones.

Where apparatgeist theory is particularly relevant is in its focus on how users incorporate technologies into their everyday lives. It allows us to concentrate on how users, and non-users, create meaning. This inclusion of non-users is important when constructing a 'view' of technological use in digitality, as non-users are affected by the social consequences of technology, regardless of their conscious involvement. The consequences of technology permeate the social consciousness, which inevitably filters down through to non-users as well. This is less an issue with youth, however, as the non-users are in the minority. In the dataset utilised for this chapter, 84.1 per cent of respondents reported owning an iPod or mobile MP3 player, with higher ownership for those under 30 (86.7 per cent ownership), as compared to older respondents (79 per cent ownership).

New standards of sociability, or norms, are developing that impact users and non-users alike, both positively and negatively. When a new technology is introduced into either the human–human or human–music relationship, new social relationships must be negotiated, with the aim of finding a new form of symbiosis (DeNora, 1999). For example, the social isolation that mobile music players have been perceived (perhaps unjustly) as promoting is an oversimplification of contemporary conditions, as youth in particular do not generally perceive these devices in such a way.

The concept that social relationships must evolve to negotiate the use of a new technology is not a new one, but is reminiscent of the writings and ideologies of Marshall McLuhan (1964). McLuhan's technologically deterministic theory that the medium is the message has had a profound effect on the landscape of media and communication studies, in that we now understand that the focus is not only on *what* is playing, but also *how* it is being played. It generates focus on the technology when examining its place in society and how people use it to alter their relationship with media. Although McLuhan was writing before the advent of mobile MP3 players, aspects of his theory are still applicable today.

McLuhan described technology as an extension of the body and pointed out that, as such, it requires 'new ratios or new equilibriums among the other organs and extensions of the body' (1964: 54). If technology is an extension of ourselves, we can freely use it, thereby forming new meanings and understandings of the devices and, in turn, new relationships, both inter- and intra-personally. This way of examining technology acknowledges the subjective experiences and relationships of the user. Looking specifically at mobile MP3 players, and their ever-increasing miniaturisation, they become an actual physical extension of the body through the use of headphones or ear buds, but never truly invisible, with the tell-tale sign of the wires connecting device and body. The music also becomes a literal extension of the self, in the form of identity formation and presentation. In this way, both the music and device encapsulate identity. In using a mobile MP3 player, there is a sense of listening to the self, which is extended into the technology, and then reflected back through a personalised loop of sound. iPod users are essentially involved in a self-reflective extension of the self. It is widely recognised that one's musical tastes represent an integral aspect of one's identity (Bennett, 2000; Bourdieu, 1984; DeNora, 2000; Frith, 1997; Hennion, 2007); therefore, by listening to one's musical preferences on headphones, one keeps those aspects of their personality essentially a secret. This is in stark contrast to playing one's music on a stereo system, or boombox, and not only imposing your music onto others within earshot, but also revealing something about your own personality. Granted, many of the associations that have surfaced between personality and music style are based on stereotypes (i.e. people who listen to heavy metal tend to be more aggressive), and even disassociating oneself from these stereotypes becomes a revealing act, socially. In contrast, as will be explored further below, many youth tend to share their headphones with friends, allowing them a glimpse into their sonic bubble, and more 'secretive' aspects of themselves.

Redefining Musical Taste

Two ways in which youth, particularly, have negotiated the relationships between technology, music and each other are how they define genres and musical tastes through a bottom-up strategy, using descriptives instead of commercially imposed genres, and online music tagging, known as folksonomies. This diminishing use of traditional, commercial genre indications is influenced by the declining number of physical music stores and the move towards digital music downloading and streaming. Contemporary youth, who were born after the proliferation of music downloading, do not have the same ties to the materiality of music or experience of utilising record stores as their primary source for purchasing. Instead, music that is acquired online, via P2P torrent sites, YouTube, or streaming sites such as Spotify and Grooveshark, is not necessarily organised by genre, and even if it is, the genres are easily juxtaposed to promote eclecticism. Although there remains a sector of music consumers who frequent record stores, the mainstream occurrence of buying CDs in a music store has largely gone out of favour. Instead of being required to physically move from one location to another within a store to explore different genres, youth utilise interfaces such as YouTube's suggested videos and crowdsourced streaming music stations, such as Last.fm, Songza and Spotify.

While music within a genre implies a technical degree of similarity, new methods of musical organisation, such as folksonomy, look past musicality to encompass the subjective experience, such as purpose and mood. The term folksonomy, first coined by Thomas Vander Wal (2007), is a combination of 'folk' and 'taxonomy'. Essentially, folksonomy is the way in which materials posted online are tagged, or defined, and how they join a larger community. As David Sturtz notes, 'the centrally defining characteristic of folksonomies are thus their bottom-up construction, a lack of hierarchical structure, and their creation and use within a social context' (2004: 1). It is important to note that they are created by the users, as opposed to an imposed classification system.

Tagging in photo and website sharing and retrieval sites has been fairly well documented, but its use in music sites, such as Last.fm and YouTube, is less well known. What we do know is that tags are not limited to traditional genre definition, just as with photos on Flickr that carry abstract or personal tags. Quite often, songs will be tagged with abstract terms, such as 'popular', 'favourite', 'sexy', or even text-speak terms, like '<3'. For example, the following is a selection of tags used to describe Justin Bieber's track 'Baby', on Last.fm:

> 10s; <3; awesome; baby; baby by justin bieber; ballad; beautiful; black metal; brutal; deathcore; camryn; Canada; Canadian; catchy; cimx-fm; collaborations; cool; cute; dance; dance-pop; death metal; dildo-boy duet; favorite; fun; guilty pleasure; guilty pleasures; happy; hip hop; hip-hop; i love being a girl; i love this song; justin; justin bieber; justin bierbe; -baby; love; love at first listen; love it; love songs; love this song; ludacris; male vocalists; pop; pop music; r and b; r&b; rhythm and blues; ridiculous; ridiculously catchy; rnb; romance; romantic; sexy; summer; synthpop; teen pop; wait and see; what the hell happened to my music taste; wkqi-fm; wow; 2010.

Although in regard to commercial popular music genre conventions 'Baby' would be considered a pop song, many of these tags have more to do with describing one's relationship with the song, or general adjectives. This list also demonstrates one of the disadvantages of user-imposed definition systems: the loss of quality control. Another is that tags can be repeated, with slight variations, including spelling mistakes. In addition, people blatantly tag songs with obviously unrelated tags, such as 'death metal' in the case of Justin Bieber, most likely as a form of irony.

Chen et al. note that non-expert users have difficulty in describing their musical tastes 'and often change their minds during the search process' (2010: 2). While genre still remains one of the ways in which youth search for music, mood and artist bio round out the top three search functions. They also found that people tag music for different reasons: some are serious about knowing more about music; others annotate music for personal use and retrieval; and some wish to contribute their personal knowledge.

This online descriptive-based preference is influencing the ways in which youth describe their preferences offline as well. In discussing musical tastes with high school-aged youth, they were more comfortable using descriptives, as opposed to established genres. For example, these youth utilised terms such as 'fast' or 'slow' to describe the type of music they enjoyed, demonstrating function over genre. Fast songs were described as beneficial for 'getting ready to go out' or preparing for a social activity, such as a party. Slow songs were more conducive to relaxing endeavours, such as studying or sleeping. Music that is expounded under such broad terms, however, remains highly subjective (Avdeeff, 2011). Interestingly, the distinction between fast and slow songs, and who is perceived to be listening to them, was gender-dependent, as observed in the following responses:

Female/15: Like, most guys don't really like slow songs and stuff.

Female/15: At least a lot of lassies listen to sad songs, and a lot of ladies just like fast songs.

Male/16: Guys listen to stuff that's not soapy and cheesy.

Male/13: Sometimes girls like slow music, and boys will like fast music, sometimes, like DJ stuff and that: boys might listen more to that. Sad songs, or slow songs might be a girl thing.

Music Playback Devices and Emerging Sociabilities

For most young people in developed nations, digital culture and social media are embedded into everyday life. Having grown up immersed in digitality and its inherent nature of perpetual contact, it is more than a way of life, it *is* life. Many of these youth have spent more of their lives connected to the internet, and digital technologies, than not. For them, these technologies have become an indispensable aspect of the more mundane aspects of everyday life. They may not always be 'with' people, in a geographical or physical sense, but their sense of interconnectedness with a larger social world is clear.

New ways of organising music online, and on mobile media, are potentially altering the ways in which people define their musical tastes to become more eclectic, rather than bound by traditional definitions. Thinking back to McLuhan's (1964) concept of new technology and the negotiation of relationships, youth are adapting to the unstructured nature of online music retrieval, with subjective genre definitions moving to the forefront, reflecting the idiosyncratic nature of social media. For youth, it is not about *how* they define their tastes, but *what* the media can do for them: what emotions it can evoke, moods it can alter and, perhaps, social capital it can impose. For McLuhan, as a new technology is incorporated into the media relationship, it faces a period of negotiation, during which it can be adapted into the social fabric of its users. To update McLuhan's theory, in digitality, we must look at how digital technologies alter the person-to-media-to-technology triangular relationship. As today's youth largely grew up in a period characterised by the rise in popularity and the technological development of mobile MP3 players, we are afforded the opportunity to see how technology has been incorporated into aspects of sociability. Moreover, we have witnessed how the development of mobile technologies has reflected (and perhaps also helped create) the social needs of consumers.

Within the general public, there is a perception that mobile music devices, with their headphones and earplugs, have the potential to be socially isolating devices. The headphones can signal a desire to withdraw from social situations and become encapsulated in a personalised sound bubble. Since the advent of the Walkman, it has been argued that the use of headphones represents a desire to be alone, to close oneself off from the world. Shuhei Hosokawa has described the process of listening to music, via headphones on a Walkman, as the 'ultimate object for private listening' (1984: 168). Hosokawa's Walkman users of the 1980s utilised the symbol of their headphones to signify that they were harbouring a secret – what they were listening to and, ultimately, the meaningful connections to music, which they forged with their shielded musical choices.

The headphones of the Walkman era might very well have symbolised a desire for autonomy, but the 21st century brought a shift in social perceptions, with a desire for media engagement 24/7. This innate desire to document, share and collaborate on everyday occurrences is not particular to music, but can be seen in all aspects of contemporary youth culture. This desire is most obviously seen with the rise of the smartphone and its ability to photographically document an event, no matter how mundane, and then upload it to a social media site, such as Facebook, Twitter or Instagram. The ability to share music on social media sites is lagging behind, slightly, but with increased exposure to streaming sites such as Spotify and Last.fm, and posting listening selections to your social media feed, it is only a matter of time before musical taste becomes as openly shared as an Instagrammed photo of one's breakfast.

The negotiation of sociability and technology, in regard to mobile MP3 players, has occurred mostly offline. For youth, the presence of ear buds or headphones is not socially isolating, but a way to foster conversation and share tastes. Of course, there is always the ability to remove oneself from the outside world with ear buds but, for youth, the visual of the headphones is not indicative of wanting to be alone. The desire for perpetual contact creates a sense that social isolation is strange and not to be promoted.

For the youth interviewed in this study, it was clear that the physical technology of mobile MP3 players was not seen as a barrier for conversation. In general, they would not hesitate to engage in conversation with someone who was listening to their MP3 player, and listeners would not be bothered by the distraction. The technology has been integrated into their relationships, almost to the point of being an extension of themselves. As with the internet, they were not cognisant of the technology, only what it could do to enhance social interactions and settings. When asked if they felt that iPods were making people less social, most felt it was quite the opposite, with responses including:

> *Female/14*: Uff, No! Are you kidding me? Everyone, like, you're just sitting there and they're like 'what are you listening to'. And you're like 'Oh, you gotta listen to this!'... And then you put it on speaker, or something, and everyone just starts to dance.

> *Female/14*: You can do both at the same time. When you're sitting with someone they might want to listen to it, too. Then you socialise and talk about what you're listening to.

> *Female/15*: I think it kinda can gets you talking because people will be, like, 'Do you like this song? Do you have this song? This song's good, you should get it.' It kinda gets you talking.

It should be noted, however, that this way of using technology was not limited to high school aged students but was nevertheless statistically more dominant in the youngest of the respondents. These results allude to my previous point that further distinctions are needed, as opposed to the generalised categories of 'youth' and 'adult'. There were respondents at the upper range of the youth category who also capitalised on the social aspects of MP3 players, such as connecting through a nonverbal acknowledgement that you are both technology users, but they were not as prevalent. As noted by one 28-year-old female: 'In some ways, people connect to others when seeing a fellow iPod-er on the street/subway/gym.' Also, older youth respondents were more likely to bring their music devices to social settings, to plug into external speakers for enjoyment, en masse. A 26-year-old female mentioned that she 'find(s) MP3 players can actually be a social tool. I bring mine with me to friends' houses to share music with them and vice versa.'

A listening method that was common amongst high school-aged youth respondents, which has, in the past, been perceived as a socially isolating technique, was engaging in conversation with others while maintaining one ear bud in place. The one-ear-in, one-ear-out technique was prevalent amongst these youth, as noted by these selected responses:

> *Male/17*: You have one ear in, and one ear out, kinda deal.

> *Male/16*: Yeah, you can still talk to people, but you have background music going.

These youth did not perceive their conversation mates as ignoring them, or paying them any less attention. For the most part, they saw this way of listening and talking as a way to combine two interests: socialising with their friends and listening to their preferred choice in music. It could be argued that part of this change in perception is due to the technology, itself. As headphones miniaturised into ear buds, the technology became less visible and less of a hindrance to conversation.

Social Media and Artist Intimacy

As we have seen, incorporating technology, such as the internet, social media and mobile music devices, into the social interactions of youth is associated with increased social contact. This contact can occur in close geographical proximity, as in sharing ear buds, or unbound by geographical constraints, be it through social media, smartphones, or the like. Changing social taboos and norms have created a culture in which youth are expected to be 'always on' and constantly connected. Going back to the concept of invisibility, the time spent with these devices is virtually impossible to quantify, as they are rarely turned off. Digital technology has become a way of life, as it elucidates life for most contemporary youths (Cockrill et al., 2011).

Just as the relationship between musical taste and genre is being blurred, so is that between youth and digital technologies, which can then be extrapolated to the digital relationship between fans and artists. Following an artist on Twitter allows for direct and real-time interaction between fan and consumer. It is almost expected of artists to have a Twitter account that they personally maintain, in order to engage fans. It is frowned upon when it is clear that the artist is not posting their own tweets, as fans expect full disclosure from the artists they support. As of March 2013, Twitter has over 500 million registered users, with 200 million active users, and 500 million tweets being sent, on average, each day (Holt, 2013).

With the dematerialisation of music, coupled with digital download-ing, youth look to YouTube and Twitter as a means to discover and interact with new music (Tepper & Hargittai, 2009). Popularity is less dependent on the traditional chart system and more on Twitter men-tions, Facebook likes and YouTube hits. Dominated by the culture of the clip, contemporary pop fans look to YouTube and Twitter as their musical gatekeepers.

Devoted fans, via social media, demonstrate a new exchange value (Adorno, 1991) relevant to pop music, in that it becomes less about what you pay for records and more about your personal involve-ment with the band and/or artist. Artist personality and openness are rewarded with fan appreciation and YouTube views, which ultimately translates into profits in the live music sector, as fans expand their online relationship offline (Hanna et al., 2011; Nuttall et al., 2011). This loss of barrier between artist and fan is not new, but has been significantly reconfigured with the success of Twitter. We can situate the development of this phenomenon as a progression and merging of reality-based singing competitions, such as *X Factor* and the *Idol* franchise, with music-focused social networking sites, such as MySpace. The former illuminates the importance of the artist's back story and personality, in an effort to promote popularity, while the latter affords fans and artist a venue to interact on a mainstream platform. One could argue that music magazines previously filled the role of bringing artist and fan together, but they are still mediated through a series of writers and gatekeepers; why read an interview with an artist when you can read their own thoughts in real time?

Conclusion

This chapter has explored the role of technology in mediating the relationship between youth and music, as well as youth with each other. The triangular relationship between youth, music and technology represents a continuing desire to engage with one another. Regardless of the intended function of a technology, the participatory mindset of the young people in this study ensures that the social consequences of that technology will be explored. To that end, it has been demonstrated that these youth are: redefining their musical tastes, as influenced by the tagging function in social media sites; changing social taboos to include the use of ear buds within casual conversation; and highly involved with mobile music devices. Throughout, a distinction has been made between those under and over the age of 30; and, while this study lays the groundwork for understanding the relationship between age and technological engagement, future research would benefit from further age cohort distinctions, as the data hint at different levels and types of engagement even within these two groups – for example, those under 20 are the most highly engaged with digital media technologies, while those over 50 tend to utilise digital media technologies as transference from previous technologies.

As the technologies and interfaces that people utilise to engage with music continue to converge, it will be interesting to track how this affects sociability. Currently, smartphones are a highly converged form of media, containing the ability to download, store, stream and share music, as well as the social media apps required to maintain perpetual contact with artists and friends alike. As these individual apps converge, and smartphones become the dominant musical playback device, it is possible that new negotiations will be created, in which the relationship between music and sociability may again be altered. What those changes will bring is still unknown, but a constant is that music will remain a dominant form of identity formation and communication.

Note

1. Surveys were conducted through SurveyMonkey.com. They were primarily distributed online, through email listings, social media sites, and blogs.

A substantial number of responses were acquired from blog postings by David Hepworth of *The Word* magazine and Leander Kahney of *Wired* magazine. The survey comprised five sections: general activities, music activities, music technology habits, internet activities, and genre preference. Respondents were asked to select, on a scale from 1 to 5, how often they participated in various activities. Email interviews were sent to those who provided an email address. The interview consisted of seven statements, related in content to the five survey categories, to which recipients were asked to respond. Overall, there was a lack of youth involvement in the online survey, so in-person surveys and interviews were conducted in two high schools: Prestonpans Secondary School in Edinburgh, UK and Lakes District Secondary School in Burns Lake, BC, Canada.

References

Adorno, T (1991) *The Culture Industry: Selected Essays on Mass Culture*. London: Routledge.

Avdeeff, M (2011) 'Finding Meaning in the Masses: Issues of Taste, Identity, and Sociability in Digitality'. PhD thesis, University of Edinburgh.

Bennett, A (2000) *Popular Music and Youth Culture: Music, Identity and Place*. London and New York: St Martin's Press.

Bijker, W (1995) *Of Bicycles, Bakelites, and Bulbs: Toward a Theory of Sociotechnical Change*. Cambridge, MA and London: MIT Press.

Bijker, W & Law, J (1992) 'General Introduction', in W Bijker & J Law (eds) *Shaping Technology/Building Society: Studies in Sociotechnical Change*. Cambridge, MA: MIT Press, 2–16.

Bijker, W, Hughes, T & Pinch, T (1987) *The Social Construction of Technological Systems: New Directions in the Sociology and History of Technology*. Cambridge, MA and London: MIT Press.

Bourdieu, P (1984) *Distinction*. Cambridge, MA: Harvard University Press.

Buckingham, D (2006) 'Is there a Digital Generation?', in D Buckingham & R Willett (eds) *Digital Generations: Children, Young People, and New Media*. Mahwah, NJ: Lawrence Erlbaum, 1–13.

Chen, Y, Boring, S & Butz, A (2010) 'How Last.fm Illustrates the Musical World: User Behavior and Relevant User-Generated Content', Workshop on Visual Interfaces to the Social and Semantic Web. Hong Kong, China, 7 February.

Cockrill, A, Sullivan, M & Norbury, H (2011) 'Music Consumption: Lifestyle Choice or Addiction', *Journal of Retailing and Consumer Studies*, 18: 160–166.

DeNora, T (1999) 'Music as a Technology of the Self', *Poetics*, 27: 31–56.

DeNora, T (2000) *Music in Everyday Life*. Cambridge: Cambridge University Press.

Frith, S (1997) *Performing Rites*. New York: Oxford University Press.

Grimley, M & Allan, M (2010) 'Towards a Pre-Teen Typology of Digital Media', *Australasian Journal of Educational Technology*, 26(5): 571–584.

Hanna, R, Rohm, A & Crittenden, V (2011) 'We're All Connected: The Power of the Social Media Ecosystem', *Business Horizons*, 54: 265–273.

Hennion, A (2007) 'Those Things That Hold Us Together: Taste and Sociology', *Cultural Sociology*, 1(1): 97–114.

Holt, R (2013) 'Twitter in Numbers', *The Telegraph*, 21 March 2013: http://www.telegraph.co.uk/technology/twitter/9945505/Twitter-in-numbers. html (accessed 15 June 2013).

Hosokawa, S (1984) 'The Walkman Effect', *Popular Music*, 4: 165–180.

Katz, J (2006) *Magic in the Air: Mobile Communication and the Transformation of Social Life*. New Brunswick, NJ and London: Transaction.

Katz, J & Aakhus, M (2002) *Perpetual Contact: Mobile Communication, Private Talk, Public Performance*. Cambridge: Cambridge University Press.

Keen, A (2012) *Digital Vertigo: How Today's Online Social Revolution is Dividing, Diminishing, and Disorienting Us*. New York: St Martin's Press.

McLuhan, M (1964) *Understanding Media: The Extensions of Man*. London: Latimer Trend & Co.

Nuttall, P, Arnold, S, Carless, L, Crockford, L, Finnamore, K, Frazier, R & Hill, A (2011) 'Understanding Music Consumption through a Tribal Lens', *Journal of Retailing and Consumer Services*, 18: 152–159.

Palfrey, J & Gasser, U (2008) *Born Digital: Understanding the First Generation of Digital Natives*. New York: Basic Books.

Sturtz, D (2004) 'Communal Categorization: The Folksonomy', paper presented to INFO622: Content Representation, 16 December.

Tapscott, D (2009) *Grown Up Digital: How the Net Generation is Changing Your World*. New York: McGraw-Hill.

Tepper, S & Hargittai, E (2009) 'Pathways to Music Exploration in a Digital Age', *Poetics*, 37: 227–249.

Vander Wal, T (2007) 'Folksonomy: Folksonomy Coinage and Definition', posted on vanderwal.net: http://www.vanderwal.net/folksonomy/html

Winner, L (1993) 'Upon Opening the Black Box and Finding It Empty: Social Constructivism and the Philosophy of Technology', *Science, Technology & Human Values*, 18(3): 427–452.

9
Understanding Everyday Uses of Music Technologies in the Digital Age

Raphaël Nowak (Griffith University)

When American student Shawn Fanning and his uncle John Fanning created the peer-to-peer application Napster in 1999, they probably knew little about the extent to which this innovation would change the face of music consumption on a global scale. Indeed, ever since the massive success of peer-to-peer applications that have all followed the path opened by Napster, much has been said and written about the nature of change brought by the digital age of music technologies in music consumption.

Throughout this chapter, I scrutinise the various changes brought about by the advent of digital technologies on music consumption practices, focusing on individuals' mobilisation of sound carriers such as CDs, digital music files (MP3s) or vinyl discs. I will develop two intertwined arguments: first, that contemporary forms of music consumption are characterised by the heterogeneity of listening practices; and second, that this heterogeneity of music consumption forms a 'circuit of practices' (Magaudda, 2011) that subsequently reshapes the meaning of each music technology. As a result, individuals' everyday experiences with music are both differentiated and embedded within the materiality of music technologies through which they access music.

The first part of the chapter will examine the nature of the cultural changes that have occurred since the advent of the digital era of music technologies. It will detail the recent history of technologies, as well as the discourses that have framed these changes and the maturation of the digital era. The second section will look at precisely how individuals access music in the digital age through various forms of technological artefacts, and discuss the notion of a 'circuit of practices'. The concluding section of the chapter will focus specifically on the materiality of music interactions and how this poses new questions concerning the input of music technologies' materiality in questions of music consumption.

Identifying Changes Created by the Digital Era in Music Consumption

This section of the chapter contextualises the advent of digital technologies within a historical, cultural and discursive framework. Generally, the latest innovations in terms of music technologies are either analysed as the ending of a business model or praised as the beginning of a new collaborative culture (depending whose interests are defended). More than a decade after the advent of digital technologies, neither the decline of the music industry nor the rise of a total collaborative model of music distribution has emerged.

How to Look at Music Digital Technologies?

When portraying what has happened since the advent of Napster and during the first decade of the 2000s, cultural theorists and various commentators have tended to focus on the possibilities of new technologies rather than on their actual adoption and diffusion throughout users' everyday lives. One instance of this is the description of new music technologies as offering individuals an endless scope to access music. This point is made by Canadian-English journalist, blogger and science fiction author Cory Doctorow, who argues that 'the whole point of digital music is the risk-free grazing' (2003, in Tepper & Hargittai, 2009: 232). Such comment establishes a link between the availability of music online and the capacities, skills and knowledge that internet users have to access it.

Similarly, English sociologist Chris Rojek argues that downloading music online provides 'music for the people at no more than the cost of an Internet connection' (2005: 358). Such a positive account on online and illegal downloading tends to overestimate the practices of individuals when it comes to accessing music content. Rojek (2005) even pushes the argument further by contending that new music technologies are a source of cultural democratisation. He states that downloading 'also reflects a powerful moral conviction that the web is a common resource for consumer empowerment, social inclusion and distributive justice' (2005: 366). Thus, according to both Doctorow (2003, in Tepper & Hargittai, 2009) and Rojek (2005), individuals who download music online not only enjoy endless possibilities, but are also animated by political convictions.

These arguments are sometimes associated with the concept of 'digital revolution' (see Knopper, 2009; Kot, 2010; Kusek & Leonhard, 2005). A revolution usually suggests a complete change of regime and a clear demarcation between a 'before' and an 'after', which is not exactly what happened in the case of music consumption in the digital age of technologies. The purpose of this chapter is not to diminish the impact of digital technologies in contemporary societies, but rather to emphasise that the term revolution is not adequate to depict the state of music consumption in contemporary society, for two main reasons: digital technologies have been commodified by music industries, and they coexist within a network of materiality. In fact, they complement other forms of music technologies within 'circuits of practices' (Magaudda, 2011).

The approaches underlining the possibilities of digital music technologies, and eventually defending the notion of a 'digital revolution' in relation to music consumption, tend to isolate these technologies from their cultural adoption and economic developments. In fact, these approaches create a gap between what technologies *enable* individuals to do, and what individuals actually *do* with them or how they *use* them.

Grounded empirical approaches suggest that individuals still develop particular strategies to access music content (see Tepper & Hargittai, 2009) and that individuals' predispositions matter in terms of how they create a repertoire of music preferences (see Rimmer, 2012). Rather than browsing through endless possibilities and unlimited music content, individuals negotiate their cultural practices by relying on a pre-existing repertoire of preferences, on particular references with which they are familiar – such as friends, websites and others. In that regard, new digital music technologies don't erase these logics of consumption. In fact, the impact of new technologies can only be measured when inscribed within an everyday usage and individuals' adoption of them. The next section presents a brief overview of the state of music consumption within the last decade, in order to understand how digital technologies have been diffused and incorporated within logics of music consumption.

The Commodification of the Digital Age and Coexistence of Music Technologies

The digital age of recorded music commenced with the advent of the compact disc (CD) in 1982. This format replaced both the vinyl disc and magnetic cassette tapes and met unprecedented success in terms of sales (Coleman, 2003). The advent of digital music files (MP3 files and then others) coupled with the democratisation of the internet in the 1990s marked the beginning of music downloading. In 1999, Napster became the first peer-to-peer application and quickly met with international success. By 2001, 50 million people had used Napster to download music illegally (Bergmann, 2004: 8). The application also opened the path for further technological evolutions in terms of online downloading.

When online exchanges hit a peak – especially after the advent of Napster – the practice was declared illegal. Music artists/bands such as Metallica, Madonna and Dr Dre sued internet users over copyright infringement. Online downloading was seen as the reason for the fall of CD sales. However, from the point of view of the creator of Napster, Shawn Fanning, peer-to-peer applications cannot be held responsible for these changes in the fortune of the music industry:

> As Napster grew and ultimately hit its peak, if you look at CD sales [they] were up as long as Napster was popular. The point at which Napster started filtering (blocking certain songs, after a court order in March 2001) is the point at which the record industry announced that the constant increase in their CD sales suddenly changed. (Fanning, 2001, quoted in Coleman, 2003: 182)

While the music industry argued for a correlation between online downloading and the decrease in CD sales, Fanning clearly rejects this position and rather defends the idea that consuming music through CDs or digital music files represents two different things. In fact, these two forms of consumption don't necessarily have to be opposed: they can complement one another.

Initially, Napster and its fellow peer-to-peer applications were subversive by definition, as exchanges of music content occurred between individuals and outside the scope of music industries and without any retribution for copyright holders. However, after fighting online downloading for a few years, lobbying for stronger copyright infringement laws and labelling downloading users as 'pirates', the music industry gave in and decided to adopt digital music technologies as a new business model. Digital technologies slowly started to be commodified. Indeed, besides the increasing number of physical devices commercialised (such as MP3 players and iPods), legal selling platforms of digital music files developed (such as Amazon and iTunes). The commodification of digital technologies obliterated the subversive potential of such technologies. As such, from the beginning of the 2010s, the overall traffic of illegal downloading started to decrease (see IFPI, 2011, 2012).

Following the decline of the dominance of the CD, the state of music consumption has become more complex and uncertain. Illegal downloading of digital files may have participated in the fall of CDs but has not signified the downfall of the music industry. Rather, the advent of digital technologies has given birth to a heterogeneous model of music consumption. The loss of revenue induced by illegal downloading and incurred by the music industries doesn't mean that listeners don't spend money on music anymore. Instead, they diversify their purchases related to music. For example, they can invest in internet access, a new computer, new speakers, external drives and so on to store and play their digital music files (see Combes & Granjon, 2007; CREDOC, 2010; Magaudda, 2011). Moreover, recent quantitative inquiries point towards a heterogeneous way of consuming music. While digital music files (primarily MP3s) represent the core of everyday interactions with music, other physical objects such as CDs and vinyl discs still draw a great interest from many individuals (see American Assembly, 2012; IFPI, 2011, 2012; UK Music, 2009). Of course, CD sales have declined over the past decade, but all these artefacts are still manufactured and sold.

The most striking example in terms of physical sound carrier is the vinyl disc, which is said to have undergone a 'revival', due to its 'iconicity' and 'performativity' (Bartmanski & Woodward, 2013; see also Hayes, 2006). IFPI (2012) reports that vinyl disc sales have increased since 2006, and even doubled within five years (from fewer than 50 million copies sold to more than 100 million). A year earlier, IFPI contended: 'Physical records, such as CDs and vinyl, account for 71 percent of worldwide sales; digital music sales comprise 29 percent' (2011: 2). Despite the spectacular emergence of illegal music downloading in the early 2000s, the appeal of other forms of music technologies has remained.

To summarise, the reception of music is currently characterised by a multiplication and coexistence of various music artefacts that all possess their own features and characteristic forms of appeal for listeners. The outcome of the heterogeneous state of music consumption lies in the interconnectedness of music technologies and their subsequent redefinition. The next section of this chapter considers listeners' own accounts of their everyday uses of music and the ways in which they utilise various kinds of music technology.

Accessing Music in the Digital Age

This section is concerned primarily with how the differentiation of modes of music consumption translates for individuals in an everyday context. In particular, the focus is on the different ways in which individuals discover and access music, in relation to the various technological artefacts at their disposal. Indeed, due to the variety of music technologies that individuals mobilise in their everyday interactions with music, they possess the means to diversify the ways they find out about music and access new content. In an era when music is increasingly 'ubiquitous' (Kassabian, 2013), the material conditions that create this ubiquity must be researched in order to provide an understanding of the role of music in contemporary society.

Digital Technologies and the 'Circuit of Practices'

Italian sociologist Paolo Magaudda (2011) argues that music consumption needs to be studied from the standpoint of 'practices'. In that regard, Magaudda contends that the advent of digital technologies has not 'de-materialized' consumption, but rather 're-materialized' it. The modality of such a state of consumption lies in a 'circuit of practices' (Magaudda, 2011). Magaudda writes: '[T]oday new and old objects and devices remain relevant and indispensable to support or compete with the consumption of intangible music formats' (2011: 31). Indeed, digital music files cannot be consumed alone. They require a set of practices that include the materiality of particular objects, such as a computer, portable devices, external drives and so on.

Magaudda's ideas are supported by my own empirical research. Drawing on 24 semi-structured interviews with individuals aged between 21 and 32 years, conducted in Brisbane and on the Gold Coast (Queensland, Australia) in 2010 and 2011, my study sought to understand the meaning of music in individuals' everyday lives. My findings largely suggest that objects matter a lot when engaging in interactions with music. For instance, two interviewees – Laurie and Latika – talk about their use of different media and material objects to discover music with which they were not previously familiar:

I listen to the radio and if something catches my attention, I look it up [on the internet].

(Laurie, 23, Medical student)

I find out [about music I don't know of] through radio, video clips as well, and just my own research on the internet.

(Latika, 25, Medical student)

In each of the above extracts, the emphasis is placed on how both Laurie and Latika listen to the radio on an everyday basis. The radio is a medium utilised to access music that has just been released, or that they don't know of. In including the activity of listening to the radio within a 'circuit of practices' that includes the use of the internet, Laurie and Latika can quickly obtain the information they seek about music listened to on radio stations. Once they obtain the name of the artist and the title of the song, they can choose to download the song legally, illegally, buy a CD, watch videos online and so on. In other words, the circuit of practices around listening to the radio enables them to pursue and extend the relationship with an artist they discover.

It is interesting to note that, in regard to how Laurie and Latika listen to the radio, the status of this media changes through its integration in a 'circuit of practices' and subsequent interconnectedness with other music technologies. As Magaudda underlines, this process of consuming music is not necessarily new but is now altered by the presence of digital technologies:

> The material devices and other accessories needed for the reproduction of music also existed in the pre-download period, but today the ways of appropriating these objects and technologies have become even more central in the whole practice of music consumption. (Magaudda, 2011: 31–32)

The internet – and digital technologies in general – are an essential part of Laurie's and Latika's circuits of practices. Digital technologies provide immediacy of information that enables them to take full benefit of their music discoveries. In other words, they don't have to neglect any sound that comes to their ears and that pleases them. They have the possibility to trace the sounds, obtain the information and access the music. As a result, the status of the radio is defined by those musics that individuals discover during their activity of listening to radio stations. Through their integration into circuits of practices, radios facilitate music discoveries even more than was the case before the advent of digital technologies and the internet.

Digital technologies enable individuals to experiment with music in a few clicks. It is not necessarily about 'free-grazing' or access to unlimited music content, but more in line with music discoveries they make through other means, such as radio stations, magazines, friends and so on (see Tepper & Hargittai, 2009). The proximity between media and music content is synonymous with immediacy. This concept is emphasised by digital technologies as well as by their multiplicity, which primarily takes the form of computers and smartphones but is also embodied in various websites (YouTube, Last.fm and so on) and applications (Spotify, Shazam and so on). For instance, in the following extract, interviewee Anne emphasises this notion of immediacy in regards to how she comes to like music:

> I tend to connect with things right away. Within the first 10 seconds of a song, I know whether I like it or I don't like it, on whatever basis, whether it's drums, guitar, vocal styling, whatever it is. I think sometimes you can tell when the lyrics don't match the song, because it just feels weird, and if it feels weird, I don't listen to it anyway.
>
> (Anne, 22, Bachelor degree student)

As emphasised by the above extract, Anne identifies musical elements (see Lewis, 1992) that explain how she incorporates music into her repertoire of preferences. With the help of digital technologies, Anne has the possibility to browse through an important amount of content and experiment with it. Then she can maximise how she discovers music, by experimenting with more content and including it in her repertoire of preferences or not.

Digital technologies certainly facilitate the discovery of more content than was the case during the age of the CD. In introducing the immediacy of the access to information about music and music content, digital technologies also introduce a different consumption logic to the pre-existing one. However, this new logic doesn't replace previous ones as much as it complements them. As such, the use of digital technologies introduces a gradual mode of interactions with music in everyday life.

The Gradualism of Practices – from Digital-Core to Physical-Peripheral

The convenience of digital technologies explains how individuals often mobilise them to seek information about artists, discover music they don't know about, and access music in a broader context of taste and listening preference. Digital technologies represent the core of everyday music consumption. However, despite their important role and quasi-ubiquity in individuals' everyday lives, these digital technologies are complemented by other pre-existing music technologies such as CDs and vinyl discs. In other words, even if individuals are now likely to own an important amount of content on digital files, and therefore to listen to music on their computers or portable devices, these forms of interaction with music are, in themselves, not *enough*. The reasons why individuals engage with material objects and therefore still purchase CDs and vinyl discs of their favourite albums lie in the different types of musical experiences that each material object induces. They gradually move from the convenience of digital music files towards physical sound carriers (vinyl discs or CDs for instance). Hence, at the periphery of their consumption practices lies the mobilisation of physical sound carriers such as CDs and vinyl discs. For instance, as interviewee Sascha explains:

> *Sascha*: If it's just one song that I want, I'll just buy it from iTunes... If it's a special album to me, or a special release with bonuses – for example, when they released those remastered Beatles albums – then I'd buy that from the shop, but most of the time when I want bits and pieces of music, then I'll just download it from torrent.
>
> *Raphaël*: So you have different sources according to what you want to get?
>
> *Sascha*: Yeah depending on what I want to get, if I'm not sure of an artist, haven't heard an album before, I'll just download it. But there's been amount of times (sic) in the previous years when downloading was not possible and I had to buy a whole album of an artist when I only wanted one song and the rest of the album would be shit and you don't know before you've heard it.
>
> (Sascha, 23, Bachelor degree student)

The gradual model of consuming music corresponds to the scale of music preferences that defines Sascha's repertoire. From the music he only owns on digital files to the music he owns on CDs, Sascha operates a reflexive categorisation of his music preferences according to how he wants to interact with it. Digital technologies represent the core of Sascha's interactions with music, while physical devices are at the periphery, but clearly mark his preferences for certain artists. The interest of having a physical sound carrier (here, a CD) of his favourite artists or albums lies in the aesthetic experience afforded by the object itself. While digital technologies are not aesthetically representative of individuals' favourite artists, other music technologies such as CDs and vinyl discs denote the aesthetic vision of music artists and display a set of preferences. In other words, interacting with CDs means experiencing more than the sound of music itself, but also a visual and material aspect that digital music files don't afford.

Sascha interacts with music through various technologies depending on how he appreciates the music. Thus, the gradualism of his musical interactions corresponds to the scale of his music preferences and is represented by the differentiation of music technologies mobilised to access music. Sascha distinguishes three categories of preference: the artists he only owns a few songs of on digital files (whether they are exchanged, purchased or illegally downloaded); the artists he owns albums of on digital copies; and the artists he owns albums of on CDs. His 'circuit of practices' (Magaudda, 2011) is not only utilitarian (what music technology is available in what context of interactions with music) but also aesthetic (what music technology embodies and represents his musical preferences). Depending on how he develops a particular taste for certain artists, he will consequently change the technology he utilises to interact with these particular artists.

Despite the fall in sales, CDs tend to gain a different status in relation to the advent of digital music files. The convenience, immediacy and immateriality that characterise digital music files also serve to emphasise the material and aesthetic qualities of CDs. While the CD used to be the standard sound carrier used to access music, it now shifts towards a more fetishised and aesthetic form of interaction with music. The study led by UK Music (2009), for example, emphasises how young people develop new forms of attachment to physical music technologies such as CDs. In the following extract, interviewee Anne (quoted in the previous section) explains the importance of owning CDs of some of her favourite artists:

> When you buy the Iron Maiden albums [on CDs], the whole collection and you put them together; on the side it makes a picture. It enhances the listening experience to know the complete set or to know the complete story from start to finish, to see how it finishes.
>
> (Anne, 22, Bachelor degree student)

Anne's discourse emphasises the aesthetic quality of CDs. Her interest in owning Iron Maiden's albums on CDs lies in the aesthetic display that the whole set affords. Such a relationship with music and materiality shows her commitment to that particular band. Anne only purchases CDs of her favourite artists, while she settles for digital music files to interact with other artists. The aesthetic qualities of CDs offer a more 'comprehensive' form of interaction with music than those offered by digital files. Anne then has the possibility to interact with the entire artistic and aesthetic vision of her favourite artists. In this regard, her taste for these musics goes beyond accessing and interacting with sounds.

Due to the proliferation of music technologies, individuals develop heterogeneous forms of music consumption, drawing on the use of different technologies and resulting in a 'circuit of practices' (Magaudda, 2011), in order to differentiate their interactions with music and distinguish their preferences for and levels of commitment to different artists.

In an age defined by the ubiquitous presence of digital music files, other types of music technologies become a testimony to listeners' preferences for particular albums or artists. Thus, listeners can display their music collection and make it visible to friends, family and to themselves. The visual aspect of CDs and vinyl discs acts as an aesthetic statement. Music doesn't necessarily have to be listened to; the aesthetics of artists remain an important visual element that is present in their everyday life, through CDs, vinyl discs, and eventually posters or t-shirts.

The forms of attachment that individuals develop with physical music technologies also take the form of support for their favourite artists. In the following extract, interviewee Wayne emphasises his connection with the Australian hardcore scene:

> *Wayne*: In the punk scene or hardcore, it's very hard for Australian bands to make it. There's only one band who's doing well in the metal scene in Australia and that's Parkway Drive, they debuted [at] number 2 in the charts few weeks ago... A lot of local bands actually put a lot of effort into the presentation of the releases with the cardboard sorts of envelopes, they get really good artists to do the covers. It's a kind of bonus, a way to say 'thank you for supporting us'.
>
> *Raphaël*: Does it matter to you – the artwork, etc.?
>
> *Wayne*: It does, because that CD is going to be on the shelves and people are going to see Winston McCall [Parkway Drive's singer]. It's like adding style to your room or whatever, because it's colorful, it's art and because humans are visual creatures as well, we always look at the exterior before we go and listen to what's on the inside.
>
> (Wayne, 23, bartender)

Like Anne, Wayne likes to own CDs of his favourite artists. Beyond the attachment to the object for its aesthetics, Wayne also wants to support his favourite bands by purchasing their albums. In comparison to digital music files that can eventually be obtained for free via illegal downloading or exchanges with friends, purchasing an album on CD or on a vinyl disc is also an act of support for the artists. Individuals are aware of the collapse of music sales and want their favourite artists to keep making music. Owing a CD or vinyl disc serves not only as a form of aesthetic fulfilment for music listeners, but also an economic retribution to artists for their work. This type of relationship and attachment to physical music technologies existed long before the advent of digital music files, but the advent of these latest technologies emphasises this relationship.

To summarise, contemporary 'circuits of practices' define the consumption of music as being embodied in material artefacts. The various objects that individuals mobilise in their everyday life represent the gradualism of their music preferences. From the 'core-digital' that includes all types of music and all sorts of preferences, to the 'peripheral-physical' that only includes favourite artists and denotes an aesthetic attachment to music, individuals diversify and differentiate their interactions with music in everyday life.

The Multiple Materialities of Music Consumption

In the last section of the chapter, I will focus my attention on the notion of a 'circuit of practices' as a framework to analyse contemporary music consumption, and discuss some of its implications for further sociological investigation. As previously argued, a contemporary 'circuit of practices' (Magaudda, 2011) contains various types of digital music technologies as well as other, 'older' sound carriers, such as CDs and vinyl discs. Music consumption is therefore conditioned by an array of technologies that individuals utilise to access music. Each individual pattern contributes to create a better understanding of the material and aesthetic diffusion of music in contemporary societies. As Magaudda argues, 'three dimensions ... contribute to shape practices as socially shared patterns of activities ...: (1) that of meanings and representations; (2) that consisting of objects, technologies and material culture in general; and (3) that represented by embodied competences, activities and "doing"' (2011: 22). The increasing heterogeneity that characterises music consumption raises a number of sociological issues.

Quantity and Quality of Musical Interactions

As discussed in the previous section, the gradual form of music consumption – from digital-core to physical-periphery – corresponds to different preferences for artists. Thus, individuals listen to digital music files of all sorts of artists. The core of individuals' interactions with music occurs through the use of digital music files because of their convenience and immediacy. Individuals can listen to full albums, discographies as well as singles, and playlists mixing different artists, albums and genres of music. Then physical sound carriers represent a complementary and peripheral form of musical interactions and afford an aesthetic component that is both the cause and the result of an attachment for an artist. Such differentiation in terms of practices raises the question of both 'quantity' (core) and 'quality' (peripheral) of musical interactions.

Presenting music consumption through the lens of 'circuits of practices' is not synonymous with an equivalent use of different music technologies. Hence, when considering the notion of quantity, it is clear that digital technologies supersede other physical devices. Interviewee Dave summarises this particular digital circuit of practices as follows:

> *Dave*: I never used to be big into music, but towards the end of high school, I got into bands that my friends were into. I'd listen to them online and to bands that are similar and also these days, what I hear on the radio, and then online, as I said before, I check bands that are similar.
>
> *Raphaël*: So how do you look for similar bands?
>
> *Dave*: On YouTube, you might have suggestions or things like that, if I look at a website like the Wikipedia page about the band, it says what influences they have, etc.
>
> (Dave, 21, Bachelor degree student)

Undeniably, digital technologies are massively diffused throughout the everyday lives of many individuals. However, digital music files and digital technologies do not offer a 'complete' type of interaction with music for individuals. For this reason, many individuals turn to CDs or vinyl discs to qualitatively complement their everyday interactions with music. This is the sense of interviewee Robert's statement:

> I don't have vinyls and the only reason why I don't is where I financially am at the moment; my dream has always been to buy a very good amplifier and speakers and a good record player, a good turntable, and then I want to start a collection of vinyl... I really like the crackling; it's a very warm sound...
>
> (Robert, 28, retail assistant)

When looking at the consumption of music through the notion of quality, it is clear that physical sound carriers such as CDs and vinyl discs hold a greater importance than digital music files, due to the type of experience they induce. Individuals may own more content on digital files (core) than on CDs or vinyl discs (periphery) – and their collection of CDs or vinyl discs may even be quite slim – but it is the aesthetic meaning of these objects that is important along with the type of interaction with music that this affords, one that is different from the quality of the interaction experienced with digital music files.

Contemporary music consumption is made more complex due to the heterogeneous forms of consumption of music that individuals develop through various music technologies. Such heterogeneity poses both notions of 'quantity' and 'quality' of music interactions at the core of sociological analyses.

Music, Technologies and Everyday Life

The contribution of this book chapter largely draws on Magaudda's theory of the 'circuit of practices' (2011) as a framework to analyse the current state of music consumption. Many previous publications have focused on the interactions that individuals have with music, without specifically addressing the actual material conditions of these interactions. That is the case, for instance, in both Tia DeNora's (2000) and Antoine Hennion's (2003, 2007) studies. Throughout this chapter, I have rather emphasised the access to music technologies – particularly sound carriers – to explain the ways in which individuals interact with music on an everyday basis.

The implications of such a sociological approach are numerous. First, the heterogeneity of music consumption suggests that individuals are reflexive in their choices of both music technologies and music content. By developing individual patterns of music interactions, individuals attach music to particular activities of their everyday lives. In mobilising music technologies as intermediaries to their soundtrack of everyday activities, individuals also subsequently attach meanings to the music to which they listen that correlate with the conditions of their interactions with music. In other words, variables such as space and time account for how music is defined and listened to. Second, music has been analysed in this chapter through the conditions of its materialities. Hence, the sound of music is played back using a set of technologies that change its aesthetic nature through the very characteristics of the technologies (such as the quality of the sound); through the attachment that individuals have for the materiality of music technologies; and through the diffusion of music they induce in their everyday lives. For instance, vinyl discs can only be listened to in a particular place, whereas digital music files can be uploaded on mobile devices and listened to everywhere.

Hence, focusing on the heterogeneity of contemporary music consumption raises further sociological questions for investigation. From everyday interactions with music, how do individuals engage with different technologies and content in accordance with their everyday activities? What are the consequences of such modes of music interaction for the aesthetics of music? Lastly, what types of narratives do individuals develop around music in their everyday lives? Each of these questions deserves proper investigation elsewhere; they can, however, only be raised when music technologies are given proper scrutiny within studies of music consumption.

Conclusion

This chapter has analysed contemporary music consumption. By looking at the increasing heterogeneity of modes of consumption, it has been argued that individuals gradually diversify the ways they interact with music in everyday life by using different types of technologies that correspond to their music preferences. Indeed, the ubiquitous presence of digital technologies is explained by their convenience and immediacy. These new technologies represent the core of individuals' consumption of music. However, they are also complemented by other physical sound carriers such as CDs and vinyl discs. These objects are only peripheral in individuals' consumption, but they qualitatively matter for the aesthetic experiences they induce.

Overall, the materiality of music technologies plays a considerable part in contemporary consumption and contributes to diffuse music within individuals' everyday lives. Different 'circuits of practice' anchor music within its materialities and offer an insight on how digital technologies have been included within individuals' repertoire of practices.

References

American Assembly (2012) *Copyright Infringement and Enforcement in the US, Columbia University*: http://piracy.ssrc.org/wp-content/uploads/2011/11/AA-Research-Note-Infringement-and-Enforcement-November-2011.pdf (accessed 26 October 2012).

Bartmanski, D & Woodward, W (2013) 'The Vinyl: The Analogue Medium in the Age of Digital Reproduction', *Journal of Consumer Culture*, Online First, doi:10.1177/1469540513488403.

Bergmann, F (2004) *Napster and the Music Industry*, Project/Open, Version 1.4: http://www.fraber.de/gem/Napster%20and%20the%20Music%20Industry%20010617.pdf (accessed 21 July 2009).

Coleman, M (2003) *Playback: From the Victrola to MP3, 100 Years of Music, Machines and Money*. Cambridge, MA: Da Capo Press.

Combes, C & Granjon, F (2007) 'La Numérimorphose des Pratiques de Consommation Musicale. Le Cas des Jeunes Amateurs', *Réseaux*, 5(145–46): 291–333.

CREDOC (2010). *La Diffusion des Technologies de l'Information et de la Communication dans la Société Française*: http://www.arcep.fr/uploads/tx_gspublication/ rapport-credoc-2010-101210.pdf (accessed 26 March 2012).

DeNora, T (2000) *Music in Everyday Life*. New York: Cambridge University Press.

Hayes, D (2006) '"Take Those Old Records Off the Shelf": Youth and Music Consumption in the Postmodern Age', *Popular Music and Society*, 29(1): 51–68.

Hennion, A (2003) 'Music and Mediation: Toward a New Sociology of Music', in M Clayton et al. (eds) *The Cultural Study of Music*. London: Routledge.

Hennion, A (2007) 'Those Things that Hold us Together: Taste and Sociology', *Cultural Sociology*, 1(1): 97–114.

IFPI (2011) *Digital Music Report 2011: Music at the Touch of a Button*: http://www. ifpi.org/content/library/DMR2011.pdf (accessed 28 January 2012).

IFPI (2012) *Digital Music Report 2012: Expanding Choice, Going Global*: http://www. ifpi.org/content/library/DMR2012.pdf (accessed 24 May 2012).

Kassabian, A (2013) *Ubiquitous Listening: Affect, Attention, and Distributed Subjectivity*. Berkeley, CA: University of California Press.

Knopper, S (2009) *Appetite for Destruction: The Spectacular Crash of the Record Industry in the Digital Age*. New York: Free Press.

Kot, G (2010) *Ripped: How the Wired Generation Revolutionized Music*. New York: Scribner.

Kusek, D & Leonhard, G (2005) *The Future of Music: Manifesto for the Digital Music Revolution*. Boston, MA: Berklee Press.

Lewis, G (1992) 'Who Do You Love? The Dimensions of Musical Taste', in J Lull (ed.) *Popular Music and Communication*. London: Sage.

Magaudda, P (2011) 'When Materiality "Bites Back": Digital Music Consumption Practices in the Age of Dematerialization', *Journal of Consumer Culture*, 11: 15–36.

Rimmer, M (2012) 'Beyond Omnivores and Univores: The Promise of a Concept of Musical Habitus', *Cultural Sociology*, 6(3): 299–318.

Rojek, C (2005) 'P2P Leisure Exchange: Net Banditry and the Policing of Intellectual Property', *Leisure Studies*, 24(4): 357–369.

Tepper, S & Hargittai, E (2009) 'Pathways to Music Exploration in a Digital Age', *Poetics*, 37(3): 227–249.

UK Music (2009) *Digital Music Attitudes and Behaviour Report*, The Leading Question: http://www.ukmusic.org/assets/media/uk_music_musically_09.pdf (accessed 20 July 2010).

Part 3
Bodies, Spaces and Places

In Part 3, the final part of this collection, we have sought to draw attention to bodies and places. There has been a tendency both in scholarship and in popular discourse concerning the internet to frame 'cyberspace' as a 'bodiless province' (Fernback, 1999: 203), yet how can we get outside of our bodies? Although the interactions mediated online can and do play out across great distances with an immediacy unimaginable not that long ago, our bodies are still tethered to keyboards and mice and touch screens. We see and hear and feel through the social web, sweating and clicking and dancing and shuffling and laughing at videos of cats. Key questions for Part 3 include:

- What role does the internet play in mediating embodied exchanges, such as sport and dance?
- To what extent do young people have a role in creating new spaces for themselves online?
- And, returning to the questions with which we began in Part 1 of this collection, what can we learn from mediated youth cultures about the blurring between online and offline conceptualisations of bodies, spaces and places?

This part outlines and examines the significance of digital media for the construction, articulation and representation of bodies and their relationships to space and place. These final four chapters by Pavlidis & Fullagar, Werner, Berriman and Bird round out this collection on mediated youth cultures, providing insights into how media facilitate a variety of posturings, including gender, sexuality and 'play', for young people.

Reference

Fernback, J (1999) 'There is a There There: Notes Toward a Definition of Cybercommunity', in S Jones (ed.) *Doing Internet Research*. London: Sage, 203–220.

10
Women, Sport and New Media Technologies: Derby Grrrls Online

Adele Pavlidis (Griffith University) & Simone Fullagar (Griffith University)

Sport has long been viewed as a public 'good' – a space for the creation and enactment of the 'good, healthy citizen'. Yet this public 'good' has also been gendered masculine: competitive, public and 'tough', with women's participation historically marginal to men's. In Australia in recent years, the participation of women and girls has fluctuated, with decline or stagnation in more traditional organised sports (netball, basketball) and growth in other areas, such as roller derby and football. However, women's sports are still largely invisible in the popular sport media. In this chapter we focus on roller derby as one particular women's sport that has undergone a global revival, mobilised through 'new' youth-oriented media forms. We examine four diverse websites that form part of the 'social web' of derby: two official league sites, a blog and a Facebook group. The reinvention of roller derby is intimately connected to the alternative mediated spaces made possible by the social web. Roller derby players and organisers have used online spaces for various ends: to promote the sport community, to make visible the relations of power between those involved, to create and maintain boundaries of inclusion and exclusion within the sport, and to express 'creative' aspects of identity. This chapter provides examples of the strategies and tactics used to establish and maintain roller derby as a 'women's only' sport and some of the challenges and possibilities inherent in this highly mediated space.

Roller derby is an exciting embodied pursuit that allows women the opportunity to push their bodies to their physical limits. To summarise, roller derby is a team sport played on roller skates. Each team has one 'jammer' and four 'blockers'. Jammers score points by skating past the opposing team's blockers, while the blockers attempt to block both the opposing team's jammer and blockers, using their shoulders and hips to knock players down or out of bounds. But roller derby is more than a 'sport'; it also creates a leisure space where women 'play with' traditional notions of passive, heterosexual feminine identity and belong to different mediated communities. The popularity of roller derby presents an opportunity to better understand the nexus between creativity and sport which may provide insights into how to counter the persistent gender inequities in women's sport and leisure participation.

In this chapter we introduce some of the key challenges for women in sport and identify some of the persistent inequalities within this sphere of social life. In the mainstream media, women are marginalised to the extreme. In Australia, less than 7 per cent of televised sport is of women's sport (Lumby et al., 2009). This is telling, especially considering that television viewing is the predominant leisure time behaviour in many developed countries (Dunstan et al., 2010). We provide some background on roller derby and how it has provided women an alternative to the sports previously available to them. We ask: How have women used the internet and new media communication technologies to promote the sport *and* create a space for the articulation of different sporting identities for women? Roller derby not only pushes women's physical capacities, but also encourages them to be creative and to take control of the organisation and governance of sport. The DIY nature of roller derby has been enabled by the internet without the hierarchies and restrictions of more traditional sport business models that are highly professionalised and commodified through globalised media agreements (see Rowe, 2013). However, despite the possibilities inherent in this form of 'user-created' production, there are still tensions in roller derby that challenge the notion that a coherent 'roller derby' exists for all women.

Sport and the media have had a long and complex relationship. Cultural studies has demonstrated the role the media plays in representing and influencing our beliefs, attitudes and values (see, for example, Hall, 1977; Turner, 1993). In sport, it could be said that the media play an even bigger role as they directly influence decision-making processes about how sport is organised and presented, when it is played, who is made visible/invisible and the sort of commentary surrounding the event (Rowe, 2013). Large media conglomerates control most of the sport media and as such have huge investment in the way sport is portrayed. Particularly in regard to gender, the media have been shown to present women in dissimilar and unequal ways to men, undermining their strength, skill and capacity as athletes (see, for example, Daddario, 1994; Fink & Kensicki, 2002). Women are associated with appearance rather than performance (Jarvie & Thornton, 2012: 229). While roller derby was invented as a sporting spectacle for television in the 1960s, today it is primarily represented through new communication technologies and a diversity of images and texts on the social web. This has meant that to a large extent the sport has so far avoided the 'logic of the media' (Jarvie & Thornton, 2012: 230), where content is driven by the economic imperative *and* theatrical and popular appeal to mass audiences.

Roller derby was a popular sport spectacle in the 1960s and 1970s, with paid professional skaters, faux violence, television coverage and a tough image. The first incarnation of the game occurred in the late 1920s and since then it has been reinvented several times, with its latest re-emergence quickly gaining momentum across the globe (e.g. Mabe, 2008). In 2001 a group of women in the US reclaimed the sport, creating a different emphasis, different rules, a flat track and overt connections with third wave feminist groups such as the Riot Grrrls[1] (Storms, 2010). The roller derby of the past was played by both men and women equally (Mabe, 2008). The 'new' version was, initially, exclusively played and organised by women with a strong youth-oriented focus on DIY (Do it Yourself) (Beaver, 2012), music subcultures (Pavlidis, 2011) and alternative feminine identities (Finley, 2010). Roller derby refined itself both as a sport and as an empowering space for women to express alternative identities.

Women, Sport and Roller Derby

Sport is fun, a challenge and provides those who watch and participate with pleasure. It makes visible the 'tensions, interrelationships and connections between corporeality and the social world embodied selves inhabit' (Woodward, 2009: 5). Sport is also often viewed as a site of 'community' and social capital (Putnam, 1995). Around the world sport is celebrated and athletes are revered for their skill and strength. Young people look up to athletes as role models (Biskup & Pfister, 1999) and this has contributed to the use of sport as a vehicle for positive youth development (Fraser-Thomas et al., 2005).

Yet this public 'good' has also been gendered as masculine: competitive, public, hierarchical and 'tough', with women and girls' participation being historically marginal to men's. Institutionalised sports confirm patriarchal, techno-capitalist, modernist styles of living (Woodward, 2009: 67), often privileging competition and winning over cooperation and creativity. Hargreaves writes:

> In sport, 'masculine' identity incorporates images of activity, strength, aggression and...implies, at the same time, an opposite female

subjectivity associated with passivity, relative weakness, gentleness and grace. (1986 in Theberge, 1987: 388)

Historically this has meant that in the main women have been marginalised in sport, struggling for fair and equal access in relation to promotion, participation and pay. In sport 'men usually are active subjects while women fill passive roles, often as wives, sweethearts and admirers' (Theberge, 1987: 388). There have been some exceptions, such as gymnastics and netball, which have been deemed 'appropriate' for women. Gymnastics (and ice-skating), with a focus on aesthetics and grace, have traditionally been seen as 'feminine' and appropriate for women (Trangbæk, 1997). Netball too has been found to promote ideals of 'compliant femininity'; netball is seen as a 'girls' game', adhering to social expectations about 'appropriate female behavior' (Taylor, 2001: 57).

Over time, with the rise of feminism and a greater emphasis on equality between men and women in law, women have begun to enter into the area of sports in greater numbers and in an increasing range of sports. Yet this increase in women's participation has not automatically generated an equitable environment (see Clasen, 2001). Even where women have entered into traditionally 'male' sports, such as tennis or boxing, they have continued to be sexualised via hyper-feminine clothing, make-up and jewellery. For professional women in sport there is often a focus on their private lives in the media and official commentary, undermining their skills and capability as athletes. More recently still we have seen the rise of women's participation in 'alternative' sports – for example surfing, snowboarding, skateboarding and roller derby. These 'alternative' sport practices have been seen as spaces to defy mainstream values and norms, *including* those that marginalise women (see, for example, Heywood, 2008; Pomerantz et al., 2004; Thorpe, 2005). Although most of these 'alternative' sports still privilege the masculine, roller derby is one that positions women at its centre.

Women of all ages are coming together internationally to create small, place-based roller derby leagues, with hundreds already established in countries around the world. Each league develops between two and four teams that then play each other. These teams train together *and* compete against each other, and although the overall goal is to win, there is a real focus on fun, expression and style. As roller derby continues to grow there is pressure on the women involved to model the sport on traditional sport-management structures. Despite the women's desire to compete against other teams and their need for funding to support this type of growth, at present they are unwilling to compromise the very things that attracted them to the sport in the first place. They are unwilling to compromise their independence and the freedom to choose the ways they use and display their bodies. However, this desire to protect the sport and the women involved can limit some of the opportunities made possible in the first place.

The sport of roller derby cannot be reduced to one single sport identity or meaning (competitive or creative expression); rather, it is produced through a multiplicity of subjectivities, some of which are synchronistic, with diverse women coming together to not only play the game, but also to manage this fast-growing, international sport on their own terms. Being a 'new' sport, the management and organisation of roller derby are influenced by the game itself. In a sport where women risk their bodies and where gender identities are 'in play', the stakes – for control, power and meaning making – are high. Roller derby can provide an alternative space for women to use their bodies differently and it allows multiple subject positions to be explored. In particular it allows the expression of youthful, strong, tough selves. As suggested by Frith (2005, in Kehily, 2007) the notion of 'youth' is more than just an age category; it also describes an attitude or a social institution. Alternative sports such as roller derby, also termed lifestyle sport (Wheaton, 2004), youth sport, adventure sport (Breivik, 2010), extreme sport (Donnelly, 2006) and subcultural sport (Atkinson & Young, 2008), have a majority of young (and also male) participants. However, contemporary roller derby, as primarily a women's sport open to all ages, allows for an opening up of definitions of 'youth', gender, and of strength, in a sporting context.

Yet it is the potential value of this space that makes roller derby so contentious. This emphasis on the value of the sport is implicated in some of the tensions present as the sport continues to grow. Roller derby is a contested space and its emergence as a women's sport continues to be fought out, on the track, within formal and informal organisations, and, central to this chapter, via virtual spaces on the internet. Women who play roller derby present themselves as 'youthful', 'tough', 'strong' and 'sexy'. Pain and injury are celebrated via online spaces sometimes called 'halls of pain'[2] and the 'femme' is privileged, with fishnets, tight shorts and make-up being regular parts of league uniforms. In this way roller derby cannot really be described as embodying 'compliant femininity', although this idea itself is subject to spatial and temporal change. Take the recent proliferation of 'tough' women in popular media (Inness, 2004). In some ways this is an extension of the changing image of the 'ideal' feminine body. As noted by Sassatelli, the 'ideal' body has changed, from

> the cult of slimness of the 1970s and the soft voluptuousness of the 1960s. A new composite ideal of the female body – strong and attractive, muscular and long-limbed, toned and blooming – ultimately contradicts the traditional association of femininity with inactivity and passivity. (Sassatelli, 2010: 165)

Despite the changed 'ideal' feminine body, bodies in roller derby still challenge this norm. Bodies in roller derby are not always toned, lean, blooming. Demographic research done by the Women's Flat Track Derby Association (WFTDA) found that the average age of players is around 31 years (WFTDA, 2011). This is traditionally the age women start having children in developed countries, yet here women are starting a physically demanding, potentially 'dangerous' and 'youthful' sport. These women are of different shapes and sizes, ages and abilities.

In some ways women in roller derby challenge dominant imaginaries of women in sport and society. Women present themselves as strong, rough, fit and sometimes threatening through the use of make-up and costumes as well as their physical prowess on roller skates. Research into women's participation in sport has shown that when women 'make the effort to refuse what they have been told they are and to reach towards their potential in the area of body movement' (Wearing, 1998: 110) they often have an increase in self-confidence, empowerment and liberation from restrictive gender norms. Theberge writes that 'the liberatory possibility of sport lies in the opportunity for women to experience the creativity and energy of their bodily power and to develop this power in the community of women' (1987: 393). This inclusion of *creativity* and bodily power is central to roller derby.

The Internet, Sport and Roller Derby

> TV is for old school derby. Twitter, RSS, Live Blogging, streaming video are the best way to feel close to the action when you can't afford to make that trip across country for a tournament! (Western Regionals, 2008)

As this quotation attests, roller derby is a sport that has been reinvented in the contemporary era of new digital media forms. This 'digital' context has profoundly shaped its cultural forms of play, spectating and fandom in a global context. Roller derby communities consist of local and globalised networks of players, coaches, referees, officials and fans. The use of digital communication technologies, although by no means unique to roller derby, has opened up a space for creative articulations of the sport and has enabled women the opportunity to promote and grow their sport without relying on public funding or commercial support. Over the past 12 years there has been a proliferation of websites dedicated to supporting, producing and circulating roller derby identities that are both individual and collective. This visual and textual realm of derby culture also includes a range of cultural artefacts such as clothing and music, as well as a range of sport-specific rules and official documents. The roller derby phenomenon is aptly described by Urry in relation to the 'increased mediatization of social life as images circulate increasingly fast and with added reach so as to form and reform various imagined communities' (2007: 9). Derby has become a sport where the boundary between the 'real' and the 'virtual' is inevitably blurred.

There has been a plethora of research into the everyday cultural meanings, practices and deployment of digital technologies that have accompanied the growth of the internet. Since the early 1990s researchers working in the areas of sport (MacKay & Dallaire, 2012; Ruddock et al., 2010; Wilson, 2008), feminism (Driscoll, 1999; Luckman, 1999), media, and subcultures (Gibson, 1999; Hodkinson, 2003; Kahn & Kellner, 2003, 2004; Williams, 2003) have brought 'virtual' spaces and representations to the fore of their work. Initially a site for 'consumption', the internet now enables users to produce as well as consume text, ideas, images, sounds and narratives (Castells, 2003; Manovich, 2009). In particular, research examining riot grrrls (Garrison, 2000) and cybergirls (Driscoll, 1999) highlights how the internet has been used by women to produce alternative femininities that circulate within a globalised geography.

In the more specific area of sport sociology, research has begun to examine how the internet figures within individual and collective identity formation, and most of this research utilises a (post)subcultural studies framework (Wilson, 2008). Leonard writes that 'sports studies continues to lag behind in terms of analysis and critical interrogation of new media' (2009: 2). This 'lag' is being addressed on several fronts, including examinations of 'traditional' masculine sports (Dart, 2009; Oates, 2009), 'lifestyle'/'subcultural' sports (Wilson, 2008) and, more recently, (re)presentations of gender and sport online (MacKay & Dallaire, 2012). As discussed earlier, women in sport are given dramatically less coverage within mainstream media compared with to men. For this reason the proliferation and accessibility of blogs, social network sites and user-produced content has been vital for the promotion and celebration of women and sport as well as the opportunity for women to challenge and rewrite gender and sport identities. Niche media, as opposed to mass media (Thorpe, 2008), and zines, such as those produced and circulated by members of the Riot Grrrl scene (Harris, 2003), have also been a site for the production of alternative femininities (see Chapter 5 of this collection for more on young people's production of zines).

A recent example of the way women are using the internet in sport is explored in an article by MacKay & Dallaire (2012), who examine a blog produced by the 'Skirtboarders', a female skateboard crew based in Canada. The authors view gender as performative and examine how women (re)present themselves online via images and text. In the 'Skirtboarders' blog MacKay & Dallaire found multiple narratives of femininities being presented, *including* 'stereotypical femininity' (2012: 15). Our analysis below also examines the narratives of femininity being presented in relation to roller derby in addition to highlighting the way women in roller derby have used the internet as a way of adhering to, and challenging, traditional notions of 'sport'.

Our analysis identified four diverse websites: an Australian league's official website (Sun State Roller Girls),[3] a UK league's official website (London Rollergirls),[4] an online collaborative blog (Live! Derby! Girls!)[5] originating in the US, and a Facebook group ('Things I learned from Derby')[6] with members from all over the globe. These sites were selected as they evoked some of the ways in which roller derby communities have used virtual spaces to produce and circulate their own 'version' of sport – feminine *and* 'tough'. The selection was informed by the first author's immersion in derby cultures over several years. Most importantly, they were all 'public' websites that could be accessed by anyone wishing to view their content and without password access. Following the ethical guidelines outlined by the Association of Internet Researchers (Ess & Association of Internet Researchers Ethics Working Group, 2002) we avoided 'lock and key' sites where greater privacy is assumed. No attempts were made to deceive participants on the sites; rather, an observational method of 'lurking' was taken – reading without taking part in online discussions or making comments of any sort.

Roller Derby Online – Official League Sites vs. User Created Content

Sites of Empowerment and Belonging?

Roller derby league websites commonly articulate the trope of women's 'empowerment' by evoking a collective sense of belonging and the complex pleasure/pain of individual involvement. Yet the tensions between and among different roller derby leagues highlight the intense affects at play within competitive roller derby communities. There are several 'versions' of roller derby currently vying for authority, with each version having slightly different rules and regulations, and, more importantly, a different style.[7] Each version is currently resisting being territorialised by normative sport frameworks, yet risks splintering and exclusion. The virtual identity of roller derby as a 'singular' sport community is continually undermined through intense conflicts and differences that can be read against each other.

Closely modelled on traditional sports, with a strong emphasis on empowerment and fairness, is the Sun State Roller Girls' website (Australia). The section titled 'About Sunstate Roller Girls' reads:

> [We] are a not-for-profit organisation dedicated to developing and promoting the sport of women's Flat Track Roller Derby in Brisbane by facilitating the development of athletic ability, sportswomanship and goodwill among league members... We promote the empowerment of women in a safe and organised environment that fosters the health, well-being and personal growth of skaters. We honour diversity and encourage self-expression and are committed to building a network of friendship and support among skaters. We seek continuous improvement in our sport and are committed to democratic principles...

Similarly, the London Rollergirls' website is also highly professional. It includes information about upcoming events and a very clear section on 'what is roller derby'. It states:

> We are the London Rollergirls: an all-female, skater-owned-and-run roller derby league based in London, England. Formed in April 2006, we were the first roller derby league established in the UK and are proud to have spearheaded the introduction of this awesome sport to the United Kingdom and Europe. The women that make up the league are not easily defined as there is no prototype for a Rollergirl. You do not need to be tattooed or punk, you do not need to be a sports fanatic but both girls fit in fine and both have a home within the London Rollergirls league. We are comprised of a diverse collection of women of various interests and lifestyles.

The London Rollergirls' mission statement evokes feelings of pride and belonging within a diverse collective that celebrates difference. The website states, 'both [tattooed and highly athletic] girls fit in fine and both have a *home* within the London Rollergirls league'. The deployment of 'home' is appealing; it draws us into an intimate connection with the organisational body of roller derby where there is no 'normal' femininity. The risky pleasures of derby are framed within the safe comforts of a home for all. At the same time the 'official' sites normalise and re-territorialise derby as a cultural space that becomes known and sanctioned in particular ways. Official league sites make visible only the 'empowering' affects (the pleasure of overcoming pain or gendered limits) while the movement of more difficult felt relationships within the sport (frustration, anger or shame) remain unacknowledged. Yet the unsettling, difficult affects surface within other virtual spaces to disrupt the static official derby narrative of empowerment and belonging.

Virtual Boundaries and the Derby Body Politic

The weblog Live! Derby! Girls! is one site where different views are circulated. The blog's title banner reads, 'Live derby. Girls, girls, girls', along with flashing lights reminiscent of strip clubs and Motley Crue songs. The blog has 20 contributors, all 'derby girls', all literate and articulate. The site embraces the 'derby confession' with stories of overcoming adversity, tales of sexual encounters and many entries about not belonging. The most popular blog entry is entitled, 'Overcoming the Dark Side of Roller Derby', and the blogger, TrACDC,[8] opens with the following:

> I'm about to do something taboo... I am about to admit, right here on the interwebs, that roller derby isn't all camaraderie and fishnets. (Live! Derby! Girls!, 2011)

This blogger confesses that the women in roller derby have not always been supportive. She states:

> Who do you think it was that gossiped about the demise of my marriage and said extremely unflattering and unforgiving things about me? A derby... Who made me feel like shit about my lack of derby engagement when my life was falling apart and I was sitting at home with a broken hand? A derby. Who made out with my girlfriend after the after party? You better believe it was a derby. Did these experiences affect how I relate to my team and perform on the track? I want to say they didn't, but they did. (Live! Derby! Girls!, 2011)

In response to this blog, over 50 comments were posted in the days and weeks following. The responses ranged from impassioned accounts of a destructive 'dark side', shame-filled assertions of personal failings, angry claims of exclusion and an outpouring of grief and loss:

> I loved derby... I always thought I'd leave with an injury or because I had another path to choose or because I simply stayed long enough. I didn't think I'd leave because I had fallen and shattered into a million pieces. I hope that I can get over it and let it go. Because I don't love derby anymore. And I miss that.

Derby culture is produced through highly ambivalent emotions where love, passion for the sport and commitment to the imagined community exist alongside the complex feelings of not belonging. By engaging in the social web, the women involved mark out their entitlement to belong in different ways. To speak out against roller derby, or to express negative affects (of 'not love', or hate), is to be positioned as 'other' within the public sphere. This otherness evokes displeasures that are defined against the pleasures of becoming a roller derby grrrl that Ahmed (2004) argues signify one's 'entitlement' to belong. The virtual space of derby culture is claimed through enjoyment that is 'witnessed' by others (Ahmed, 2004). Those who show the most enjoyment, the most pleasure – those who *love* roller derby the most – are the most entitled. Against the claims of 'happy diversity' within the vision statements of major leagues exist sites produced by disaffected players who make visible the complex affective economies that are intertwined with the power relations of women's sport.

Extending Probyn's (2005: 85) argument about television as a key cultural site where emotion is produced, we view new communication technologies as another complex interactive and 'felt' space. In particular, Facebook is an important contemporary site where individual and collective identities are produced and negotiated (boyd & Ellison, 2007). 'Things I learned from Derby' is a public Facebook group with over 4,500 fans and is a space where anyone can contribute to an ongoing discussion. Daily comments are made on this Facebook page and it provides an example of how social network sites circulate and, in the case of roller derby, intensify affects through stories of pleasure and pain. In this context pride, anger and passion are validated, while sadness and shame are not (Carlson, 2010; Finley, 2010). On both the Facebook site ('Things I learned from Derby') and the blog (Live! Derby! Girls!) described earlier, 'Shut up and skate' is a common response given to any expression of 'girly' emotion such as sadness or hurt.

Interactive websites create a collective space where different derby identities are enacted via the rules and gender norms that regulate this 'alternative' sport via the affective power relations that include/ exclude. Comments on the blog act as a 'skin', a shifting boundary regulating who is 'in' and who is 'out' of the roller derby body politic; an online participant is 'pounced on' by others for saying something against the status quo. Anyone who expresses too much 'hurt' is 'out'. Women who demonstrate they have a thick skin, who can handle pain (and derive pleasure from pushing and working on the body) are 'in'. A recent comment by the administrators of the group stated: '[T]here is no entitlement to anything. There is only earning.' Over 80 people 'liked' this post and five women commented, expressing an emotional response to this highly charged issue – enthusiasm, sorrow and anger. Text and images evoke the subjection of the individual derby body through sport practices that involve pain, pushing oneself beyond gendered limits and intense competition. Moreover, derby websites enable, and also regulate, the flow of meaning for individuals through the discursive boundaries (or skin) of the collective roller derby 'body politic' (Gatens, 1996).

Discussion and Conclusions

As noted at the beginning of this chapter, sport is often conceptual- ised as a common 'good'; sport is a space where social values around teamwork, winning and strength are played out. Women have histori- cally been marginalised from this space, but in the past few decades this trend has slowly been challenged. Yet despite growing opportunities for women to participate in sport, their inclusion is often dependent on their willingness to ensure that they still appear 'feminine' – for example, wearing pink as their team colour (Caudwell, 2006). Roller derby, as a 'new' sport for women, has attempted to position itself dif- ferently from traditional sports through the use of parody, an emphasis on playfulness and the use of new communication technologies to promote and organise itself. Through the use of the social web women in roller derby have had the 'power' to re-write the norms of sport and femininity.

Through the social web, roller derby has very quickly spread across the globe. The internet has provided a space for women to quickly and easily share information, support each other, and allow multiple voices to be involved in shaping this new international sport. Since 2001 over

900 roller derby leagues have been established (Women's Flat Track Derby Association, 2011) and over 35,000 unique 'derby names' registered with the international register (Two Evils, 2012). However, using the internet to grow and nurture roller derby is not without challenges. The interactive digital interface demonstrates the productive working of power through affective relationships within the virtual space of derby culture. Websites operate through a different register of meaning, one that does not simply 'represent' a women's sport culture, but is as intense as the sport experience itself. Women are 'empowered' to (re)write the sport in varied, sometimes conflicting ways. By writing about, in and through the dark side of derby culture, women's marginalised voices work to 'trouble' the truth claims of empowerment and inclusion of diverse identities on the official league websites.

Yet 'troubling' these truth claims about who and what roller derby is, or is not, and embracing diverse identities in the sport, is not without risk. Earlier we quoted Woodward who wrote that sport 'de-materializes the body' and 'overwhelms traditional modes of perception' (2009: 133). Sport provides people with opportunities to use their bodies in 'youthful', pleasurable, exciting ways, yet for women their participation has been restricted and marginalised. Roller derby, in the few examples above of the way the sport has used the social web, demonstrates one way in which women have sought to overcome some of the constraints to their leisure participation. To a large degree it is through the social web that women in roller derby have been made visible and their sustained participation in the sport has been made possible. The social web has allowed women in roller derby the ability to destabilise the dominance of traditional media representations, allowing participants to exercise greater capacity to represent themselves in diverse ways. Yet it is these same technologies that uncover the 'dark side' of roller derby. It is important to acknowledge the cultural significance of new media technologies in the everyday lives of women in roller derby – not just the growth of roller derby, but also the ways roller derby and the relations of power between those involved are played out in virtual spaces.

Acknowledgements

This chapter includes excerpts from A. Pavlidis & S. Fullagar (2012) 'Becoming Roller Derby Grrrls: Exploring the Gendered Play of Affect in Mediated Sport Cultures', *International Review for the Sociology of Sport*, first published on 5 June 2012, doi:10.1177/1012690212446451.

Notes

1. The use of 'grrrl' is a 'feminist reclamation of the word girl with a less polite and more assertive political stance' (Rosenberg & Garofalo, 1998: 809).
2. See for example http://ratcityrollergirls.com/news-and-photos/hall-of-pain
3. http://sunstaterollergirls.com
4. http://www.londonrollergirls.com
5. http://livederbygirls.com/ This was the correct URL when accessed (12 June 2011); however the website has been taken over by a commercial enterprise completely unrelated to roller derby. This very much speaks to the fleeting and fluid movements of online content and the way meanings can very quickly change. Traces of the blog and its content can be found on other blogs, for example: http://fivepointgrandslam.blogspot.com.au/2011/07/overcoming-dark-side-of-roller-derby.html
6. http://www.facebook.com/pages/Things-I-learned-from-Derby/349318613615
7. Two of the main leagues that are vying for authority within the roller derby community are the Women's Flat Track Derby Association (http://wftda.com) and Modern Athletic Derby Endeavour (http://www.skatemade.org). These leagues have slightly different rules, and different values and ways of organising competition.
8. Women in roller derby take on a 'derby name' or moniker for themselves. A list of registered names around the world can be found on the international list, http://www.twoevils.org/rollergirls

References

Ahmed, S (2004) *The Cultural Politics of Emotion*. Edinburgh: Edinburgh University Press.
Atkinson, M & Young, K (2008) *Tribal Play: Subcultural Journeys through Sport*. Bingley: Emerald Group.
Beaver, TD (2012) '"By the Skaters, for the Skaters": The DIY Ethos of the Roller Derby Revival', *Journal of Sport & Social Issues*, Online before Print, doi:10.1177/0193723511433862.
Biskup, C & Pfister, G (1999) 'I Would Like to Be Like Her/Him: Are Athletes Role-Models for Boys and Girls?', *European Physical Education Review*, 5(3): 199–218.
boyd, d & Ellison, N (2007) 'Social Network Sites: Definition, History, and Scholarship', *Journal of Computer-Mediated Communication*, 13(1): 210–230.
Breivik, G (2010) 'Trends in Adventure Sports in a Post-Modern Society', *Sport in Society*, 13(2): 260–273.
Carlson, J (2010) 'The Female Significant in All-Women's Amateur Roller Derby', *Sociology of Sport Journal*, 27(4): 428–440.
Castells, M (2003) *The Internet Galaxy: Reflections on the Internet, Business, and Society*. Oxford: Oxford University Press.
Caudwell, J (2006) 'Femme-fatale: Rethinking the Femme-inine', in J Caudwell (ed.) *Sport, Sexualities and Queer/Theory*. New York: Routledge, 145–157.
Clasen, PRW (2001) 'The Female Athlete: Dualisms and Paradox in Practice', *Women and Language*, 24(2): 36–41.

Daddario, G (1994) 'Chilly Scenes of the 1992 Winter Games: The Mass Media and the Marginalization of Female Athletes', *Sociology of Sport Journal*, 11(3): 275–288.

Dart, JJ (2009) 'Blogging the 2006 FIFA World Cup Finals', *Sociology of Sport Journal*, 26(1): 107–126.

Donnelly, MK (2006) 'Studying Extreme Sports', *Journal of Sport & Social Issues*, 30(2): 219.

Driscoll, C (1999) 'Girl Culture, Revenge and Global Capitalism: Cybergirls, Riot Grrls, Spice Girls', *Australian Feminist Studies*, 14(29): 173–193.

Dunstan, D, Barr, E, Healy, G, Salmon, J, Shaw, J, Balkau, B, et al. (2010) 'Television Viewing Time and Mortality', *Circulation*, 121(3): 384–391.

Ess, C & Association of Internet Researchers Ethics Working Group (2002) *Ethical Decision-Making and Internet Research: Recommendations from AOIR Ethics Working Committee*: http://www.aoir.org/reports/ethics.pdf (accessed 1 March 2012).

Fink, JS & Kensicki, LJ (2002) 'An Imperceptible Difference: Visual and Textual Constructions of Femininity in *Sports Illustrated* and *Sports Illustrated for Women*', *Mass Communication & Society*, 5(3): 317–339.

Finley, NJ (2010) 'Skating Femininity: Gender Maneuvering in Women's Roller Derby', *Journal of Contemporary Ethnography*, 39(4): 359–387.

Fraser-Thomas, JL, Cote, J & Deakin, J (2005) 'Youth Sport Programs: An Avenue to Foster Positive Youth Development', *Physical Education & Sport Pedagogy*, 10(1): 19–40.

Garrison, EK (2000) 'U.S. Feminism-Grrrl Style! Youth (Sub)Cultures and the Technologics of the Third Wave', *Feminist Studies*, 26(1): 141–170.

Gatens, M (1996) *Imaginary Bodies: Ethics, Power and Corporeality*. London: Routledge.

Gibson, C (1999) 'Subversive Sites: Rave Culture, Spatial Politics and the Internet in Sydney, Australia', *Area*, 31(1): 19–33.

Hall, S (1977) 'Culture, the Media and the Ideological Effect', *Mass Communication & Society*, 315–348.

Harris, A (2003) 'gURL Scenes and Grrrl Zines: The Regulation and Resistance of Girls in Late Modernity', *Feminist Review*, 75(1): 38–56.

Heywood, L (2008) 'Third-Wave Feminism, the Global Economy, and Women's Surfing: Sport as Stealth Feminism in Girls' Surf Culture', in A Harris (ed.) *Next Wave Cultures: Feminism, Subcultures, Activism*. New York and London: Routledge, 63–82.

Hodkinson, P (2003) '"Net.Goth": Internet Communication and (Sub)Cultural Boundaries', in D Muggleton & R Weinzierl (eds) *The Post-Subcultures Reader*. Oxford: Berg, 285–298.

Inness, SA (2004) *Action Chicks: New Images of Tough Women in Popular Culture*. New York: Palgrave Macmillan.

Jarvie, G & Thornton, J (2012) *Sport, Culture and Society: An Introduction* (2nd ed.). New York: Routledge.

Kahn, R & Kellner, D (2003) 'Internet Subcultures and Oppositional Politics', in D Muggleton & R Weinzierl (eds) *The Post-Subcultures Reader*. Oxford: Berg, 299–313.

Kahn, R & Kellner, D (2004) 'New Media and Internet Activism: From the Battle of Seattle to Blogging', *New Media & Society*, 6(1): 87–95.

Kehily, MJ (2007) *Understanding Youth: Perspectives, Identities and Practices*. London: Sage Publications.

Leonard, DJ (2009) 'New Media and Global Sporting Cultures: Moving Beyond the Clichés and Binaries', *Sociology of Sport Journal*, 26(1): 1–16.

Live! Derby! Girls! (2011) 'Overcoming the Dark Side of Roller Derby': http://live derbygirls.com/2011/02/13/overcoming-the-dark-side-of-roller-derby (accessed 12 June 2011).

Luckman, S (1999) '(En)gendering the Digital Body: Feminism and the Internet', *Hecate*, 25(2): 36–47.

Lumby, C, Caple, H & Greenwood, K (2009) *Towards a Level Playing Field: Sport and Gender in Australian Media*: http://www.ausport.gov.au/__data/assets/pdf_file/0007/356209/Towards_a_Level_Playing_Field_LR.pdf (accessed 12 June 2011).

Mabe, C (2008) *Roller Derby: The History and All-Girl Revival of the Greatest Sport on Wheels*. Denver: Speck Press.

MacKay, S & Dallaire, C (2012) 'Skirtboarder Net-a-Narratives: Young Women Creating Their Own Skateboarding (Re)presentations', *International Review for the Sociology of Sport*, Online Before Print, doi:10.1177/1012690211432661.

Manovich, L (2009) 'The Practice of Everyday (Media) Life: From Mass Consumption to Mass Cultural Production?', *Critical Inquiry*, 35(2): 319–331.

Oates, TP (2009) 'New Media and the Repackaging of NFL Fandom', *Sociology of Sport Journal*, 26(1): 31–49.

Pavlidis, A (2011) 'From Riot Grrrls to Roller Derby? Exploring the Relations Between Gender, Music and Sport', *Leisure Studies*, doi: 10.1080/02614367.2011.623304.

Pomerantz, S, Currie, DH & Kelly, DM (2004) 'Sk8er girls: Skateboarders, Girlhood and Feminism in Motion', *Women's Studies International Forum*, 27(5–6): 547–557.

Probyn, E (2005) *Blush*. Sydney: University of New South Wales Press.

Putnam, RD (1995) 'Bowling Alone: America's Declining Social Capital', *Journal of Democracy*, 6(1): 65–78.

Rosenberg, J & Garofalo, G (1998) 'Riot Grrrl: Revolutions from Within', *Signs*, 23(3): 809–841.

Rowe, D (2013) 'Reflections on Communication and Sport: On Nation and Globalization', *Communication & Sport*, 1(1–2): 18–29.

Ruddock, A, Hutchins, B & Rowe, D (2010) 'Contradictions in Media Sport Culture: The Reinscription of Football Supporter Traditions through Online Media', *European Journal of Cultural Studies*, 13(3): 323.

Sassatelli, R (2010) *Fitness Culture: The Gym and the Commercialisation of Discipline and Fun*. New York: Palgrave.

Storms, CE (2010) 'There's No Sorry in Roller Derby: A Feminist Examination of the Collective Identity Formation of Women in the Full Contact Sport of Roller Derby', *New York Sociologist*, 3: 68–87.

Taylor, T (2001) 'Gendering Sport: The Development of Netball in Australia', *Sporting Traditions*, 18(1): 57–74.

Theberge, N (1987) 'Sport and Women's Empowerment', *Women's Studies International Forum*, 10(4): 387–393.

Thorpe, H (2005) 'Jibbing the Gender Order: Females in the Snowboarding Culture', *Sport in Society*, 8(1): 76–100.

Thorpe, H (2008) 'Foucault, Technologies of Self, and the Media: Discourses of Femininity in Snowboarding Culture', *Journal of Sport & Social Issues*, 32(2): 199–229.

Trangbæk, E (1997) 'Gender in Modern Society: Femininity, Gymnastics and Sport', *The International Journal of the History of Sport*, 14(3): 136–156.

Turner, G (1993) *Nation, Culture, Text: Australian Cultural and Media Studies*. Hove: Psychology Press.

Two Evils (2012) *International Roller Girls Master Roster*: http://www.twoevils.org/rollergirls (accessed 5 June 2012).

Urry, J (2007). *Mobilities*. Cambridge: Polity Press.

Wearing, B (1998) *Leisure and Feminist Theory*. London: Sage.

Western Regionals (2008) *Western Regionals – Almost as Good as Being There*: http://www.rollerderbyblog.com (accessed 1 October 2011).

Wheaton, B (2004) *Understanding Lifestyle Sport: Consumption, Identity and Difference*. London and New York: Routledge.

Williams, JP (2003) 'The Straightedge Subculture on the Internet: A Case Study of Style-Display Online', *Media International Australia*, 107: 61–74.

Wilson, B (2008) 'Believe the Hype? The Impact of the Internet on Sport-Related Subcultures', in M Atkinson & K Young (eds) *Tribal Play: Subcultural Journeys through Sport*. Bingley: Emerald Group, 135–151.

Women's Flat Track Derby Association (2011) *Media Kit. 1–8*: http://wftda.com/files/wftda-media-kit.pdf (accessed 5 June 2012).

Woodward, K (2009) *Embodied Sporting Practices: Regulating and Regulatory Bodies*. New York: Palgrave Macmillan.

11
Getting Bodied with Beyoncé on YouTube

Ann Werner (Södertörn University, Sweden)

In 2006 while I was conducting research about music use and gender among teenage girls in a Swedish town, one of the girls I was working with sent me an e-mail with a link to a YouTube video clip of a toddler dancing to Shakira's song 'Hips Don't Lie'. Before Facebook, distributing URL links in e-mails was a common method for spreading viral videos, and because YouTube was a completely new website at the time, the video interested me. Later, in conversation with the girl in her home, I asked her about the clip and she said that she thought it was a funny video of a cute child, so she sent it to all her friends who might enjoy it. YouTube has grown in popularity since 2006 and is a platform for participatory media culture where millions of people from all over the world upload videos for others to view and comment on. While some of the videos posted on YouTube mirror overt commercial interests, others are part of a 'do it yourself' (DIY) culture where people conduct practical jokes, play music or dance. This type of online user culture is part of an increase in the number of people who produce their own media and broadcast it to others. Within British cultural studies of youth, combinations of music, style and play have been identified as three core ingredients of the lives and cultures of young people (Hebdige, 1979; McRobbie & Garber, 1975/2006). In subcultural research, for example, the elements of music, style and play/playfulness have been seen as meaningful expressions of symbolic resistance and/ or expressing ideology (Hall & Jefferson, 1975/2006). The video of the toddler dancing to Shakira can therefore be considered as yet another way of assembling and communicating music, dance and humour through a mainstream music culture that is shared by many young users all over the world. The video clip is also part of one phenomenon on YouTube where users – mainly young girls and boys – film themselves imitating dances of globally successful artists like Shakira, Britney Spears, Beyoncé or Lady Gaga. Their performances are negotiated by other users in the commentary field on the YouTube interface, with the videos taking on a new meaning that is not necessarily contained in the individual video clips. In this way, the dress-up play of imitating and dancing can be regarded as a global youth culture framed by the possibilities and constraints of YouTube. It involves a process of mediation where bodies interact with media technology, music, dance styles and other users.

The spaces where such negotiations in youth culture take place, the objects and technologies used by young people to share cultural texts and the content of these texts will look different depending on which decade, which country and which young person one examines. The styles investigated by early youth culture research are not universal; gender, ethnicity and class are all important dividers of youth cultures, now and then (Phoenix, 1997), but the practice of negotiating music, style and play prevails. Central to these negotiations is always the body, even though the body and its importance for culture have not always been recognised in cultural studies (Featherstone, 1991). The body is that which moves in dance or dresses up in new clothes; the body can ride a motorcycle or hang out at the club. The body also experiences the sounds and lyrics of music, imitates singers or performs in a band and when fashion is discussed, the body – and its possibilities – are often imperative. That the body of a toddler moves in certain ways, dissimilar from a teenager, is crucial for the cuteness and funniness of the video. Shakira's body dancing to the same song moves differently from both the toddler and the teenager, and evokes different responses.

This chapter investigates the intersections of youth, gender, race and new media in clips where people parody and imitate the dances of Beyoncé. The dancers' embodiments take part in constructing an image of how a young body should look and move, not only on YouTube but in contemporary youth culture as a whole. The video clips are seen as part of a larger online hypertext: they are accompanied by comments in the commentary field and linked to other videos by both users and the YouTube interface. The sound and image in the video, how dancers are presented on YouTube and perceived by commentators, and how their videos are linked, are all factors taken into account in this chapter. The videos that were chosen all portray teenagers, young adults and children dancing to Beyoncé's music and imitating her dance moves in a homelike environment. The young bodies are seen as more than just a surface where meaning is inscribed. Bodies are entities that take part in youth cultural production and are never neutral, but always at the centre of formations of gender, race and age.

Questions posed in the chapter are: What bodily expressions of gender, race and new media do the video clips of people dancing like Beyoncé – and their comments and links – create on YouTube? What bodies and which moves are seen as desirable and what ideas about gender and race does this construction of the desirable (re)produce? The expressions on YouTube can be seen as intertextual with their intersections of gender, race, age and the media technology that come into being through references to music and dance history. But they are also a construction of actual physical bodies that are able to do some things and not others, that feel some things and not others. Embodiment on YouTube is understood as both discursive and material where the figures, the personas we meet, are constituted of flesh, ideas, and material social conditions (Braidotti, 2003: 44).

YouTube and Home Dancing as Youth Culture

As a platform for commercial, non-profit and participatory video culture, YouTube has been growing quickly since its release in 2005 and is now the most popular place to share video clips. YouTube's slogan 'Broadcast Yourself' suggests that everyone can be a participant actor in a video on the site but fewer than 1 per cent of the site's users actually upload their own videos, according to Geert Lovink (2008: 11); the rest of the users are there to watch.

YouTube has often been described as a participatory online culture. As a cultural form that allows the consumer to influence the production, it blurs the line between consumer and producer (Jenkins, 2006). YouTube is indeed a place for home-style videos although the commercial content in video clips and advertisements on the site has been steadily increasing since YouTube was bought by Google in 2006, making it far from a non-profit business. Rather, it is part of a multimillion dollar business that does not sell content, but rather advertising space and information about the users and their tastes. Its popularity and content have been debated in terms of risk and innovation. The risks considered to exist on YouTube range from cyberbullying to lawlessness in general, and the innovations are described as being situated within both the 'wacky' and funny content and the new media technology software (Burgess & Green, 2009: 16). The site's associations with cutting-edge culture as well as the mundane and everyday cannot be contested, and a large proportion of the users are young adults, or teenagers; 17 per cent are between 15 and 19 years old (Chau, 2010: 66). Obviously, YouTube holds relevance in youth culture today, offering a space for a wide variety of cultural expressions provided by or/and for youth containing music, style, play and so much more. It is also worth noting that YouTube is more than a platform for youth culture and a social network. The content of YouTube is diverse and YouTube does not produce or exercise complete control over its own cultural product (Burgess & Green, 2009: 5). YouTube must therefore be seen as a medium with multiple channels, viewer groups and cultural expressions. As mentioned, one expression consists of young people and children imitating popular artists' songs and dances in the milieu of their home, then broadcasting the video clips.

The following sections of this chapter are based on an analysis of 31 clips where people dance like the artist Beyoncé in a homelike environment accompanied by one of three of her songs – 'Crazy in Love' (2003), 'Get Me Bodied' (2007) or 'Single Ladies' (2008) – and the comments made to these clips by YouTube users.[1] The criteria for selecting them and the comments and links that followed were: 1) that the milieu looked like a home, in order to not include professional dancers performing tutorials in dance studios; 2) that the dance moves performed were inspired by, or were copies of, Beyoncé's moves in the music videos for one of the three songs; and 3) that one of the afore-mentioned three Beyoncé songs was played in the background. Most of the videos do not contain the whole song, or the whole dance routine, and they were found by searching for the title of the song and the word 'dance' on YouTube in 2007 and 2008.[2] All of the dancers are children, teenagers and young adults, or appear to be so. This was not a criterion when selecting the video clips but it seemed that few adults or older persons made home dance videos at the time. The video clips were analysed as a genre, where genre is seen as a way of using language in connection with a social activity (Chouliaraki & Fairclough, 1999: 56). The video clips are therefore on one hand in the same genre but can be divided into sub-genres. Three sub-genres were identified by studying the visual language in the clips collected. All video clips performed the same group of dance moves and in the majority of them the performers did this with seriousness and aspirations to move as much like Beyoncé as possible. Some performers dressed like her, and set up formations like hers – with background dancers for example. But other performers did not seem to try to look or move as much like Beyoncé as possible; instead, they exaggerated the moves and ridiculed the costumes; with ironic smiles and bursts of laughter these performers made clips for laughing rather than admiration. By looking at these two modes as two sub-genres they are understood as different forms, but not necessarily as containing different ideas about gendered, raced bodies. Finally there were a couple of videos by young children in the selection of the 31 clips. These provoked laughter, because the children could not properly imitate the dance moves even though they tried, but also reactions appropriate to admiration of the children as children – not as dancers. Because of the different social activities to which these three types of clips' visual language connected them, they are here considered three modes of embodiment. All of the material – video clips and comments – was studied in terms of how moves, clothes and words constructed ideas about gender, race and bodies. Inspired by discourse analysis, these different expressions of cultural language were mapped in all sub-genres and compared with the broader cultural understandings and social practices the textual processes performed, interpellated in the dancers, for example through intertextual chains (Chouliaraki & Fairclough, 1999: 51). The expressions of gender and race are linked to wider discourse by using previous research on gender and race to compare ideas articulated in the material.

Different Modes of Embodying Beyoncé

The dances of Beyoncé that are performed in her music videos and on stage are often intertextually flirting with previous cultural texts, as is common for music videos (Vernallis, 2004). Many music videos entail the re-working of previous dances, looks and narratives from artists of previous eras, movies or fashions. This intertextuality is often conducted with humour; when Marilyn Monroe-style dresses are re-used by, for example, Madonna, they refer to a certain time and quality while also drawing this time and quality into the present. Beyoncé frequently embodies feminine figures from cultural history through dance and style in this manner. These feminine figures (Braidotti, 2003) are shaped as discursive ideas about women coming to life through embodiment in the flesh and in the context of material social conditions of R&B and hip hop cultures from North America. Some feminine figures appearing in Beyoncé's music videos are: the femme fatale from American cinema ('Ring the Alarm' and 'Dance for You'), the belly dancer of orientalism ('Baby Boy') and the stripper from burlesque cultural revival ('Naughty Girl'). Embodied femininity is a key feature in Beyoncé's music videos and her dance moves are creations of – and are creating – feminine bodies, both for Beyoncé and for other dancers taking on her moves in their own video clips. This does not imply that all the dancers on YouTube are girls or women, or embody femininity in similar ways to Beyoncé, but their embodiment is in dialogue with hers. Grosz (1994: 120) has argued, drawing on Deleuze, that the physical body is a part of a larger ensemble, or machine, a network of alignments with other bodies and other things. This body machine is the body we can see or experience since no body can be understood without the things with which it is aligned, like movements and clothes, and ideas about health and beauty. The body is a site of signification (but not only of signification) and it is to be understood in relation to what it is aligned with, for example figures of femininity, dance moves or media technologies such as the YouTube interface. When a dancer takes on Beyoncé's moves from these particular songs and music videos, the dancer's body machine is constructed through alignment with Beyoncé, but also with the comments made on YouTube by other users and with the other video clips to which YouTube links the dancer. This way of understanding the construction of bodies denies the idea that bodies are expressions of intentions or a psychical interior of a single subject.

The young bodies constructed in home dancing clips on the interface of YouTube can become different types of embodiment through their different alignments, in the clip itself and through the comments and links. In the video clips collected on YouTube the dancers are, as previously explained, understood as embodying Beyoncé's dance moves in three primary modes: as parodies, as serious imitations, or (when young children between 1 and 10 dance) as displays of cuteness and play. In the parodies, dancers make fun of the original dances, for example through exaggeration and funny costumes. In the serious imitations and the videos of cute play, no tricks from the genre of parody are used and the dancers seem to try their best to imitate the original moves, with varying results.

The young bodies perform quite differently in these three modes of video, and they are also discussed differently in the commentary fields. Many comments touch upon the subjects of gender, race and age but dancers are understood as aged, gendered and raced, depending on the mode of the video. In the interface of YouTube the video clips are also linked together. In the right column of the interface, 'recommended' video clips are automatically generated by the site and the recommended clips are often similar to the clip that has just been watched. Video clips of small children dancing are linked to other clips of small children dancing, while videos of pretty girls dancing are linked to other videos of pretty girls dancing and in this way the mode of the video determines how it is linked. The three modes of home dancing found in these clips will be discussed in the following sections of the chapter.

Parodies

Parody is a popular genre on YouTube where home-made video clips commonly steal, appropriate and/or re-use form and content recognisable from western popular culture and from other amateur video clips produced for YouTube in a humorous style (Juhasz, 2008: 138). Humour is at the core of parody and to re-use one or several cultural texts may be a way of paying homage while also making fun of certain elements in the texts. Producing parodies of Beyoncé's dances has also been a popular activity outside of YouTube. For example, in the television programmes *Glee* and *Saturday Night Live*, performers embody her dances in parodies, simultaneously mocking and celebrating the original.

Where the original ends and the parody and re-use begin is impossible to determine. Beyoncé herself re-uses dance moves from previous popular culture texts and when imitations are distributed through different media platforms, professional music videos sometimes imitate amateur videos from YouTube (Vernallis, 2010). Thus it is not a simple question of one original and a few copies but a network of embodiments aligned with each other. In the sample of home dancers dancing like Beyoncé, a small but interesting part of the video clips were overt parodies. The video clips in the sub-genre parodies were performed by dancers who dressed in costumes that exaggerated and/or ridiculed the costumes of Beyoncé's performances, and/or dancers who exaggerated and ridiculed the dance moves.

All of the parodies in my sample were performed by persons who identified themselves as male in their comments and alias on YouTube and/or they presented themselves in terms of masculinity, passing as white westerners. Therefore the imitations of the dances in moves and costume gave the impression of an unsuccessful drag show, mocking Beyoncé, and some appeared as more successful attempts by men to imitate her. But the embodiment of these young men as men mocking cultural expressions of femininity was also created through the comments they received: their parodies were popular in the sense that they received a lot of positive feedback in the commentary field and a lot of people watched them. Comments most commonly stated how funny they were: 'hilarious'[3], 'crazy' and 'out there'. When a user asked 'you're boys, right?' the question was directly followed by a 'that's so funny' response from another user, ensuring that the gender identity play of the dancers is seen as a good-humoured parody and not a performance that seriously questions the man/woman dichotomy. More ambiguous performances of gendered bodies were also found in the sample, and will be discussed below.

Lange (2011) has argued that the everyday video-making with friends as a social activity is a motive for young consumers to participate in YouTube video clips. She draws this conclusion from fieldwork with a group of young boys who had made videos together for years. Lange (2011) does not suggest that the content is unimportant for the producer but her findings support the sociality of the act of producing. In the parodies of Beyoncé's dance moves, as in Lange's fieldwork, the production process is homosocial as it is young boys/men socialising with each other, and being applauded by women and men, girls and boys. Participating in cultural production online is sometimes seen as a positive learning process for young people or a way of bringing people from all over the world together (see, for example, Mazzarella, 2005). But in the parodies it was a process bringing young white men together in their mocking of dances originally performed by a black woman.

One might ask which bodies are included in the learning and togetherness when young men make parodies and comment on YouTube, especially when the parodies mock dances originally performed by a black woman. The parodies in my sample performed by men all featured two or more young white boys/men and they were all filmed in the US or in the UK. Thus while the dance videos on YouTube that contain school recitals, home dancing and professional tutorials are all dominated by girls and women as performers, the parodies of Beyoncé's dance moves showed the opposite pattern and portrayed a world of young men having a good time.

Imitations

Although the parody in many ways is symptomatic of YouTube videos, and parodies and pranks often rate among the most popular video clips, the Beyoncé dancers *without* overt parody elements were more common in the sample of videos collected.[4] The video clips I refer to as imitations are all the clips where young people performed the dance steps from Beyoncé's three songs without overt exaggerations and ridicule. They did not wear funny costumes but were often dressed in everyday clothes like jeans or a dress and a small number seriously tried to dress as Beyoncé does in her videos. Most of the imitations were done by girls, either alone in their room, in a pair with a friend or in groups of three. While the parodies were almost always performed by white men, the imitations were most often performed by girls who were presented as black or African-American, although there were also white and Asian girls.[5] The imitations and the discussions about them in the commentary fields were preoccupied with ranking looks and likeness. The performers who managed dance moves and attitudes that resembled Beyoncé's were encouraged. The dancers who did not fully achieve likeness often excused their presentation, claiming that it was 'the first time', or 'I'm just goofing around', when in fact the dancing was close to the original moves and the dancer was obviously 'trying hard'. They were still regarded as imitations, and not parodies, because they did not exaggerate or ridicule the dances in any obvious way. On the contrary, these dancers looked like they tried their best to achieve likeness.

Girls that were considered 'hot' or 'sexy' by the YouTube users were also complimented for this in the feedback they received. Open sexual invitations directed towards girls dancing alone were common from users presenting themselves as men or boys. Home dance videos on YouTube have often been found to contain dimensions of ranking and competition when they are compared with other videos and with texts from commercial popular culture to determine which one is better (Peters & Seier, 2009: 201). The ranking criterion is not always explicit, nor is it the same as would be used to rank a professional dance. In fact, video, humour and presence are often valued qualities. In the case of the dance imitations that were not overt parodies, the looks of the dancer and her/his performance of the moves were the main ranking criteria. And the shape of their bodies played into both of these two rankings.

In striving for likeness, the dancers have to imitate some of the core dance moves that involve dropping your behind to the ground, shaking your behind and grinding the body in movements accentuating 'ass' and breasts. These are Beyoncé's signature moves and drawing attention to breasts and ass is a technique commonly used in female dancing in R&B and hip hop (Emerson, 2002: 129). As in many other genres, they are used as a way of embodying femininity. Booty dancing, accentuating women's asses, is common in hip hop videos, and the hyper-sexuality of the booty-shaking black female has been understood as a continuation of colonial and racialised stereotypes of black girls and women as sexually available (Durham, 2012). The connotations of certain body parts as sexual is furthered by the dancers in the clips when they imitate the moves, but the features of their bodies, such as size, shape and colour, become crucial for them in order to be perceived as performing a good imitation.

Negative comments are highly prevalent in the commentary of imitation videos, and many focus on the performance of the dance or the looks of the dancer. When white and Asian girls receive positive feedback for their looks and dances they are often perceived as good 'for being' white/Asian, not as just good. In one comment on a video showing three young white girls dancing to 'Single Ladies', the user writes, 'you do good for white girls, represent Britain!' It manages to imply that the dancers are not good per se, but rather that they are good in the category of white girls, and also that white girls can represent Britain because 'British' girls are white (Gilroy, 1987). Between the lines of such comments lurks an idea that only black women have the bodies and moves to dance these dances, an idea common in racist discourse suggesting that the black woman is more closely aligned with her body and sexuality (Durham, 2012; Perry, 2004).

The dancers who are not understood as black or African-American are all subject to the critical eye of YouTube's users, for their way of performing the dances as Beyoncé. In most areas of popular culture, whiteness is the unspoken norm that others are measured against but this racial dominance is not present in these home dancing videos, where whiteness is openly addressed. The idea that white people are stiff and without dancing skills, expressed in YouTube comments, is not a new way of imagining whiteness (Dyer, 1997: 6). It is predictable since whites are typically portrayed as rational and not overly passionate in popular culture in general, and passionate dancing connotes blackness, exotic places or possibly the working class (1997: 6). However, the girls who are black do not seem to benefit from this reversal where they are the norm of good dancing. They are also judged harshly by the users when making even the smallest mistake, and they are understood as 'you need to eat' or 'girl you're fat'. There are no excuses made when their dance moves or bodies fail. When the dancers are perceived as white or Asian, the negative comments as well as the positive ones refer to the dancers' race: 'it's not fair to these little white girls! They ass flat as hell' writes a person who argues the white girls in a clip can't dance, but it is not their own fault because they do not have the physical attributes required. Being not-black is therefore enough to be considered a bad dancer; the white and Asian girls are perceived as having the wrong bodies for the dance moves.

Some of the YouTube comments reflected a view of the girls' behaviour as risky: 'go put some clothes on with ya hot ass' or 'you're a beautiful girl but shouldn't put yourself out like this' were expressions of the idea that displaying your embodiment in dancing can be understood as an invitation; this was particularly the understanding if the dancer was a woman. None of the dancers understood as men were warned in comments about their dress or behaviour. The female imitators' embodiments as sexy or beautiful were typically also seen as dangerous (for them) and as a reason for imaginary men to prey on them. Notably, internet researchers have argued that media reports about risks to children and youth online are presented in a manner suggesting continuous 'moral panics' in an area adults feel they do not control (Ponte et al., 2009: 161). In particular, the risk of young girls meeting sexual predators online has been a topic of some interest (Weber & Dixon, 2007). In academic research, this feminine figure of the sexually vulnerable girl has been discussed in a more complex manner. The figure is a cultural idea, a way of portraying real girls as vulnerable in relation to sex and ideals of femininity, through enhancing the figure. Of course the feminine figure of vulnerable girls must through intertextual analysis be understood as a way of upholding control and hierarchy in terms of bodies and looks, where subjects are warned about being too feminine.

The greatest number of negative comments relate to the serious imitations performed by dancers understood as boys/men. When a young man dances like Beyoncé and does a good job, he successfully embodies femininity, in a serious drag performance. Such performances by biological men are variously perceived as 'gross', 'gay' or 'just wrong' by the users and associations are made between the dancers embodying black femininity and homosexuality. These video clips of boys/men seriously imitating Beyoncé are also linked to each other and to cross-dressers' video clips. Drag, according to Butler (1990: 175), is when a person performs in a manner that contradicts his/her sex and gendered identity. It is, according to Butler, a way of displaying that sex/gender is a performance and not rooted in nature or biology. Drag in this context is obviously perceived as threatening by some YouTube users, but other reactions are also present in the comments. One user claims to be jealous of the booty of a dragging young black man who has little fat on his body but a rather round ass. In a different video where a young man, looking to be in his early twenties, performs 'Get Me Bodied', another user comments that he's such a good dancer, if only he were a girl it would be sexy.

The embodiments in home dancing videos involving bodies seen as male doing serious female imitations, and girls who were white, Asian, too skinny or too fat, are variously framed in the comments associated with the videos as 'slightly wrong'. These videos all direct the user to express a perceived ideal dancer, and an ideal woman. Becoming this woman seems impossible when not even Beyoncé's own dances are considered perfect by some of the commentators. For the girls and boys dancing the imitations, the verdicts were often harsh in contrast to the young men doing parodies of the same dances whose bodies, skills and clothes were never commented on. It was as if the mere ambition to be good opened the performers up to critique, where the parodies did not. Feminine embodiment is judged in a different way than male, and this supports previous research done on girls online (Mazzarella, 2005). It is useful to keep this in mind when considering the role of smaller children on YouTube.

Cute Play

Besides the parodies and the more serious imitations, a third category of videos was classified in the sample. These were the video clips that depicted young children, all looking to be under 10 years of age – and some only toddlers – doing the dance moves to the best of their abilities. In these clips somebody other than the dancer was filming, and thus producing the clip for them. Not only were the children too young to produce these videos themselves, there were also audible sounds of background voices, laughter and camera movements revealing the presence of an adult or an older child. In these cute clips, the dancer and the producer were separated – as in a professional production where the performer and the other(s) producing the music video are different persons.

So while most parody and imitation dancers were directly in contact with their commentators, these cute clip dancers were actually often too young to even read and write and could therefore not take part in what was happening on YouTube. The feedback the cute videos received was overwhelmingly positive. Many visitors on the site watched the videos and commented on how adorable and cute, skilful for their age, and funny these children were. They were not ranked and judged like the teenage and 20-something dancers from the imitations; the clips were embraced as a genre of home dance video nobody could dislike. Notably, the comments were void of racialising the children or using gender-specific language, much like the comments on the parodies. Both boys and girls were seen as cute and funny and this approach created the children's embodiments in terms of age – not as raced or gendered bodies. By the way the children were dressed, it was possible to determine their gender in all cases: the girls wore skirts and pastel colours while the boys wore trousers – often jeans – and t-shirts. This was noted by the commentators by use of 'he' or 'she', but the comments were similar and the links recommended in the YouTube interface (by YouTube algorithms) were often to other small children, girls and boys, of all skin colours, dancing or singing. To establish children's embodiment as primarily cute and funny, the ideas and texts these clips were aligned with were TV programmes such as *America's Funniest Home Videos* and home photography – imagery where children are depicted as fundamentally different from adults, innocent and new to the world; imagery that is consistent with the idea of childhood as innocence (Cross, 2004). The lack of ranking and discussions about gender and race is in itself an indicator that children are not yet seen as proper bodies and their embodiment becomes a genre of its own.

Conclusions

The embodiment of young people and children performing Beyoncé's dances on YouTube may seem diverse at first glance; age, gender, body type and skin colour vary between the 31 video clips collected, and the comments are many. One may even understand the variety as a marker of successful participatory online culture where everybody is taking part in home dancing as a cultural and social practice. But by studying the embodiments more closely as three sub-genres visually and verbally expressing ideas about gender and race, and considering the styles of the video clips, the content of the comments and the YouTube-generated links that connect the videos to each other, another conclusion must be reached. The embodiments of the videos and the comments put together speak to an already known discursive idea about a certain femininity: an ideal racialised and sexualised black woman, with rhythm and sass. Although none of the dancers may achieve this figure, she is present with what is deemed good and bad, what videos are funny or sexy. By understanding this type of femininity as a figure shaped by both racial and gendered stereotypes, and agents' attempts to subvert those, young people dancing at home for a YouTube audience form part of a wider cultural practice that negotiates race and gender in popular culture today.

Notes

1. Originally 50 video clips and their comments were collected during 2007 and 2008, and a previous article in Swedish (Werner, 2010) is based on this

material. Some of the material was unfortunately lost in a computer crash and for this article I have revisited 31 of the clips, and the comments made on them. There is no indication that the lost sample would have changed the main conclusions in this chapter (compare with Werner, 2010).

2. There are other video clips available on YouTube today: the sample is time specific, and the amount of videos logged allowed for a qualitative analysis that maps tendencies in the video clips. This chapter discusses these tendencies and does not aspire to understand dance clips on YouTube in general, or people dancing like Beyoncé in general, which would be a much larger research endeavour.

3. All quotes are from the actual commentary fields of the video clips. Spelling has been corrected in the quotes I use.

4. Just over half of the 31 clips were categorised as imitations, a third were parodies, three were of young children and one clip had both a young child and an older imitation dancer.

5. These four were the main racial categories used in the comments on YouTube; sometimes other more specific differences were named in comments such as terms of nationality, like British or Korean.

References

Braidotti, R (2003) 'Becoming Woman: Or Sexual Difference Revisited', *Theory, Culture & Society*, 20(3): 43–64.

Burgess, J & Green, J (2009) *YouTube: Online Video and Participatory Culture*. Cambridge: Polity Press.

Butler, J (1990) *Gender Trouble: Feminism and the Subversion of Identity*. New York: Routledge.

Chau, C (2010) 'YouTube as a Participatory Culture', *New Directions for Youth Development*, 2010(128): 65–74.

Chouliaraki, L & Fairclough, N (1999) *Discourse in Late Modernity: Rethinking Critical Discourse Analysis*. Edinburgh: Edinburgh University Press.

Cross, G (2004) *The Cute and the Cool: Wondrous Innocence and Modern American Children's Culture*. New York: Oxford University Press.

Durham, A (2012) 'Check on It! Beyoncé, Southern Booty and Black Femininities in Music Video', *Feminist Media Studies*, 12(1): 35–49.

Dyer, R (1997) *White: Essays on Race and Culture*. London: Routledge.

Emerson, R (2002) 'Where My Girls At? Negotiating Black Womanhood in Music Videos', *Gender & Society*, 16(1): 115–135.

Featherstone, M (1991) *Consumer Culture and Postmodernism*. London: Sage.

Gilroy, P (1987) *There Ain't No Black in the Union Jack: The Cultural Politics of Race and Nation*. London: Hutchinson.

Grosz, E (1994) *Volatile Bodies: Toward a Corporeal Feminism*. Bloomington, IN: Indiana University Press.

Hall, S & Jefferson, T (1975/2006) (eds) *Resistance through Rituals: Youth Subcultures in Post-War Britain* (2nd ed.). London: Routledge.

Hebdige, D (1979) *Subculture: The Meaning of Style*. London: Methuen.

Jenkins H (2006) *Convergence Culture: Where Old and New Media Collide*. New York: New York University Press.

Juhasz, A (2008) 'Why Not (to) Teach on YouTube', in G Lovink & S Niederer (eds) *Video Vortex Reader: Responses to YouTube*. Amsterdam: Institute of Network Cultures, 133–140.

Lange, P (2011) 'Video-Mediated Nostalgia and the Aesthetics of Technical Competencies', *Visual Communication*, 10(1): 25–44.

Lovink, G (2008) 'The Art of Watching Databases: Introduction to the Video Vortex Reader', in G Lovink & S Niederer (eds) *Video Vortex Reader: Responses to YouTube*. Amsterdam: Institute of Network Cultures, 9–13.

Mazzarella, S (ed.) (2005) *Girl Wide Web: Girls, the Internet and the Negotiation of Identity*. New York: Peter Lang.

McRobbie, A & Garber, J (1975/2006) 'Girls and Subcultures', in S Hall & T Jefferson (eds) *Resistance through Rituals: Youth Subcultures in Post-War Britain* (2nd ed.). London: Routledge, 177–188.

Peters, K & Seier, A (2009) 'Home Dance: Mediacy and Aesthetics of the Self on YouTube', in P Snickars & P Vonderau (eds) *The YouTube Reader*. Stockholm: The National Library of Sweden, 187–203.

Phoenix, A (1997) 'Youth and Gender: New Issues, New Agenda', *Young: Nordic Journal of Youth Research*, 5(3): 2–19.

Perry, I (2004) *Prophets of the Hood: Politics and Poetics in Hip Hop*. Durham, NC: Duke University Press.

Ponte, C, Bauwens, J & Mascheroni, G (2009) 'Children and the Internet in the News: Agency, Voices and Agendas', in S Livingstone & L Haddon (eds) *Kids Online: Opportunities and Risks for Children*. Bristol: Policy Press, 159–172.

Vernallis, C (2004) *Experiencing Music Video: Aesthetics and Cultural Context*. New York: Columbia University Press.

Vernallis, C (2010) 'Music Video and YouTube: New Aesthetics and Generic Transformations', in H Keazor & T Wübbena (eds) *Rewind, Play, Fast Forward: The Past, Present and Future of the Music Video*. Bielefeld: Transcript Verlag, 233–259.

Weber, S & Dixon, S (2007) 'Perspectives on Young People and Technologies', in S Weber & S Dixon (eds) *Growing Up Online: Young People and Digital Technologies*. New York: Palgrave MacMillan, 1–14.

Werner, A (2010) 'Danssteg på YouTube: Musik, Genus, Etnicitet/"Ras"', *Tidsskrift for Kjønnsforskning*, 34(2): 236–249 ('Dance Moves on YouTube: Music, Gender, Ethnicity/"Race"', *Journal of Gender Research*).

12
'Activating' Young People in the Production of Virtual Worlds

Liam Berriman (University of Sussex)

The past decade has seen a rapid expansion of the virtual world market for children and young people. Though virtual worlds exist in a number of forms, this chapter will primarily refer to those that offer an 'open-ended' experience in which users can create avatars and are able to interact with other users in a simulated virtual environment.[1] At the beginning of 2009, industry figures estimated that there were approximately 246 million registered virtual world accounts for young people aged 10–15 and 73 million registered accounts for those aged 15–25.[2] By early 2012 this estimate had risen to approximately 852 million and 712 million, respectively. The growing popularity of virtual worlds has led many large media corporations to break into the market in recent years. Though initially launched by small independent firms, both 'Neopets' and 'Club Penguin' have subsequently been acquired in multi-million dollar transactions by Viacom (owners of Nickelodeon) and The Walt Disney Company[3] respectively. The popularity of virtual worlds has also led to a number of independent firms, such as Sulake[4] and Mind Candy,[5] emerging as key market competitors rivalling more established media corporations.

Despite the significant growth experienced by this market, virtual world use amongst young people remains relatively limited when contrasted with other online activities, such as instant messaging and watching online videos.[6] It is also important to bear in mind that statistics reporting the number of registered virtual world accounts may suppress more than they reveal, potentially disguising global and social divisions that determine which young people have the means to access these online environments. Nonetheless, rising user figures across age groups raise the possibility that virtual worlds will become an increasingly dominant form of media activity for young people in the coming years. As such, it has become increasingly pertinent to examine the relationship between this expanding industry and its growing user base.

Over the past few decades, theories of the 'active audience' (Fiske, 1990, 2002) and 'participatory media cultures' (Jenkins, 2006, 2008) have become increasingly commonplace within media and cultural studies, with academics emphasising the importance of examining everyday media interpretation and engagement (Ang, 1996; Fiske, 2002; Morley, 2002; Silverstone, 1994). Though initially formulated through research on television audiences, these terms have gained greater currency with the rise of online media. With the arrival of the so-called 'Web 2.0', a number of academics have heralded the arrival of an 'online participatory culture', in which, 'consumers of media can now be much *more active* and engaged, producing and distributing their own creative material' (Gauntlett, 2011, emphasis added) (see also Gauntlett, 2009; Jenkins, 2006; Merrin, 2009). The active media user has thus been re-framed by some academics as being able to exercise a greater degree of agency and creativity in their engagement with media.

Such discussions and rhetoric have not just been confined to academics. The notion of the 'active' media consumer has increasingly been adopted in both media marketing and design, with the consumer being characterised as playing a significant role in the development of media products and brands (Arvidsson, 2005; Lury, 2004). As Arvidsson argues:

> Consumers are ... used as *active partners* to the product development process, as a kind of co-producers. In certain sectors ... subjecting new models to consumer feedback before launching them on the market has become normal business practice ... product designers have come to rely much more on end-user feedback or even participation. (Arvidsson, 2005: 70, emphasis added)

The virtual world and online games markets have been particularly significant proponents of this approach to product development. The design of virtual worlds and online games is often a cyclical process, with new updates and product releases regularly being added to the existing service. As Kline et al. (2006) note, this has led to games designers and marketers increasingly adopting a 'user-centred approach' and positioning themselves as the *intermediaries* between the 'changing tastes, preferences and subcultures' (2006: 252) of users and the constantly evolving design of the media product.

A large proportion of research on virtual worlds to date, particularly in the UK, has primarily sought to examine them as sites of social play and learning (Carrington & Hodgetts, 2010; Marsh, 2010, 2011; Tuukkanen et al., 2010; Willett & Sefton-Green, 2003). In studies such as these, the young person as virtual world user is often at the centre of both the empirical investigation and subsequent analysis. As such, virtual worlds are primarily understood in terms of the experiences, and forms of interaction and participation, that they afford users. Research into the design and development of virtual worlds has been slightly more limited. Primarily emerging from Finland, a number of studies have sought to examine the specificities of the virtual world design process, particularly around the user-centred approach (Johnson, 2007, 2010). Though these studies have gone some way to broadening our understanding of the development of virtual worlds, they have often done so with limited consideration of the specificities of young people as virtual world users.

This chapter explores the production of virtual worlds, with a specific focus on the 'activation' of users within the design and production process. Building on existing discussions, it seeks to critically examine the enrolment of young people as 'active' media consumers by virtual world corporations. Drawing on research with designers of virtual world 'Habbo Hotel', this chapter will explore how Habbo's users are described and positioned as 'active' participants in the design of the Habbo service. This chapter also seeks to examine how the designers of Habbo position themselves as 'activators' of young people. Following on from Kline et al.'s description of the intermediary role that designers have adopted, this chapter will explore how the 'activation' of young people is practised and accomplished in the design of Habbo.

In order to address these questions, the chapter will begin with a brief overview of the Habbo Hotel case study and methodology, followed by a short discussion and analysis of the academic development of young people as 'active' media users. Building on this discussion, the chapter will then examine two examples of user 'activation' in the design and development of Habbo Hotel. The first of these will consider how the virtual world has been used as a means for designers to observe and engage with users. The second example will explore the more recent deployment of social media as a means of mobilising users. The chapter will then conclude with some critical reflections on the positioning of young people as 'active' in the design of virtual worlds.

Background and Methodology

Launched in the UK in 2000, 'Habbo Hotel' (or simply 'Habbo') is described by its parent company, Sulake, as 'the world's largest social game and online community for teenagers'.[7] At present, Habbo is available in 11 different language versions, with the most recent 'hotel' opening in Turkey in August 2012. According to Sulake's most recent figures, 90 per cent of the current Habbo user base is aged between 13 and 18 years.[8] Figures from 2009 suggest a gender split of approximately 56 per cent male versus 44 per cent female.[9] Sulake's own figures estimate that Habbo's websites currently receive 10 million unique visitors per month, with approximately 250 million registered users in total.[10] According to Kzero, an industry analytics firm, Habbo's user figures rank it the largest virtual world globally, outpacing rivals such as 'Stardoll' and 'Club Penguin' (with 200 million and 170 million registered users, respectively).[11]

Habbo, like many other virtual worlds, primarily generates income through micro-transactions, user membership schemes and in-game advertising. Habbo is free at the point of use, but in order to decorate virtual rooms and customise an avatar beyond basic apparel, users need to purchase the in-game currency 'Habbo Credits'.

The present chapter is based on qualitative interviews with six Sulake employees at the company's Finnish headquarters. The employees represent a cross section of staff directly involved in the development of Habbo, including concept designers, a graphic artist and a software architect. As Sulake's headquarters are based in Helsinki, the majority of staff are native Finnish speakers with one exception. All of the interviews were carried out in English and, although every person interviewed was a confident English speaker, it is important to note the interviews were not carried out in their native tongue. For ethical purposes, the names of all staff have been kept anonymous, and research participants are referred to by their general job role.

In addition to interviews with staff, a variety of textual data were also gathered from a range of Sulake-owned websites and social media accounts. All of the textual data collected were publicly available online, though names and details of the authors of those materials have again been kept anonymous.

Young People, Agency and 'Active' Media Consumption

Though discussions of young people's 'active' media engagement have long pre-dated online media (see Buckingham, 1994; Kinder, 1999), the arrival of the internet sparked a range of new debates and rhetorics around young people's agency and media consumption (Buckingham, 2007; Livingstone, 2003). In *Growing Up Digital* (1998), Don Tapscott heralded the arrival of the internet as initiating a fundamental re-framing in the perception of young people's media use. According to Tapscott, young people of the 'N-Generation' were swiftly adapting to new media technologies and were rapidly becoming more technologically competent than their parents. Thus, he argued, 'If parents think that their kids are catching on to the new technologies much faster than adults, they're right. It's easier for kids. Because N-Gen children are born with technology, they assimilate it' (1998: 40). Tapscott's rhetoric can largely be placed at the more extreme end of a spectrum that celebrated the arrival of new technology and viewed young people as having their agency rapidly extended by the arrival of the internet. This rhetoric has, however, attracted a significant amount of criticism, with studies challenging the extent to which young people have become media 'experts' (Livingstone, 2003) and are made 'active' as a result of new technologies (Buckingham, 2007).

Recent research has tended to offer a more cautious account of young people's media competency, although the question of agency has remained a key issue. Over the last decade, studies have examined an increasingly broad range of topics relating to young people's agency, such as identity performance through profile pages and avatars (boyd, 2007; Kafai et al., 2010) and the development of technical skills through the creation of webpages and video mash-ups (Lange & Ito, 2010; Stern, 2007). Within studies such as these, the theme of creativity has become particularly significant, as researchers have sought to explore the extent to which young people can become 'producers' of media content in their own right.[12] Here there has been a significant amount of overlap with the notion of a 'participatory media culture' as advanced by academics such as Jenkins and Gauntlett (see above). Some scholars have, however, offered a more cautious note to these discussions. Livingstone, for example, warns that the types of 'creativity' in which the majority of young people are engaged online are 'highly formatted' and 'often commercialized' (2010: 60). This is not to say that young people are not engaged in the creative forms of media production, but rather that we also need to account for young people's agency in engaging with all forms of media, including those that are 'highly formatted' and 'commercial'.

Another important reason for examining young people's agency in relation to commercial media is the increasing employment of notions of the 'active' and 'creative' consumer within the youth media market. Following Arvidsson (2005), Buckingham (2011) has examined a range of new marketing and design practices that address young people as 'active agents', such as 'immersive marketing' and 'advergaming'. Buckingham is particularly critical of the way in which young people's agency is framed within these commercial practices, arguing that

> *activity* on the part of audiences should not necessarily be equated with *agency* or power. Contemporary media phenomenon like Pokémon position children as active participants even if that activity is mediated almost entirely through commercial processes and relationships – and, as such, they may at least *feel* 'empowering' even if ultimately they are not. (Buckingham, 2011: 94, emphasis in original)

Buckingham thus argues against the presumption of agency in instances where media users are demarcated as 'active'. Indeed, one of the most persistent criticisms of defining media users as 'active' has been the presumption that they are *always* 'active' (Evans, 1990; Morley, 1993). By examining the 'activation' of users, this chapter attempts to move away from presumption of young people as always 'active' in their media engagement. As such, the following case studies will explore some of the ways in which virtual world designers describe users as 'active' and by what means they attempt to 'activate' in the design of the virtual world.

Framing Habbo Users as 'Active' Agents

Before exploring how users are described as 'active' in Habbo's design, it is important to get a sense of how Sulake staff frame users as more generally 'active' in their engagement with Habbo. One of the overriding themes of my interviews with Sulake staff was the significance placed on 'creativity' as part of the Habbo user experience. The ability to personalise an avatar and to host and decorate virtual rooms was commonly given, as an example of the creative activities in which Habbo users could engage. When asked to summarise Habbo, one Sulake staff member described it as follows:

> Habbo is a creative social space ... the main feature for me is the freedom and the creativity. Users can create their own space, their own room. In a way it's a bit like a mini-god simulator ... because you have your own space you can decide to make it an airline check-in desk, some users do that, or a mafia room, a role play, a maze or just

a chat room. Users, they go to Habbo, they have their space and they choose what direction to take their experience.

According to this interviewee, Habbo is an environment that *enables* and *facilitates* user creativity. Of particular interest here is the way in which the rhetoric of 'creativity' is mobilised to position the user as 'actively' contributing to development of their own, and others', Habbo experience. The description of Habbo as 'like a mini-god simulator' implies that the user has a degree of creative control over the way the virtual environment is shaped. There is also a repeated reference to the Habbo environment as the user's 'own space'. Though Sulake hosts and owns Habbo, the interviewee suggests that the virtual world is designed to give users a sense of ownership and control.

Another Sulake staff member framed user creativity in a slightly different way:

> [Creativity] becomes more important for more active users, I would say that new users doesn't see it so clearly that aspect of creativity. It's more a visual chat room for them, but after awhile, when you use the service more, the creative part becomes really important.

This interviewee identifies varying levels of 'activity' and 'creativity' between users, particularly between new and more established users. In this instance some Habbo users are defined and distinguished as *more* actively or *more* creatively involved in the Habbo environment than others. This may then suggest that references by design staff to 'active' or 'creative' users do not refer to the user base as a whole, but rather to a distinct subsection of users. It is important, therefore, to look not only at *how* users are described but also at *which* users are being included and excluded from a particular rhetoric. In addition to considering differences between new versus old users, we might also look at paid versus free accounts. For example, are users who pay and financially contribute to virtual worlds more likely to be considered 'active' and 'creative' contributors than those who only use 'freemium'[13] services?

Buckingham (2011) argues that industry rhetoric of 'creative' and 'active' involvement is an attempt to present young people as 'empowered' in their engagement with media. Though this may be the case, I believe we need to explore more closely the way in which the rhetoric of the 'creative' and 'active' user is mobilised and put into practice – in other words, *how* designers go about 'activating' their users within their design practices.

'Activating' Habbo Users through the Virtual World

For Habbo's designers, the virtual environment provides a key means of mediating their relationship with Habbo's users. Habbo is not only the product that they design but also a primary means of gaining *closer* access to their user base. During interviews for this study, staff would frequently report going 'in-game' at various points in the design process – whether to look for inspiration for new design ideas or to get a sense of how users were responding to recent product releases. In the following extract, a concept designer describes their experience of engaging with users during the beta testing phase of a new product release:

> When the beta was out, we used Habbo a lot with [the lead designer] and we sort of just spent time in beta and started to interview users about the beta as well, about how they feel about it. I guess that's like a skill as well. So, trying to get in there and talk face to face to the users as well, how they feel about something. And then again, I guess, the feedback, what we gather, is sort of to get the insight from that and turn that into a concept. It's a skill that you can do that as well, so that first you have to realize the problem and then you have to sort of evaluate what you can do based on that, and then turning that into a functioning concept on the site.

This quote provides some indications as to how Sulake's designers use the virtual environment as a means of 'activating' users. Through their presence in the beta, the staff member positions and establishes themself as a means by which users can contribute their thoughts and feedback on the beta release. It's interesting to note that the designer describes this as a 'face-to-face' encounter – thus, although it is a mediated encounter, it is framed as one that brings the user and designer closer together. The designer then describes how a user's feedback can be evaluated and transformed 'into a concept' which can then be incorporated into the development of the product or feature. The designer thus positions themselves as the intermediary between the user's ideas and their implementation. As such the role of intermediaries is also partly one of authority; the designer is not only a facilitator of user suggestions but also a filter, able to judge and evaluate the usefulness and viability of a user's ideas.

The designer describes this means of engaging with users in-game as a form of skill. Earlier in the interview the designer had been asked what kinds of skills were required for their role, and these were generally listed as a set of technical and organisational skills. In this instance, however, the designer suggests that being able to engage users and to act as an intermediary for their feedback is an additional skill. As Kline et al. (2006) describe, the 'intermediary' role of the designer has become an increasingly significant means of developing a productive relationship with consumers. How then is this relationship developed and on whose terms?

For the Sulake staff interviewed, developing the ability to engage with users raised a number of issues ranging from the kind of avatar used to the type of language they employed when talking with users. In the following extract a concept producer describes some of the difficulties of engaging with users in-game:

> We don't want to come across as the user's best friend, we don't want to come across as cool, uncool or anything like that, you know, we want to be as straight forward and blunt with our users as possible. So yeah we can be funny, we can be friendly but, you know, we don't want to be down with the kids *per se*. You know, because that is the kind of thing that if it works, it can work brilliantly, but in my experience, more than not, it backfires and makes you sound like a boring uncle [laughs].

In this extract several contrasts are made between how staff should and shouldn't interact with users in-game. Though great importance is placed on developing a closer relationship with users, this extract suggests that staff must also maintain a degree of distance. As such, appearing to be 'down with the kids' or acting as a 'user's best friend' are flagged as interactional boundary points. These boundary points also hint at the generational distance between Habbo's designers and users. There is a sense that by avoiding certain forms of behaviour, Sulake's designers are better able to suppress these generational differences in their engagement with users and thus avoid sounding 'like a boring uncle'.

Many of the designers interviewed chose to use avatars that didn't explicitly identify them as staff members.[14] As one interviewee described:

> I just go in ... as a random account and just start talking to users ... they don't know that I'm a staff member because that wouldn't be beneficial for my aims, which is, well one of them is seeing what users are talking about, seeing what users are doing.

Being recognised as a Sulake staff member is regarded by this interviewee as occasionally being an impediment to observing how users are engaging with Habbo. The ability to observe users' 'activities' could, in this case, potentially be obstructed by the staff member's presence. Though the Habbo user is positioned as 'active' in this instance – as both engaged in the game and providing information for the designer – both tasks are being done unwittingly. For the most part, the activation and engagement of Habbo's users in-game occurs predominantly on the terms of the designers. The Sulake staff are able to select at what points in the design process they enter the game's interface for user feedback. The terms of engagement remain limited for the user, who may or may not have the opportunity to share their opinions with Sulake staff. Negus (2002) has suggested that, although the role of the intermediary provides a point of connection between consumers and the production process, it also serves to reproduce a degree of distance between these two points.

'Activating' Habbo Users through Social Media

In this final section we turn our attention to user–designer interactions that take place 'outside' of Habbo's virtual world interface. Over the last few years Sulake has begun to implement a brand presence spanning a number of social media platforms, including Facebook, YouTube and Twitter. In this section we will restrict ourselves to looking at Sulake's presence on Twitter and examine how this platform has provided staff with an alternate means of 'activating' users.

Sulake's Twitter presence can broadly be categorised into two main account types. First, there are the 'official' Habbo and Sulake Twitter accounts, which provide regular corporate and product announcements to Twitter followers. For example, if the Habbo service experiences technical 'downtime', the Habbo Twitter account is used as a channel to provide users with estimates as to when the service will be reopened. The second group of accounts is the 'Sulake Tweeters' – individual Sulake staff members who manage their own Twitter accounts. These range from the company's CEO to members of the design and creative teams and community-orientated staff. In order to promote the Sulake Tweeters, Sulake's corporate website contains a section of self-written profiles promoting each staff member, accompanied by a single photograph. Each of the profiles follows a similar template, with staff members describing their role at Sulake, sometimes hinting at some of their interests, and finally encouraging users to follow their Twitter account.

The following are just a few extracts from the profiles of Sulake Tweeters encouraging Habbo users to follow them on Twitter:

> So Habbos, I'm here for you...to answer your questions, to listen to your crazy ideas and to help as much as I can.

> I am curious to hear your thoughts about the future. About great new ideas or things you saw at different games that you think would work in Habbo as well. Let me know and see you in Habbo!

> I am interested in your thoughts and ideas on how to make the Habbo experience more fun, meaningful, creative and social. Let me know how to bring more value to the Habbo experience.[15]

In each case the Habbo user is addressed as being in possession of opinions and ideas that are significant and of value to Sulake. The staff members invite the Habbo users to connect with them on Twitter in order to share their 'crazy' or 'great new' ideas. They can then gauge how users would like to see Habbo changed or improved and therefore 'bring more value' to the users' 'Habbo experience'. In this way, the staff members establish themselves as *channels* through which a user's opinions can be heard and potentially implemented into the virtual world's design. As opposed to being a faceless or anonymous channel, the Sulake Tweeters present themselves as individuals who can be interacted with and wish to hear the opinions and ideas of Habbo users. As such, there is a sense of 'immediacy' in the interaction offered between Habbo users and the Sulake Tweeters, with users apparently able to contact the staff members on their own terms.

The profiles of the Sulake Tweeters provide an important initial means of appealing staff to users, furnishing Habbo users with insights into each staff member's interests, areas of expertise and personality quirks. The accompanying profile photos add a further means by which staff can express their individuality to users and also allow users to put a 'name to a face'. In the majority of cases, staff members opt for a regular portrait photograph, but in some instances their faces are obscured either by a mask or are edited until the face is only partially discernible. Though staff members are referred to by their first names, it's interesting to note that a number of staff choose to disguise their faces in the photographs. Thus to some degree the Sulake staff may choose to assert a degree of privacy in sharing only limited details about their identity. Nonetheless, these profiles could be seen as an attempt to encourage users to engage with staff through the promise of a closer and more 'personalised' connection via Twitter.

According to some academics, using Twitter and other social media involves a particular form of identity performance to an imagined audience (Marwick & boyd, 2011). In the case of the Sulake Tweeters their audience is to some extent pre-formed, as the accounts appear to have been established with the intention of interacting with and 'activating' Habbo users. Indeed, the majority of tweets through the Sulake Tweeters' accounts are directed at a 'Habbo audience', either sharing Habbo-related news or responding to tweets from Habbo users. The notion of identity performance is, however, significant to the way that Sulake staff seek to activate users. As we saw in the previous section, the type of language and avatar used in the virtual world is important to how designers attempt to engage with users. However, the framing of these accounts as 'Sulake' Tweeters suggests these Twitter accounts form part of the company's public identity and may follow a similar set of guidelines to those employed in the Habbo environment. The interaction between the Sulake Tweeters and Habbo users might therefore be seen as mediated to some degree by corporate values.

It is also important to consider the potential unevenness of Twitter as a mediatory channel between Habbo users and Sulake. Although Habbo users have the ability to tweet to Sulake staff members, it remains the purview of the Sulake Tweeter to decide which tweets to acknowledge and respond to. As such, a Habbo user's ability to tweet to staff members does not necessarily equate with having the ability to be included or recognised as a contributor to the development of the Habbo service.

Conclusion

This chapter has sought to examine how young people have come to be defined as 'active' participants in the design of virtual worlds and how designers of virtual worlds seek to enrol and 'activate' users in the design process. Through research with Sulake staff, this chapter has attempted to show how the virtual world 'Habbo' and external social media platforms have emerged as significant mediatory points between designers and users. In both instances, the media platform was employed as a means of developing a 'closer' relationship with users, and staff attempted to engage users as 'active' contributors with valuable views and opinions. This process of 'activation' has, to some extent, been specifically shaped around Habbo users as 'young people'. Decisions around how to approach and engage with users have been shaped by generational differences, as 'adult' designers attempt to find an appropriate mode and means of eliciting young people's interests and ideas.

The 'activation' of Habbo users has remained, a markedly uneven process however. As Couldry (2008) has suggested, mediation is often an 'asymmetric' process. Habbo's designers are able to determine the points at which users are able to contribute to the design process through temporal management and decisions as to whether to disclose their identity as Sulake staff. Although users may be rhetorically defined as 'active' contributors, they may not always be able to exercise agency regarding when and how they participate. It remains unclear as to how Habbo's diverse range of users each experience participation. Certainly, further study is required in order to explore this in more detail. It seems unlikely that all young people share an equal chance of being able to contribute to the virtual world's design.

Due to limitations of space, this chapter has focused exclusively on those activities and forms of participation identified as significant or of value by Sulake's designers. Future discussions must also consider the ways in which users define their own and others' 'active' participation in relation to virtual worlds. This might include forms of user participation that are unobservable or overlooked by the designers, such as the use of private social media channels (e.g. Facebook or MSN) or gated online communities 'outside' of Habbo (e.g. fan forums). It might also include activities within the Habbo service that have not attracted the attention of Sulake staff.

This chapter provides just one instance of how rhetorics of the 'active' media user are shaping and informing the practices of designing young people's virtual worlds. As such, the full impact of these practices on young people's media use still requires further exploration.

Acknowledgements

With thanks to the staff at Sulake for their warm welcome in Helsinki and for sharing their time and experience. This work was supported by the UK Economic and Social Research Council (grant number ES/H013474/1).

Notes

1. This is in contrast to massively multiplayer online role-playing games (MMORGs) in which the virtual world environment is primarily (though not

exclusively) geared towards the completion of a set of gaming objectives. An example of this would be the *World of Warcraft* series.

2. http://www.slideshare.net/nicmitham/kzero-universe-q1-2012   (accessed 5 September 2012).

3. The former for $350 million in 2007 and the latter for $160 million in 2005; http://www.guardian.co.uk/business/2010/apr/25/boaki-social-networking-child-safety-online?INTCMP=SRCH (accessed 6 June 2012).

4. Finnish creators of the early virtual world franchise 'Habbo Hotel'.

5. The British firm behind the 'Moshi Monsters' franchise.

6. As part of a EU Kids Online II survey (Livingstone et al., 2011), a random sample of young people (n = 25,142) aged 9–16 were asked what activities they had done online in the past month. Sixty-two per cent reported using an instant messaging service, 76 per cent reported watching a video online and 16 per cent reported accessing a virtual world.

7. http://www.sulake.com/habbo (accessed 15 March 2012).

8. http://www.sulake.com/habbo (accessed 25 August 2012).

9. http://www.sulake.com/press/releases/habbo-hotel-and-mtv-international-partner-to-bring-the-mtv-europe-music-awards-to-the-worlds-largest-teen-virtual-world (accessed 15 March 2012).

10. http://www.sulake.com/habbo (accessed 25 August 2012).

11. http://www.slideshare.net/nicmitham/kzero-universe-q4-2011   (accessed 15 March 2012).

12. In the case of virtual worlds and online games, the issue of users as producers of content has emerged as a particularly complex issue. An example is the issue of whether the avatar and virtual property created in a game are the property of users or the corporation that owns the servers which host the game environment and its content. See Grimes (2006) and Taylor (2009) for comprehensive discussions on these issues.

13. The term 'freemium' refers to virtual world accounts that are free at the point of use. However, there is often the potential for users to subsequently pay for a 'premium' membership account that offers a range of additional features unavailable to freemium users.

14. Staff involved in Habbo's community management often use avatars with a badge that clearly identifies them as Sulake staff members.

15. http://www.sulake.com/contact/sulake-tweeters (accessed 3 July 2012).

References

Ang, I (1996) *Living Room Wars: Rethinking Audiences for a Postmodern World*. London & New York: Routledge.

Arvidsson, A (2005) *Brands: Meaning and Value in Media Culture*. London & New York: Routledge.

boyd, d (2007) 'Why Youth (Heart) Social Network Sites: The Role of Networked Publics in Teenage Social Life', in D Buckingham (ed.) *Youth, Identity, and Digital Media*. Cambridge, MA & London: MIT Press.

Buckingham, D (1994) *Children Talking Television: The Making of Television Literacy*. London & Washington, DC: Falmer Press.

Buckingham, D (2007) *After the Death of Childhood: Growing Up in the Age of Electronic Media*. Cambridge: Polity Press.

Buckingham, D (2011) *The Material Child: Growing Up in Consumer Culture*. Cambridge: Polity Press.

Carrington, V & Hodgetts, K (2010) 'Literacy-lite in BarbieGirls™', *British Journal of Sociology of Education*, 31(6): 671–682.

Couldry, N (2008) 'Mediatization or Mediation? Alternative Understandings of the Emergent Space of Digital Storytelling', *New Media & Society*, 10(3): 373–391.

Evans, W (1990) 'The Interpretive Turn in Media Research', *Critical Studies in Mass Communications*, 6(2): 145–168.

Fiske, J (1990) *Understanding Popular Culture*. London & New York: Routledge.

Fiske, J (2002) *Television Culture*. London & New York: Routledge.

Gauntlett, D (2009) 'Media Studies 2.0: A Response', *Interactions: Studies in Communication and Culture*, 1(1): 147–157.

Gauntlett, D (2011) *Media Studies 2.0 and Other Battles Around the Future of Media Research*, ebook, self-published.

Grimes, S (2006) 'Online Multiplayer Games: A Virtual Space for Intellectual Property Debates?', *New Media & Society*, 8(6): 969–990.

Jenkins, H (2006) *Fans, Bloggers, and Gamers: Exploring Participatory Culture*. New York & London: New York University Press.

Jenkins, H (2008) *Convergence Culture: Where Old and New Media Collide*. New York & London: New York University Press.

Johnson, M (2007) 'Unscrambling the Average User of Habbo Hotel', *Human Technology*, 3(2): 127–153.

Johnson, M (2010) 'User Involvement, Social Media, and Service Evolution: The Case of Habbo', in *Proceeding of the Forty-third Annual Hawaii International Conference on System Sciences*. Available from: http://doi.ieeecomputersociety.org/10.1109/HICSS.2010.425.

Kafai, YB, Fields, DA & Cook, MS (2010) 'Your Second Selves: Player-Designed Avatars', *Games and Culture*, 5(1): 23–42.

Kinder, M (1999) 'Kid's Media Culture: An Introduction', in M Kinder (ed.) *Kid's Media Culture*. Durham, NC & London: Duke University Press.

Kline, S, Dyer-Witheford, N & De Peuter, G (2006) *Digital Play: The Interaction of Technology, Culture, and Marketing*. Montreal & Kingston: McGill-Queens University Press.

Lange, P & Ito, M (2010) 'Creative Production', in M Ito et al. (eds) *Hanging Out, Messing Around and Geeking Out*. Cambridge, MA & London: MIT Press.

Livingstone, S (2003) *Young People and New Media: Childhood and the Changing Media Environment*. Thousand Oaks, CA: Sage.

Livingstone, S (2010) *Children and the Internet*. Cambridge: Polity.

Livingstone, S, Haddon, L, Görzig, A & Ólafsson, K (2011) *Risks and Safety on the Internet: The Perspective of European Children. Full Findings*. LSE, London: EU Kids Online.

Lury, C (2004) *Brands: The Logos of the Global Economy*. London & New York: Routledge.

Marsh, J (2010) 'Young Children's Play in Online Virtual Worlds', *Journal of Early Childhood Research*, 8(1): 23–39.

Marsh, J (2011) 'Young Children's Literacy Practices in a Virtual World: Establishing an Online Interaction Order', *Reading Research Quarterly*, 46(2): 101–118.

Marwick, AE & boyd, d (2011) 'I Tweet Honestly, I Tweet Passionately: Twitter Users, Context Collapse, and the Imagined Audience', *New Media & Society*, 13(1): 114–133.

Merrin, W (2009) 'Media Studies 2.0: Upgrading and Open-Sourcing the Discipline', *Interactions: Studies in Communication and Culture*, 1(1): 17–34.

Morley, D (1993) 'Active Audience Theory: Pendulums and Pitfalls', *Journal of Communication*, 43(4): 13–19.

Morley, D (2002) *Television Audiences and Cultural Studies*. London & New York: Routledge.

Negus, K (2002) 'The Work of Cultural Intermediaries and the Enduring Distance Between Production and Consumption', *Cultural Studies*, 16(4): 501–515.

Silverstone, R (1994) *Television and Everyday Life*. London & New York: Routledge.

Stern, S (2007) 'Producing Sites, Exploring Identities: Youth Online Authorship', in D Buckingham (ed.) *Youth, Identity, and Digital Media*. Cambridge, MA & London: MIT Press.

Tapscott, D (1998) *Growing Up Digital: The Rise of the Net Generation*. New York: McGraw-Hill.

Taylor, TL (2009) *Play Between Worlds: Exploring Online Game Culture*. Cambridge, MA & London: MIT Press.

Tuukkanen, T, Iqbal, A & Kankaanranta, M (2010) 'A Framework for Children's Participatory Practices in Virtual Worlds', *Journal of Virtual Worlds Research*, 3(2): 3–26.

Willett, R & Sefton-Green, J (2003) 'Living and Learning in Chatrooms (Or Does Informal Learning Have Anything to Teach Us?)', *Education et Sociétiés*, 2.

13
Flash Mobs and Zombie Shuffles: Play in the Augmented City

Susan Bird (Victoria University)

On Facebook I received an invitation from a young guy I'd met at a party. It said:

> After the success of "Dont Walk Dance", Awkward/Amazing are opening up another Portable Dance Portal at 5:55pm on the 5th of May!!!! This time it's...
> >>>>>>DANCE CROSSING<<<<<<
> Step 1. Set aside all other priorities
> Step 2. Find an MP3 player
> Step 3. Meet at the intersection of Elizabeth and Flinders St at 5.55pm on 5/5/11
> Step 4. When the little man goes green dance your little hearts out in the middle of the intersection (this is the set of lights where you can cross the street diagonally)
> Step 5. When the little man turns red return to the sidewalk
> Step 6. Repeat steps 4 and 5 for as long as you feel necessary
> Please spread the word...
> >>>>>>SEE YOU THERE<<<<<<

I jumped on the Flinders Street train at East Malvern, excited by the invitation and not wanting to be left out. I noticed a girl in my carriage, dressed in brightly coloured, alternative clothes. You don't see many people like that on my line. Carriages tend to be filled with mostly business people and school kids in uniform. This urban hipster didn't belong on the Southside.

Twenty minutes later, I was dancing with her in the intersection of two of the busiest streets in Melbourne's CBD. Like a storm appearing in the summer sky, swirls of people skipped unexpectedly into the

213

intersection as the lights changed to green. They emerged out of the peak hour suits as though drawn by an invisible thread, cavorting and pirouetting, dancing to the tunes on their MP3 players until the lights changed to red. I, caught in the current, felt a strange connection with my new friends, although no words were exchanged.

The dancing went on for about an hour – the crowd swelling to a peak of about 150. It was not a large mob, but this made it perfect. When the light turned red, the mob had the ability to melt into the sidelines, and appear again as if by magic at the sound of the walk signal. Astounded commuters stared, but continued in a frantic bee-line for the next train. I wondered whether seeing the spin of whirling dervishes made them question their hurry, and consider joining in. Perhaps life doesn't hinge on catching the next train...

This was my very first flash mob, up close and personal. According to Bill Wasik, the inventor of the phenomenon, flash mobbing was dead before the end of 2003. However, as reported by Giles Hewitt, flash mobs have taken on 'a life of their own' (Hewitt, 2003), and this was confirmed for me on the streets of Melbourne in 2011.

In this chapter I will explore flash mobs as a form of mediated youth culture that exemplifies the shifts occurring in the ways that we view and use 'real' and 'virtual' public spaces. An early writer who brought the concept of cyberspace into the popular imagination even before the advent of the World Wide Web was novelist William Gibson. In the *Sprawl Trilogy* Gibson painted a dystopian vision where 'real' world action becomes secondary to that taking place within 'the Matrix' (e.g. Gibson, 1984). The idea of the Matrix reaches its pinnacle in the movie of the same name, where humans are not even aware of their 'real' existence, but live out their lives in a virtual world. Manuel Castells, in positing a theory of what he called 'the information age', imagined that space and time would collapse as we moved into a 'space of flows' where online communication, and the exchange of information, could happen anywhere and at any time, reducing the importance of 'real' geographies (Castells, 2000). Gaming environments such as *Second Life* attempt to create an online virtual world with as many aspects as possible of the 'real' world replicated, allowing individuals to submerge themselves in a parallel universe. However, this kind of gaming is beginning to give way to gaming environments that incorporate the real in such a way as to create a layered, or augmented, experience of public space. I assert that the internet, and mobile technologies often used to access it, expand rather than diminish the importance of public space to young people, and increase the amount and types of interaction that occur there. Further, it is becoming increasingly difficult to argue that the 'virtual' and the 'real' exist as two, separate, dichotomous worlds (Brighenti, 2012; Crang & Graham, 2007; Crang et al., 2007). Ubiquitous computing technologies permeate further into public and private urban life, leaving dwellers caught in an invisible web which is often only noticeable when it stops working (Crang & Graham, 2007: 812). These technologies have the ability to track, sort and statistically analyse populations, and create Foucauldian 'territorialisation of populations' – a kind of urban control that uses statistical data as leverage in its authority over populations (Brighenti, 2012: 399). Activities such as flash mobs resist such measures of control as they draw attention to the ordering of public space and the pervasiveness of mobile technologies, making them visible and thus open to critique. They do this via disrupting the norms of behaviour in public spaces, and by illuminating the invisible thread that ties the participants together – the online world.[1]

It is not surprising that flash mobbing was invented by a media-savvy journalist. What Wasik may not have known was quite the extent to which flash mobbing would capture an imagination driven by the do it yourself (DIY) immediacy of Web 2.0. Flash mobbing has a symbiotic relationship with the internet and mobile technologies. Flash mobs very much capitalise on the blended environment of ubiquitous computing technologies. They often last for only a few minutes, but are attention-grabbing and visually spectacular, and therefore bounce around in cyberspace for a much longer period of time, being posted and reposted on YouTube, Facebook, blogs and other interactive platforms, usually by the participants themselves.

Where boundaries are blurred between online and offline, fantasy and reality, the theatrical imagery of the flash mob appeals to a generation brought up on a diet of TV, movies and now YouTube. Media devices and social media provide platforms for the quick, easy uploading of events or any attention-grabbing images. Web 2.0 is a DIY environment where anyone with access and even basic computing equipment, such as a smartphone, can become a photographer, promoter, producer or developer. While anyone can do it, the vast volume of images means that only the most spectacular can survive, be reposted and reproduced throughout the online world – anything less than amazing is quickly forgotten. Without the internet and mobile technologies, the flash mob may have remained a small, brief event in New York's history, rather than a global phenomenon. But social media sites such as Facebook and YouTube also owe their success to people's desire to create spectacles. Activities like flash mobs are at times rehearsed or involve complex

Figure 13.1 Melbourne Zombie Shuffle

preparations such as zombie costumes designed to attract attention, reanimating in endless reiterations online. In augmented public space, the mobbers become the stars of their own show.

This chapter is based on an extensive examination of the very public display of flash mobs online on sites such as YouTube, but also observation of and participation by the author in flash mobs on the streets of Melbourne, Australia. I have also conducted a series of interviews with participants in the Melbourne Zombie Shuffle, which could be described as an extended or interactive flash mob. Zombie walks are an international phenomenon but have been particularly large in Melbourne, numbering well into the thousands each year.[2]

The Origins of the Flash Mob

Bill Wasik, a journalist at *Harper's Magazine*, originally came up with the flash mob idea because he was 'bored and therefore disposed towards acts of social-scientific inquiry' (Wasik, 2006: 57). Inspired by the experiments of Stanley Milgram[3] and by what he saw as tendencies towards conformity in New York's young urban hipster crowd, Wasik created the first mob in 2003, in an attempt to see how many people he could gather in one place only for the reason that 'Tons of other people are doing it' (Wasik, 2006: 57). Wasik felt that those in New York's in-crowd were more interested in being seen at events than in their artistic content, and hated to miss out on anything new. He sent a mysterious and anonymous email to friends and acquaintances who were young and arty. Wasik's original email stated: 'You are invited to take part in MOB, the project that creates an inexplicable mob of people in New York City for ten minutes or less. Please forward this to other people you know who might like to join' (Wasik, 2006: 57). Wasik sent the email to people he felt fitted the profile he was looking for:

> My subjects were grad students, publishing functionaries, cultured technologists, comedy writers, aspiring poets, musicians, actors, novelists, their ages ranging from the early twenties to middle thirties. They were, that is to say, a fairly representative cross-section of hipsters, and these were people who did not easily let themselves get left out. I rated the project's chances as fair to good. (Wasik, 2006: 57)

The first mob was cancelled after the targeted destination, a department store, received a tip-off. Police arrived at the scene before the mob could form (Hewitt, 2003). The second mob was organised using an initial meeting point at which people received instructions on slips of paper telling them where and what the mob involved. MOB #2 involved the crowd meeting in several bars and then heading to Macy's department store. Once in the Macy's rug department, participants started discussing the purchase of a 'Love Rug' for their commune. Before the strange actions of the mob could be explained, the crowd dispersed. The whole process had taken less than ten minutes, but caused a ripple around the world.[4]

Flash mobs were such a new way of relating in public spaces that they quickly attracted attention online. Wasik himself describes the flash mob as 'a spectacle for spectacle's sake' (Wasik in Hewitt, 2003). As a journalist, Wasik knew how to play the media game, and was soon giving interviews, although he remained anonymous, being known only as 'Bill'. He states that he gave over 30 interviews in the first six weeks after MOB #1 (Wasik, 2006: 58). Many of the interviews given were for online magazines and websites (Wasik, 2006: 58). Although Wasik denies that technology was responsible for the rapid rise of flash mobbing, stating that 'technology played only a minor role' (Wasik, 2006: 58), it has been noted elsewhere that 'journalists with mobile phones and cameras sometimes outnumbered the people who gathered to participate in flash mobbings' (Savage in Nicholson, 2005). Without mobile phones and the internet, flash mobbing may have remained isolated to New York City, rather than going global within months of its beginnings. Moreover, the concept of the flash mob has also shifted from its originator's stated purpose, as a 'social science experiment' and a 'vacuous fad' (Wasik, 2006: 57) into something more significant. Flash mobs cannot be understood out of context. In New York City the 9/11 attacks on the World Trade Center created a climate of fear and conformity. Although the flash mob 'experiment' began in Wasik's mind as a comment on conformity amongst young urban hipsters, it became a form of disruptive art (Ejbye-Ernst, 2007), unsettling the overly organised post-9/11 New York City, and other locations where flash mobs took place. Reflecting on the purpose and meaning of flash mobs, Wasik stated that although the flash mob is 'silly' it 'is also, as I've discovered somewhat to my surprise, genuinely transgressive, which is part of its appeal, I think... People feel like there's nothing but order everywhere, and so they love to be a part of just one thing that nobody was expecting' (Wasik in Hewitt, 2003).

Within the bloggsphere of the mobsters themselves, flash mobs are defined via their meaninglessness. 'The power of many in the pursuit of nothing' is a common catch cry (Tom, 2003). One informant, when asked whether he felt that the Zombie Shuffle had meaning, said 'Fun. Just fun.' The flash mob, for this informant, is vacant of any specific message, but still has power. It can challenge mainstream messages in the city by operating against the usual symbolic order. Its meaninglessness can confuse people who find it difficult to understand why people engage in creative acts without a leader or a purpose. This is much like what Jean Baudrillard theorises about graffiti in his article 'Kool Killer, or The Insurrection of Signs' (Baudrillard, 1993). Flash mobs contain empty messages that 'tell us nothing' but in their very existence create meaning (Baudrillard, 1993). The term 'flash mob' was coined not by creator Bill Wasik, but by bloggerator Sean Savage of *Cheesebikini.com*. He named the mobs after a 1973 science fiction short story, 'Flash Crowd'. In the story, the main protagonist creates a riot using teleportation technology (Wasik, 2006: 58).

Another, perhaps more direct, inspiration for the flash mob is performance art created in Düsseldorf in 1963. Nicholson suggests that the first flash mob in Macy's department store is a close copy of the work of the artist group Fluxus, who carried out a project called 'Demonstration for Capitalist Realism' in a furniture store (Nicholson, 2005). The similarity between the two, Nicholson argues, is no coincidence and is evidence that flash mobbing has at its roots an anti-capitalist political outlook, although Wasik did not openly acknowledge this (Wasik, 2006).

Mobile Technologies and the City

The way that people, particularly young people, are using urban public spaces is changing. These changes are occurring in part due to the increasing use of mobile technologies such as mobile internet devices. The internet, once a discrete, separate world accessed within the privacy of the bedroom or workplace, is rapidly moving out into the public realm, and on to the streets.

The uptake of new media technologies has been very rapid, particularly in urbanised areas. The messages sent and received are not outwardly visible like billboards or graffiti scrawlings, but create a 'floating private "phone-space" in public spaces' (Nicholson, 2005). The users of the devices also increase their own visibility. Global positioning systems (GPS) allow the location of the device user to become traceable, and a flag to commercial or other interests (such as military) in the city. Resistant practices have also resulted from these new modes of communicating and being in city spaces. Although often not overtly political, flash mobs are playful practices that draw attention to new media devices, and disrupt the smooth, commercialised, over-regulated planes of the postmodern city.

As previously stated, flash mobs began in the increasingly militarised public spaces of New York City. The flash mob can be characterised as a unique form of pervasive game that uses internet and mobile technologies in its organisation, but is played out in public urban spaces. They draw attention to the technologies that are utilised in their organisation, if not overtly via their content (the subject of which can be the use of the technologies themselves, as explored later), then certainly in the necessary use of these technologies in the planning and choreographing of such precise and bizarre activities, often between strangers, in public spaces. They also cause observers to question their responses to the unexpected in public spaces. In this way, they have the potential to jam or disrupt mainstream messages which prevail in the city. These mainstream messages might be, for example, the pedestrian light that tells us when to cross a road, or the cultural norm that tells us that we should walk straight across, not dance in the intersection as we did in the 'Portable Dance Portal'. By resisting normal codes of behaviour, flash mobbers and observers are given a chance to question these codes, and to ask themselves what it is that persuades us to conform to these usually unwritten laws.

Flash Mobs and Reactions from the Mainstream

Flash mobs have come a long way from Bill Wasik's original Milgramesque experiment on New York hipsters. Flash mobs have even made their way into the Oxford English Dictionary where they are defined as

> a public gathering of complete strangers, organized via internet or mobile phone, who perform a pointless act and then disperse again (Oxford English Dictionary 2003).

Flash mobs are often wrongly conflated with gang violence or riots such as those that occurred in England in August 2011. Although in both instances mobile technologies were being used, there is no other link between flash mobs and the types of riot observed in England. Articles such as Linda Kiltz's 'Flash Mobs: The Newest Threat to Local Governments' feed into the fear of large groups organising quickly via mobile technologies to commit acts of violence and robbery (Kiltz, 2011). Kiltz writes:

> Armed with cell phones and connected through social media sites, young people banding in groups have been rushing into stores or assaulting bystanders in a slew of 'flash mob' incidents...leaving police and public officials scrambling to curtail crimes associated with these spontaneous assemblies. (Kiltz, 2011: 7)

These 'moral panics' smack of those generated around numerous youth activities over the years, which are often feared by those who do not understand them (Cohen, 2011). The media often leap onto these misconceptions as they generate dramatic headlines that increase sales.

Young people in particular are targeted by authorities in urban public spaces. In general, they are more intensely governed there than older users. This is because they are often engaged in activities that do not fit the 'designed purposes' of city spaces, and their presence in itself can be seen as a potential threat to older people. 'Hanging out' and being visible in public places, separate from family and other adult guardians, is key to establishing identity (Mesch & Talmud, 2010). The identity-forming aspects of flash mobs and the Zombie Shuffle were strongly iterated by my informants:

> [I]t is a kind of forum to push people's tolerance a little bit, and also to build up your own confidence. It has always been an exercise

in being comfortable with being different. Like being in a place and having people look at you, and even laugh and point, and little kids pulling on their dad's jacket and saying 'Daddy, what is that?' And if you have an insecurity, that could be a quite shocking experience to be pointed out for being different. But then if you can kind of go 'I am actually enjoying that exhibitionism', to kind of enjoy that, puts your ego up a little bit, and that is sort of the power in it...

The above comment exemplifies how the city is still an important 'third place' for young people to hang out and establish identity, even with the increasing popularity of social media. The internet has not taken over from the street as the site of interaction, as has been theorised by many – see, for example, the discussion of this point in 'Computer-Mediated Communication as a Virtual Third Place' (Shoukup, 2006). Social media sites can be seen as places of intense scrutiny by guardians. For example, Facebook was described by one informant as 'Mum-and-Dad-Book' because of the lack of privacy that many young users experience after 'friending' parents or other authority figures on social media programmes. The street therefore remains an important space for acting out identities for young adults, away from the constant surveillance of their elders.

This need to push boundaries in establishing identity means that young people may occupy public spaces even when they may not have anything to do, or may not have the money to afford to do anything. In many cities, legislation is enacted that specifically targets young people – such as anti-social behaviour orders, which can require people loitering to 'move along' (Walsh & Taylor, 2007). Other strategies such as playing amplified, high-pitched sounds only audible to people under 30, or Barry Manilow[5] hits piped through train station speakers, are specifically designed to make public spaces unbearable to young people (McFadyen, 2006). Flash mobs allow young people to circumvent these strategies because they exist only for brief periods. Participants use private networks and mobile devices to organise online, and appear in public for such a short time that the flash mobber both avoids Barry Manilow and cannot be charged with loitering. Flash mobs are tiny acts of rebellion that disappear quickly 'before the state can crush [them]' (Bey, 1991).

Another appropriation of the flash mob concept within mainstream media is its use as an advertising tool. In 'Ways to Showcase your Brand in a Flash with Mob Mentality', Ivy Wong (2003) asks, 'how can we harness the power of a flash mob...?' Wong suggests that flash mobs can be created for mindless followers as a PR stunt:

> [I]magine if, during the Christmas shopping season, we sent out flash mob emails asking the mob to wear a red top on Christmas Eve and dance like a turkey for a minute at noon at, of course, a client's shopping mall? Imagine the PR and traffic it would create. (Wong, 2003)

This use of the flash mob is what Wasik saw as the final stage of his original experiment: when the Ford Motor Company ran a series of 'flash concerts'. As Wasik writes: 'Ford and Sony had managed to take my fad, an empty meditation on emptiness, and to render it even more vacuous. They had become...the new and undisputed masters of the game' (Wasik, 2006: 66).

'Reality is the Impediment of the Unimaginative'

Flash mobs are resistant to definitions. They are diverse in form and content. In online discourse following a flash mob event, the mobsters continually insist that their missions are meaningless. When onlookers see a flash mob, a common reaction is to question whether the mob is organised for political or commercial purposes. Someone asked me at last year's Zombie Shuffle: 'What are they selling?' Observers are usually astounded to find that there is no leader, and no motivation except fun. Defining and analysing goes against the anarchic nature of the mob. As one mobster writes:

> The way I see it they can try all they like, as long as we stay meaningless they're stuck with nothing to report... Maybe we should all be militant communists for a day. Possibility is ours to create. Reality is the impediment of the unimaginative. It's them stuck in the network of needing to organise, label, categorize, ANALyse. We have the secret of pronoia and we will always lead this dance. (Shaw in Marchbank, 2004)

Molnár attempts to define the broad spectrum of flash mobs by dividing them into three distinct types – atomised, interactive and performative (Molnár, 2010: 10–13). The first two types described by Molnár are very similar. The only real difference is the length of time that they occupy public space. Atomised flash mobs are carried out between people who have generally only met online or communicated through media devices, such as mobile phones. They come together for a period of less than ten minutes, perform a meaningless act and then disperse. People do not interact with each other. The flash mob purist might see this form as the only true type of flash mob (Molnár, 2010: 12).

Interactive flash mobs are very similar to atomised flash mobs, except that they last for longer and can involve interaction between participants. Zombie shuffles, including the annual Melbourne Zombie Shuffle, would fit into this category. Molnár writes that interactive flash mobs can interrupt public spaces, leaving bystanders confused or 'uneasy even though participants do not perform any illegal activity or break any formal rules' (Molnár, 2010: 12). Performative flash mobs differ from the other two categories. These are usually formally rehearsed, and therefore the participants already know each other before the mob occurs. Participants may be professional performers, and could have a motive such as promoting an artistic event (Molnár, 2010: 12).

Public Space vs. Online Space?

Many utopian theorists such as Castells have suggested that cyberspace is the new public space, and that as communities develop within it, real public space will become less and less important. In contrast, however, theorists such as Crang & Graham (2007), Molnár (2010) and Brighenti (2012) have argued that the advent of mobile internet technologies has made the dichotomy between online and offline spaces redundant. Online space has permeated offline space to such an extent that they now coexist, with users straddling the two spheres effortlessly. Young people in developed world, English-speaking Western societies in particular occupy this liminal space, as 'digital natives' (Lentini & Decortis, 2010).

Speaking about the kinds of relationship that exist in the online and offline worlds, Ilan Talmud and Gustavo Mesch write: '[T]he online/ offline comparison is...becoming a faded and even false dichotomy' (Talmud & Mesch, 2010). The physical city – already awash with messages – has simply added another layer: a constantly changing, individualised one. Although the changes to city spaces created by mobile technologies are at times subtle and invisible, the 'entwining of people, place and software' creates complex, new relationships (Crang & Graham, 2007: 792). They allow young people to express their identities in different ways, such as through flash mobbing.

Much less than vanishing into the 'mainframe', online identities rely very much on participation in 'real' space activities. Apps such as Facebook centre around representations of users' experiences in 'real' spaces – enhanced by automatic real-time check-ins at venues and events powered by GPS. While at such events, users upload content to their or others' profiles via their mobile devices, updating status to reflect up-to-the-minute experiences. In this way, rather than diminishing the meaning and purpose of the physical space of the city, mobile technologies enhance and augment the city, allowing for new interactions within it. In this context, the desire for young people to occupy the public spaces of the city is just as strong as ever.

Interview participants who had taken part in several Zombie Shuffles in Melbourne explained the importance of Facebook in transforming the event from a small one, with 'four or five hundred zombies' to about eight thousand in one year and to a world record-breaking ten to twelve thousand participants in the space of another year or two. One participant informed me that he had no idea who had started the Zombie Shuffle in Melbourne, but said he had first found out about it 'on the internet'. Another told me that he felt the expansion of the event was 'almost entirely' because of Facebook: 'People saw photos of their friends doing it [on Facebook], and thought, wow! Let's do that next year! I think that's why it became so popular in one year.'

Another participant was also unclear as to how she found out about the event. However, Facebook and other internet coverage was cited as the reason for its huge growth:

> The year we went there was maybe 1000 people, which was pretty big. But I had heard by the next year it just grew exponentially, and I think that had a lot to do with people putting up photos on Facebook, and of course when you see other people doing it [you want to join in]... There were so many photos being taken! There were heaps of photographers just everywhere taking photos of the event. I think that really...adds to the buzz.

Another said that the quick rise in popularity of the Melbourne Zombie Shuffle 'would have been [due to] all of the pictures, and the comments that were surfacing, and all the coverage. It was all: "What was this? Oh my God! When was this?"'

There was also a strong sense from all informants that there had been an increasing interest in 'horror' themes among young people, and that this had created an internet 'meme'. In the words of one participant:

> I think that there does exist almost a global subconscious meme of ideas, and things become ripe, not necessarily traceable sometimes,

the same thing can happen around the world sort of because of subtle subconscious messages that are happening globally, maybe politics are bringing people to a kind of a point, and maybe a movie comes out, or a couple of things kind of present a sort of platform for an idea to kind of pop up. These kinds of global ideas are encouraged and move faster while using new media technologies, where messages can cross the world in seconds.

While flash mobs could not exist without new media technologies, physical public spaces are also essential. Molnár writes that 'the technology in itself is a requirement but not a sufficient condition for mobilizing people to meet in physical space' (Molnár, 2010: 19). She writes that what is crucial to the effective flash mob is 'its rootedness in particular geographic locales. Flash mobs tend to be strictly urban affairs, favouring large, densely populated urban centres as evidenced by the very high incidence of flash mob activity in New York, London, or San Francisco' (Molnár, 2010: 19). She also writes that areas with high concentrations of young, educated people are more likely to have flash mobs. Research shows that they are more frequent in university towns (Molnár, 2010: 21). The flash mobber is generally young and technologically savvy, such as university students, who are living in close proximity to one another:

> [T]he high spatial density of digitally networked college student and post-collegiate populations seems to be the key to the success and vitality of flash mobbing in a particular physically bound area... Flash mobs can really only mobilize people who are in relative physical proximity to each other to be able to make the leap from cyberspace to urban space. (Molnár, 2010: 22)

So although the flash mob usually originates in the digital world, it must be played out in 'real' physical space. This public space, however, is likely to be the augmented one of the 'digital native', who continues to rely on and relay information between online and offline spaces in participating in the mob.

Flash Mobs: Resistance to Hyper-Surveillance and Control via Artistic/Playful Means

Artistic and playful uses of public spaces resist the conventional ways in which mobile and surveillance technologies operate within public spaces. As Crang & Graham (2007) write, these technologies do not have to turn us into passive consumers; they can also provide spaces where marginalised groups can become visible. Rather than this visibility resulting in what de Certeau (2002) would argue was an ossification of resistant tactics which render them ineffective, the technologies can 'allow us to claim and mark our territory... Where once there were official and dominant memories inscribed on the city now these stories from below can be added' (Crang & Graham, 2007: 808). Via artistic and playful practices, 'a second politics of visibility' (Crang & Graham, 2007: 811) becomes apparent. As Crang & Graham argue, artistic practices that use mobile technologies in public spaces draw attention to these technologies and their usage, making the technologies themselves visible. In the same way, self-surveillance, or 'sousveillance', utilised by some youth cultures in public spaces, also draws attention to mobile technologies, thus prompting similar forms of questioning and critique.

Flash mobs which call attention to mobile technologies are described by Judith Nicholson in 'Flash! Mobs in the Age of Mobile Connectivity' (Nicholson, 2005). One of these, in Berlin in 2003, involved people meeting in a crowded street before shouting 'yes, yes!' into their mobile phones, applauding and dispersing (Nicholson, 2005). In another, also in August 2003, participants were to meet in a furniture store and call another person on their phone and admire the furniture. Nicholson explains how both of these mobs called our attention to the issue of mobile phone use in public spaces. She asserts that flash mobs were

> not shaped simply by the incorporation of mobile phones [but] also seemed to function as parodies or commentaries on mobile phoning in public spaces. Flash mobbing shaped and was shaped by a worldwide shift in mobile phone use from private communication characterized primarily by mobile phoning in the 1980s and 90s to more collective uses dominated by mobile texting in the late 1990s and early 2000s. This shift was evident in a corresponding change in sentiments and concerns regarding direct one-to-one mobile phone use versus indirect one-to-many mobile phone use. (Nicholson, 2005)

Flash mobs not only provide parodies and commentaries on the use of mobile devices in public space, but also are ways that young people reclaim these spaces. As de Souza e Silva explains, games which use mobile technologies create 'an imaginary playful layer that merges with the city space, connecting people who previously did not know each other'. In this way, augmented environments support playful communities that have a very real and visible presence on the streets of the city.

Molnár also discusses the way flash mobs are a commentary on the commercialisation of public space, and create alternative ways that young people can utilise the city. She writes that

> those who see interactive flash mobs as part of the ... 'urban play-ground movement' attribute a strong anti-consumerist element to [them]. They argue that flash mobs combine whim and serious social commentary: they want to create fun but also to 'reclaim' public space that is otherwise often choked with tourists and overtaken by commercial uses. They contend that these urban games 'arise out of an underlying frustration with consumer culture and simply, a desire to have unabashed childish fun'. In a society where choices for social entertainment are largely limited to activities that involve some form of consumption, flash mobs offer free and non-commercial enter-tainment while 'reframing' public space and breaking the mundane routine of urban life. (Molnár, 2010: 12)

Playful performances such as flash mobs encourage onlookers and par-ticipants to question the rigidness of laws and norms that govern street behaviour. Why do the activities of the mobsters stand out as unusual or disruptive? Are our streets overly controlled or commercialised? These questions may raise political issues; however, unlike the participants in a protest, the flash mob does not seek to provide answers or solutions to such questions. They merely throw out a possibility of change.[6]

The Melbourne Zombie Shuffle had originally finished outside Crown Casino in the CBD. I asked some participants whether they felt that this was in part political.[7] One informant answered that he thought that the decision to end at the Casino was political, and added 'it just seemed to be the logical place to go...if you're brain dead!' Two informants stated that it would be 'awesome' to see 1,000 zombies inside the Casino, play-ing on the poker machines, 'not doing anything wrong', but causing a general disruption to the space. This form of quasi-political action fits with the newer and more diverse ways that young people in Australia are expressing themselves politically. Australian youth have diversified the ways that they are engaging with political issues, such as the use of public space. As Gelai writes, 'young people are...beginning to embody more autonomous and individualised forms of participation' (Gelai, 2011). Traditional forms of protest, involving chanting a political slogan in a unified voice, are unappealing to many young people, who would rather express themselves more individually, and aided by the acces-sibility of the internet are able to do so with ease. One informant told me that she felt that the Zombie Shuffle 'definitely had a political slant' although she did not feel that this would be 'the general consensus' on the event. The political content for her was derived from what she saw as the symbolism of zombie imagery:

> [Z]ombies are a symbol of society's numbness, and its de-sensitivity, and its mindless programming. It can be really sad being on public transport at peak hour and just watching all the people, all the zombies, you know, not talking...being non-human, almost, just being these empty vessels...stuck in their routine...

Conclusions

In this chapter I have discussed flash mobs from the perspective of a participant and observer. I have also drawn on data generated via unstructured interviews with a number of participants in the Melbourne Zombie Shuffle. I have provided a detailed description of the phenomenon and contextualised it by engaging in an analysis of changes occurring in urban public spaces since the 9/11 attacks on the World Trade Center in New York. Further, I have explored ways in which mobile technologies are affecting the use of public spaces and asserted that mobile technologies have eroded the real/virtual dichotomy. People, particularly the young and educated, now exist in a reality augmented by mobile technologies, which blurs boundaries between online and offline worlds. Within this augmented reality, new technologies are often taken for granted, or go unnoticed.

In the postmodern city, public space is becoming increasingly privatised, over-regulated and commercialised. This surface-driven, reflective space is less accessible to young people, who may not have the financial resources to legitimately participate within it. Flash mobs provide room for involvement by playfully resisting increasing controls on public space. They draw attention to the technologies of power, upending them, resulting in sousveillance. The empty reflections of the mob paradoxically do not attempt to challenge the hollowness of capitalism, but simply bounce off urban space.

Participating in the mob, I become the performer, front and centre in a world that is often marginalising. The dominant city traffic becomes momentarily lost in our chaotic flow, a prop in the mob's play. By joining the mob, I free myself from the shackles of expected behaviour. Ironically, I also respond to a desire to fit in, and realise – *I* am an *über*-cool, Southside hipster.

Acknowledgements

Thanks to my informants who gave me invaluable insights into flash mobs and the Melbourne Zombie Shuffle. Thanks also to Andy Bennett for his helpful comments.

Notes

1. A number of flash mobs have specifically involved drawing attention to the technology behind their planning – see Nicholson (2005), who cites two flash mobs which involved calling people on mobile phones as part of the action of the mob. She argues that the link between mobile phones and flash mobs began with the culture of 'one-to-many' communication that is associated with texting.
2. The Melbourne Zombie Shuffle could be described as an 'extended flash mob' in that it lasts for several hours. The Melbourne Zombie Shuffle Facebook page simply describes the event as 'Melbourne's biggest gathering of the undead'. There are few constraints on the activity beyond turning up at a specified location dressed as a zombie, and marching on a set route through the city. Zombie marches began in the year 2000 at a gaming convention. Early zombie marches had as few as six participants, but many world records have recently been set and surpassed, with the latest record for the biggest zombie march set at around 30,000 participants in 2012. Melbourne has been a record holder, in 2010, with about 7,000 zombies taking part.
3. The now famous experiments on obedience by Stanley Milgram during the 1960s were written up in his article 'A Behavioral Study of Obedience' (Milgram, 1963). In these experiments destructive obedience was tested where subjects were asked to give another participant an electric shock if they got the answer to a quiz wrong. The participants receiving the shock, however, were actually actors and the shocks fake – the experiment was designed to test how far the participants would go in giving electric shocks when asked by a person who they thought of as holding authority. Milgram himself expected some level of obedience, but was surprised at how far the participants went in obeying the instructions of a man in a white lab coat. He was inspired to test obedience when he noticed the responses of the Nazi war criminals who claimed that they were simply 'following orders' when executing millions of innocent people.
4. A search of flash mobs on YouTube today yields about 51,200 results. YouTube: http://www.youtube.com (accessed 19 August 2012).
5. Barry Manilow is an easy listening singer who was very popular in the 1970s. His music is generally unappealing to young people. An Australian city council has used Manilow's music to 'repulse the miscreants' and it has been described by a councillor as a secret and successful weapon.
6. At a traditional protest the strength lies in a unified voice – flash mobbing does not rely on everyone thinking the same thing, but on simply a non-acceptance of the status quo.
7. This site has some significance to politically active Melbournians. One of the largest protests in Melbourne's recent history was the three-day S11 protest against the World Economic Forum in September 2000, which was held

outside Crown Casino. This protest remains important in the minds of many as definitive because of the violence directed towards protesters by police.

References

Baudrillard, J (1993) 'Kool Killer, or The Insurrection of Signs', in *Symbolic Exchange and Death*. London: Sage.

Bey, H (1991) 'Waiting for the Revolution', in *TAZ: The Temporary Autonomous Zone, Ontological Anarchy, Poetic Terrorism*. Brooklyn: Autonomedia.

Brighenti, AM (2012) 'New Media and Urban Motilities: A Territiologic Point of View', *Urban Studies*, 49: 399–414.

Castells, M (2000) *The Rise of the Network Society: The Information Age: Economy, Society, and Culture* (2nd ed.). Oxford: Blackwell.

Cohen, S (2011) *Folk Devils and Moral Panics: The Creation of the Mods and Rockers* (ebook). New York: Routledge.

Crang, M & Graham, S (2007) 'Sentient Cities: Ambient Intelligence and the Politics of Urban Space', *Information, Communication and Society*, 10(6): 789–817.

Crang, M, Crosbie, T & Graham, S (2007) 'Technology, Timespace and the Remediation of Neighbourhood Life', *Environment and Planning A*, 39: 2405–2422.

De Certeau, M (2002) *The Practice of Everyday Life*. Trans. S Randall. Berkeley, CA: University of California Press.

De Souza e Silva, A (2006) 'From Cyber to Hybrid: Mobile Technologies as Interfaces of Hybrid Spaces', *Space & Culture*, 9(3): 261–278.

Ejbye-Ernst, J (2007) 'Contemporary Urban Performance-Intervention: An Aesthetic Perspective', *Limits of Aesthetics*, May–June: http://aestetik.au.dk (accessed 19 August 2012).

Gelai, H (2011) *Contextualising the Changes in Young People's Participation in Australia*. Youth Affairs Council of Victoria Policy Paper: http://yacvic.org.au (accessed 7 May 2013).

Gibson, W (1984) *Neuromancer*. New York: Ace Science Fiction.

Hewitt, G (2003) 'Flash Mobs: A New Social Phenomenon?', *ABC Science*: http://www.abc.net.au (accessed 19 August 2012).

Kiltz, K (2011) 'Flash Mobs: The Newest Threat to Local Governments', *Public Management*, December: http://icma.org/pm (accessed 18 August 2012).

Lentini, L & Decortis, F (2010) 'Space and Places: When Interacting with and in Physical Space Becomes a Meaningful Experience', *Personal Ubiquitous Computing*, 14: 407–415.

Marchbank, T (2004) 'Intense Flows: Flashmobbing, Rush Capital and the Swarming of Space', *Philament*, 4.

McFadyen, W (2006) 'Manilow, a Secret Weapon', *The Age*, 13 August: http://www.theage.com.au (accessed 19 August 2013).

Mesch, G & Talmud, I (2010) *Wired Youth: The Social World of Adolescence in the Information Age*. Hove: Routledge.

Milgram, S (1963) 'A Behavioral Study of Obedience', *Journal of Abnormal and Social Psychology*, 67(4): 371–378.

Molnár, V (2010) 'Reframing Public Space through Digital Mobilization: Flash Mobs and the Futility (?) of Contemporary Urban Youth Culture', *Theory, Culture, and Society*: http://isites.harvard.edu (accessed 19 August 2013).

Nicholson, JA (2005) 'Flash! Mobs in the Age of Mobile Connectivity', *Fibreculture Journal*, 6.

Shoukup, C (2006) 'Computer-Mediated Communication as a Virtual Third Place: Building Oldenburg's Great Good Places on the World Wide Web', *New Media & Society*, 8(3): 421–440.

Tom (2003) *Disperse Now*: http://flashhack.blogspot.com.au/ (accessed 20 August 2012).

Walsh, T & Taylor, M (2007) '"You're Not Welcome Here": Police Move-On Powers and Discrimination Law', *UNSW Law Journal*, 30(1): 151–173.

Wasik, B (2006) 'My Crowd: Or, Phase 5: A Report from the Inventor of the Flash Mob', *Harper's Magazine*, 312(1870): 56–66.

Wong, I (2003) 'Ways to Showcase your Brand in a Flash with Mob Mentality', *Media: Asia's Media & Marketing Newspaper*, 19 September.

Glossary

ANOVA (analysis of variance): A statistical test that compares the difference of means between two groups. If a significance rating is above 0.05, then the results are not statistically significant. A significance rating below 0.05 indicates that the two groups are statistically different from each other.

Crowdsourcing: The act of outsourcing work tasks to members of the general public. As a business model, it has enabled companies to utilise the (most often free) labour of the general public. As the boundaries continue to blur between producers and consumers, crowdsourcing has occurred most effectively through the internet. Tasks range from small requests for creative solutions to problems through to large requests for labour for work projects.

Creative crowdsourcing relates to projects more explicitly in the creative realm and involves creative artists seeking contributions from the general public to anything from ideas for book or music cover art through to sourcing large community art projects. Some of the best-known examples of this include *PostSecret*, *It Gets Better*, and *Learning to Love You More*. Such projects commonly enable would-be artists or activists to engage in artistic or political activity. But it could also be seen as exploitative as the curators of these large projects have the most to gain.

Cyberbullying: When someone is being bullied online or through other digital media devices. Moral panics around cyberbullying are often targeted at young people as victims and bullies.

Dematerialisation: In regard to music consumption, dematerialisation refers to the loss of the physical object, such as the CD or record, in favour of digital storage, such as the MP3.

Digitality: Originally coined by Nicholas Negroponte, digitality is the circumstance of living in a digital world, characterised by the proliferation and use of digital technologies.

Discourse: Discourse can have a number of meanings, and what it refers to is different in different contexts and areas of scholarly research. Sometimes it refers to a set of terms or special use of language associated with a particular area of society, as found in phrases such as 'legal discourse' or 'educational discourse', which describe the collection of words and their meaning unique to the law and education. Influential theorist of history Michel Foucault used the term in a more specific and complex way. For Foucault, 'discourse' refers to a system made up of the interaction between three elements: 1) the processes of knowledge production (such as scientific inquiry, which has rules about what counts as knowledge and how we can come across it), 2) the language used to describe that process and the knowledge produced by it, and 3) the influence (or power) that the knowledge and language *working together* have in relation to the organisation of resources and rights in a given historical context. Using this more complex sense of the word, 'educational discourse' refers to how teachers and researchers go about understanding the way students learn and how to assess that learning, the language they use to describe how they do that and what they find out, and the influence this has on the development of government policy regarding the provision of education.

Foucault was particularly interested in how the being recognised as a person – something denied many people in both ancient and contemporary times, such as slaves, criminals, women, the mentally ill – was reliant on how one was classified by discourses of subjectivity – processes of producing knowledge, language and influence regarding who can and cannot count as being a person. This more complex sense of 'discourse' has been very influential in the humanities and social sciences. In speaking about autobiography as a discourse rather than a genre, Julie Rak argues that autobiography is one of the systems of knowledge production and language that has influence on how individuals might claim to *be* a person and in so doing claim the rights associated with it.

Hypertext: A hypertext is a text that is not singular, but connected to other texts with links, often on the web. A hypertext is not linear and takes on multiple meanings, depending on which links the reader follows.

Intertextual: An intertextual text refers to or contains other texts in its own content. For example, a TV show that contains parodies of famous movies, like *The Simpsons*, is intertextual.

Late modernity: The period of history in which many sociologists would claim we are currently living, characterised by the information revolution and global capitalist economies.

Metadata: A set of data that describes and provides information on other data. Web pages, for instance, include information on the language they are in, the tools used to create the page, and so on.

Moral panic: A media-driven public anxiety around a problem that is perceived to threaten moral standards. Stanley Cohen's seminal 1972 book *Folk Devils and Moral Panics* focused on the media representation of the mods and rockers in 1960s Britain and explored the amplification of deviant youth practices associated with violence.

Music tagging: A system of tagging was originally used online for file-sharing sites, such as Flickr, whereby users uploaded photos and tagged them with subjective terms, primarily for future retrieval. Music tagging refers specifically to tagging music online, usually on social media sites such as YouTube and Last.fm.

Participatory online culture: An internet culture where the content is created by the same group of people who consume it.

Patriarchy: A system of power in which men are dominant over women.

Perpetual contact: A term popularised by film historian James Katz, perpetual contact refers to a form of sociability whereby people are differently social, but not less so. Perpetual contact is a product of the proliferation of mobile phones, and the desire to be in constant contact with others. Katz coined the term to suggest an ultimate, pure form of communication, akin to a melding of the minds.

Prosumer: Portmanteau of producer and consumer, drawing attention towards the notion that a) consumption (of goods, of culture) is also a form of production; and b) consumers are increasingly empowered to become producers through the social web.

Reflexive project of self: Giddens (1991) theorised that individuals are constantly working on narrative of self – even in seemingly mundane moments – and that each activity or encounter contributes to this reflexive project of self.

Soundscape: The sounds that make up one's sonic environment. Canadian composer and music writer R. Murray Schafer coined the term.

Virtual world: An online environment in which users create an avatar that acts as their proxy within a navigable, simulated space. Virtual world users are frequently able to customise their avatar's appearance, allowing them to create a personalised 'in-game' presence. Avatars often have a human-like appearance but can also be animals, robots, monsters, and so on. Virtual worlds are primarily social forms of media that are designed to enable users to chat, interact and play collaboratively with other users.

Zines: Zines emerged as a type of media in the form of 'fanzines' in the mid-to late 20th century. A reworking of the word 'magazine', the word 'fanzine' described a publication produced *by* members of a group of people with a common interest, distinguishable from the professional and commercial publications produced *for* their consumption. Beginning with the newsletters of science fiction enthusiasts during the golden age of the short story and serialisation of fiction in magazines in the 1930s and 1940s, fanzines have been used by football fans in the United Kingdom, and punks in the United States and the United Kingdom, to circumvent the commercialisation of information and reporting on their chosen interests, and to connect members of an interest group as a fan community. In the case of the punks in England in the 1970s, fanzines were a vital means of distributing information about gigs and new record releases, many of which were not covered by the established music press. With the rise of the internet as a site for fan communities to share information and discuss their shared interest, fanzines became less prominent, but the appeal of handmade, small-circulation publications has continued. Zine culture takes zines themselves as the common point of interest, although zines are still a vital space of publication for information-sharing in punk, queer and vegan communities.

Index

Printed and bound by CPI Group (UK) Ltd, Croydon, CR0 4YY